I0800972

IMAGES
of America

TOWNS OF MOUNT LASSEN

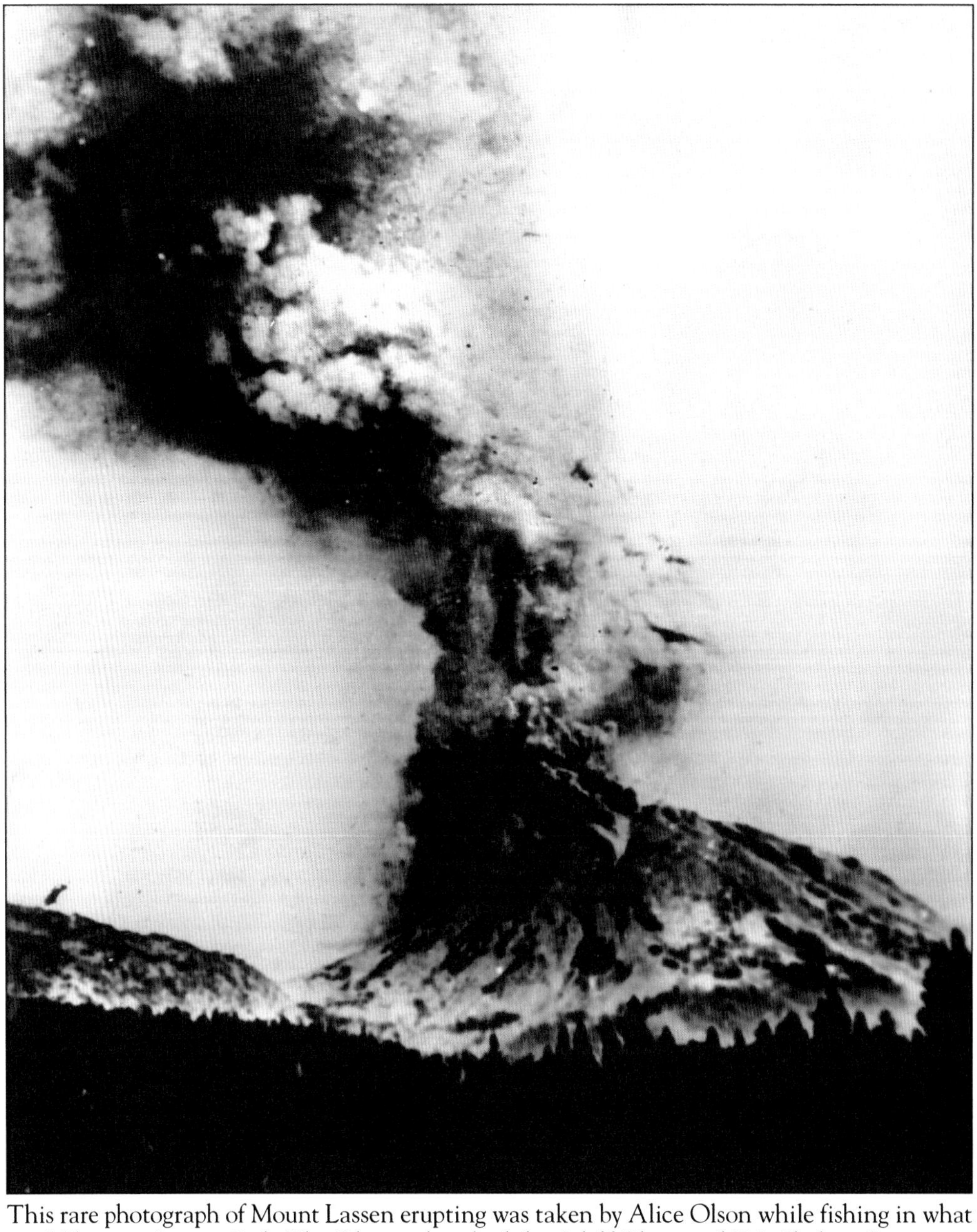

This rare photograph of Mount Lassen erupting was taken by Alice Olson while fishing in what would become Lassen Park. The Olson cabin, built by Adolf Olson and T. J. Shelton Sr., was on the south shore of Grassy (later Horseshoe) Lake and served as a sheep camp. Landing on the left ridge, just above the tree line, is a piece of the mountain the size of a house. Those living within the perimeter of the mountain fled to safer areas in the valley for safety.

ON THE COVER: Shown here is the cookhouse that sat just below the trestle and flume. "There is mud four inches thick when it rains," wrote Mary Shelton (head cook) in her autograph book. Shown from left to right are John Shelton, Mary Shelton holding Anne Bandy, Tom Shelton, Danny Shelton, John Westrope, Don Westrope, "Doc" Shelton, Jim Shelton , Dyas Shelton, John Redner, and Charlie Shelton holding daughter Doris. (Courtesy of author.)

IMAGES
of America

TOWNS OF MOUNT LASSEN

William Shelton

ARCADIA
PUBLISHING

ISBN 978-0-7385-4270-6

Published by Arcadia Publishing
Charleston, South Carolina

Printed in the United States of America

Library of Congress Catalog Card Number: 2006935605

For all general information contact Arcadia Publishing at:
Telephone 843-853-2070
Fax 843-853-0044
E-mail sales@arcadiapublishing.com
For customer service and orders:
Toll-Free 1-888-313-2665

Visit us on the Internet at www.arcadiapublishing.com

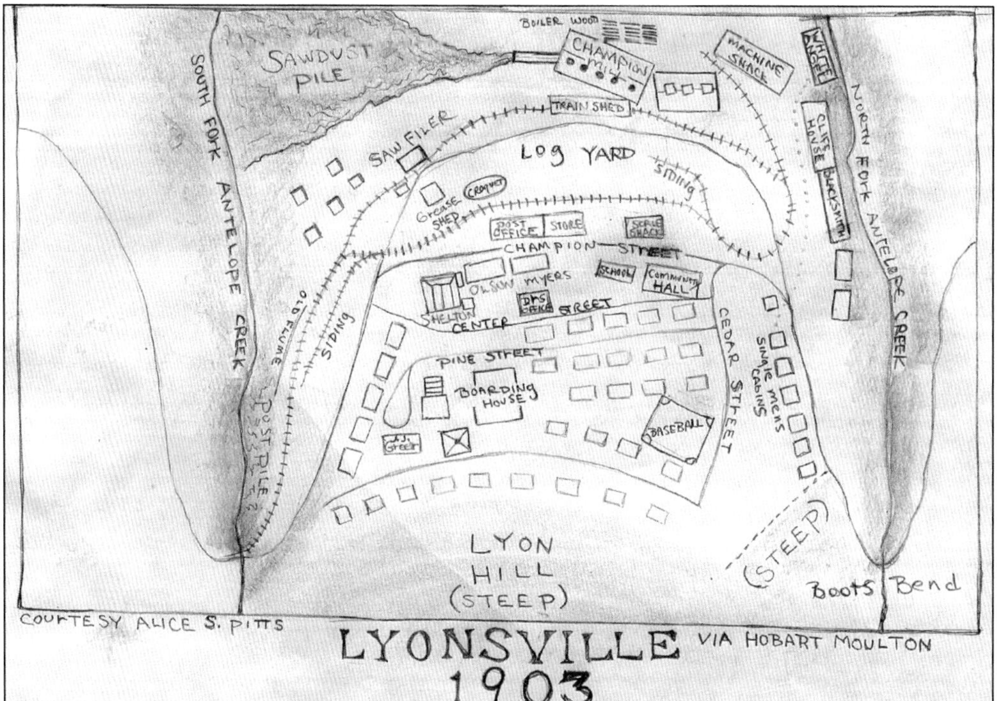

Lyon Hill was pushed up by early, violent eruptions of Lassen. This abrupt hill drops off to a large flat expanse, deep in volcanic soil and bordered by creeks on either side. From the steeps looking down, this same soil was forced down the right side of the hill to what would become Boots' Bend, situated on the north fork of Antelope Creek. As the force of the earth pushed up, a rocky slope with volcanic posts and rock piles was created, bordering the south fork of Antelope Creek along the base of Lyon Hill. As the earth continued to push up with great pressure, the hill grew higher. This map was made up in the 1960s from the recollections of many people who had lived there.

Contents

ACKNOWLEDGMENTS

The material for any book has to be gathered, researched, sorted, compiled, and written. Throughout my life, I have felt something tugging at me in many ways. Many roads diverge, and by chance we find our way through.

I am thankful to my great-great-great-grandparents, William and Miranda Gurnsey; the Westropes, who were among the first Californian pioneers; my great-great-grandparents, Hannah and James Gray; and my great-grandmother, Emma "Redwing" Shelton, who taught me *Yahi* words and the old ways around Mill and Deer Creek Canyons. Hannah Gurnsey Gray was the first saver of things in our family, from the 1901 Hogsback Homestead deed to her parent's portrait, which developed into a family collection.

Thank you to photographers of a century ago Reinhart and Dorothy, R. F. Stinsen, Scripture and Weston, Valentine the Rambler, and their masterpieces mounted on cardboard as early as 1860. Many photographs in my collection were passed down and guarded by generation after generation and form a history of the entire region. Unless otherwise noted, the images in this book are from my collection.

To my great-aunt Alice Shelton Olson of Red Bluff, who homesteaded on Grassy (Horseshoe) Lake and named Jakie Lake for her son, Jakie Olson, in what would become Lassen Volcanic National Park. Her vast collection was left to my father and passed on to me.

I thank my parents, Charles and Camille Shelton, for encouraging my interest in family history and local history. With much thanks, I acknowledge family members and friends who enriched my life with the stories, photographs, and artifacts that made this book possible.

INTRODUCTION

From the earliest beginnings and through the continual eruptions of Mount Lassen, many of the prominent rock formations known today, such as Black Rock, Camel Rock, Immigrant Rock, Cragston Rock, and the Pinnacles, were formed. The torn landscape from the valley floor to Lassen was formed over centuries and is strewn with volcanic stones. One arm of this formation is the Hogsback Ridge, much of which is lava and cinder cone. There are places today that contain hot springs, mud pots, and postpiles with perfect, four- and five-sided posts.

The Forty-niner influx of settlers in the mid-19th century spread to the Lassen environs. Those pioneers brought craft and trade skills and new technologies to push industry in the mountainous terrain. But even more so, they brought with them a simple way of life. The Hogsback was the original road from Red Bluff to Lassen. The site of the town of Lyonsville sits high above the Hogsback Ridge and between the north and south forks of Antelope Creek. In the beginning (or as far back as can be traced, which is 1862), a trail ran from the lower south fork of Antelope Creek all the way to Lassen, which the Native Americans called *Waganupa*. This was a narrow foot trail used by the Yahi Native Americans for seasonal migration when traversing from the valley where they lived during the winter to the mountains for the summer season.

Darwin B. Lyon, the town's namesake, was superintendent of the Sierra Lumber Company in Red Bluff when the town was founded. In 1862, pioneers had settled on the escarpment on the spot that would become the town site for Lyonsville. The original settlers built a crude cabin and designed a box flume to carry water from Antelope Creek, several hundred feet above Boots' Bend, to the house. The new box flume actually bypassed the original flume. In time, the residents left the area, and the town was left to ruin by 1918. The flumes endured the seasons, and its structural remnants could be found for years thereafter.

A narrow-gauge railroad was laid down to service the area. Lyonsville was now linked and new Champion Mill, which the townspeople referred to as "the Champ," was built for the thriving lumber industry. A sawdust pile was dumped hundreds of feet over the bank to the south fork of Antelope Creek, spilling over the trail used by the Native Americans and in the end becoming hundreds of feet deep. At Lyonsville's peak, more than a thousand people resided in the town, worked the railroads, and logged the woods for a prosperous half-century.

All that remains today are the brick boiler foundations of the old Champion Mill; thousands of square nails, bolts, and railroad spikes; and the gigantic sawdust pile hidden in the thick woods where a civilization disappeared as if it had never existed. The cemetery where many early Lyonsville pioneers repose is a mile and a half from the town. The cemetery is mostly under brush and overshadowed by trees, the same as the skeletal stone, brick, and mortar foundations of the old Champion Mill.

From Lyonsville to Lassen, there are many settlements and homesteads dating from 1860 to 1900—and some within the national park. Prior to the volcanic eruptions within the park boundaries, there were summer homesteads for cattle and sheep grazing that were privately owned and operated. The practice was abolished by the federal government under the Park Act to preserve the land.

Mount Lassen, or *Waganupa* as the native people call the mountain, holds an abundant history captured in these photographs of lakes, cabins, people, and eruptions. It is, after all, one of North America's dormant volcanoes and a scenic wonderland.

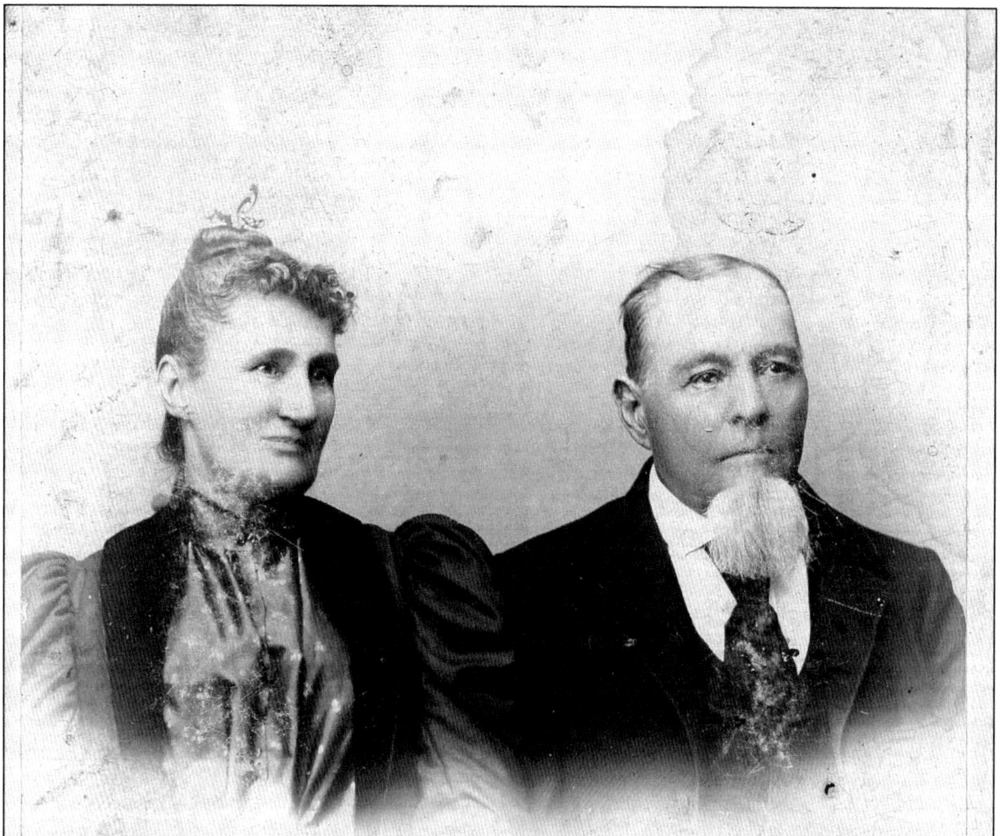

Will Gurnsey and Miranda Parsons came from New York in 1849 by wagon, settling in what is now Taylor Valley. The Gurnseys had three children: Will Jr., Hannah Jeanette, and Mary Miranda. This pioneer family is the namesake for Gurnsey Creek and Gurnsey Avenue in Red Bluff, where Gurnsey and his son-in-law J. S. Hunt built a house to found the new town of Huntsville, which never materialized.

One

Mount Lassen

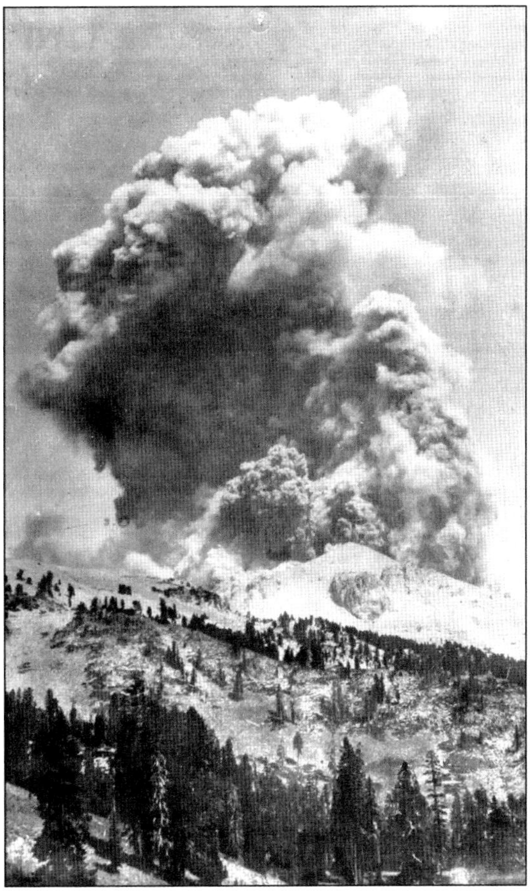

This spectacular photograph of Lassen erupting was taken by Alice Olson, who was on a fishing trip within the perimeters of what would become Lassen National Park. The Olson cabin, built originally by Thomas Shelton and Charles Avery, sat on the backside of the mountain on the far side of Horseshoe (also called Grassy) Lake.

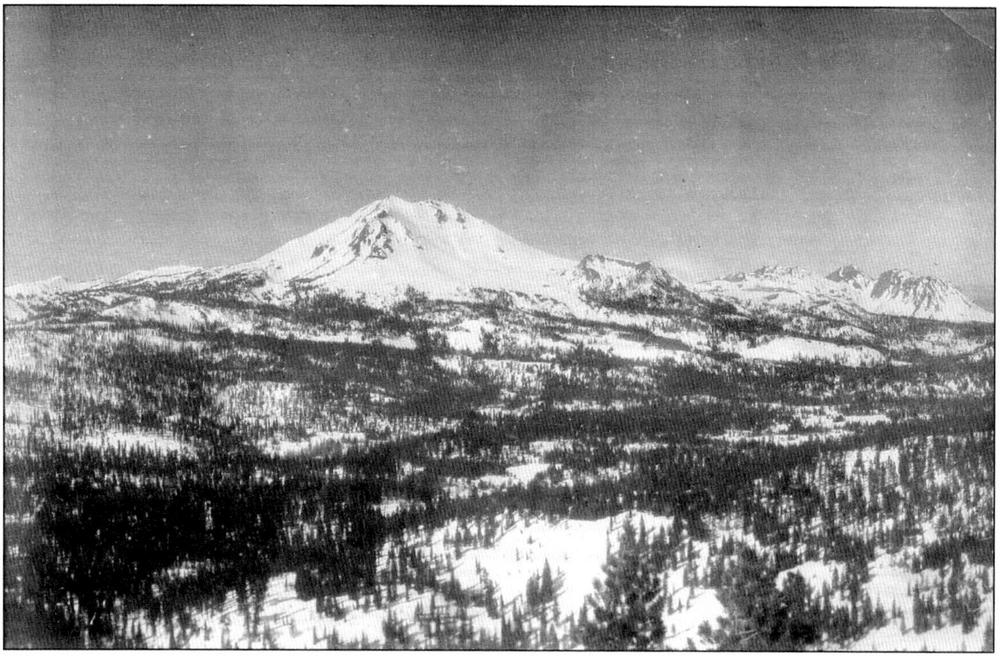

Waganupa, or *Wowonopu* as the Yahi and Yana Native Americans called it, supposedly holds magic powers and big medicine. Mount Lassen, visible for hundreds of miles, had languished there for as long as the Native Americans could remember, and they waited for the wrath of the volcano to be unleashed again. Legend has it that the volcano had been created as a means for the Native American spirits to ascend to their final resting place.

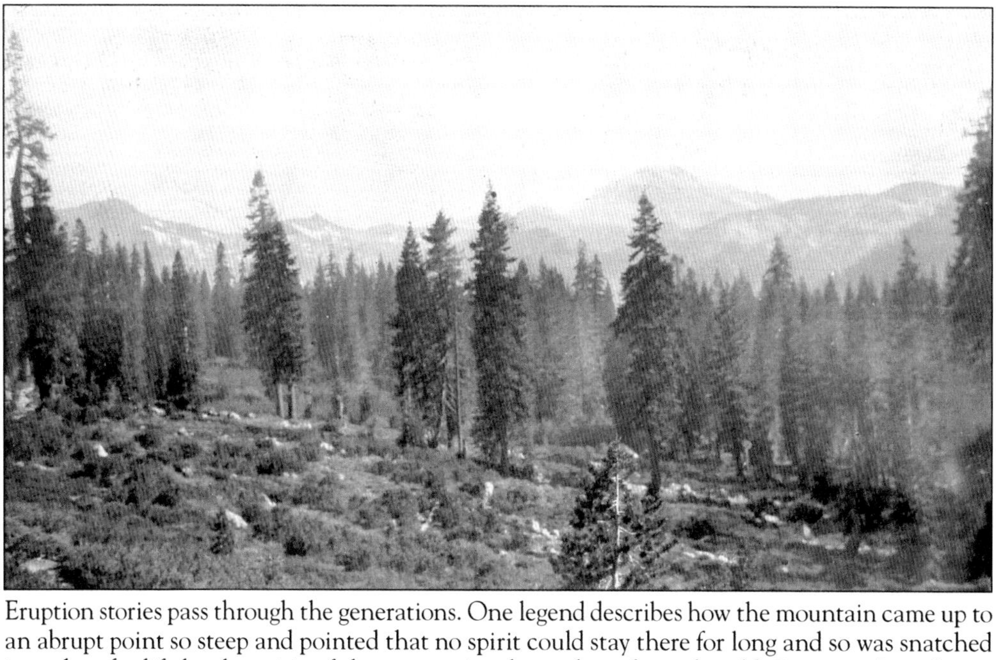

Eruption stories pass through the generations. One legend describes how the mountain came up to an abrupt point so steep and pointed that no spirit could stay there for long and so was snatched into the afterlife by the spirit of the mountain, shown here from the old Gurnsey place. James Gray wrote of one eruption, "We watched as the lava covered our land and cabin."

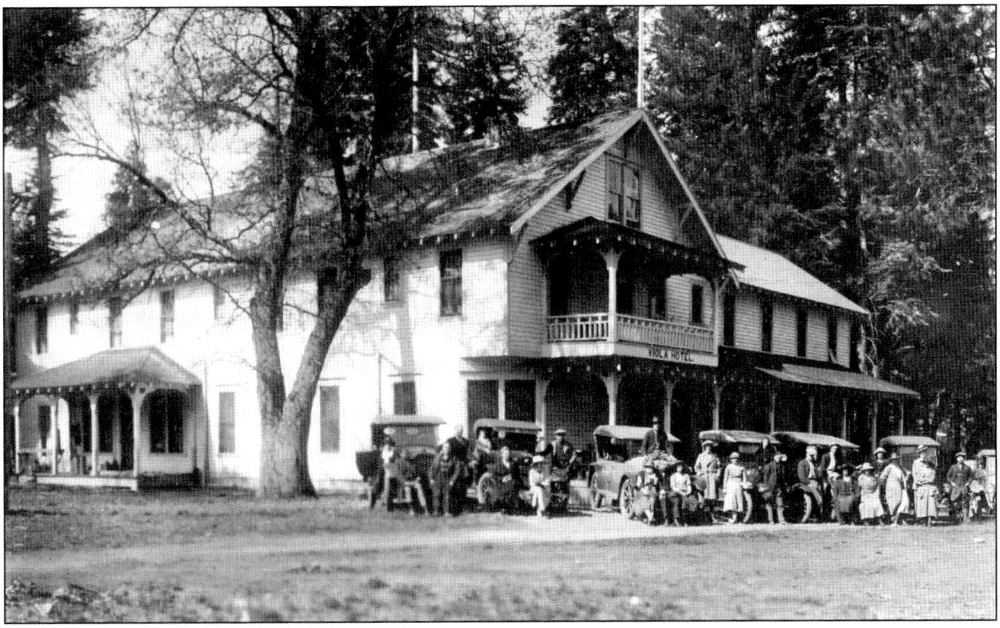

Sitting just a short distance away from the current park entrance was the Hotel Viola, which predates the national park. Frequented by tourists visiting the park, the Hotel Viola had been a favorite stopping place for stagecoaches on the way to Prattville, now under Lake Almanor.

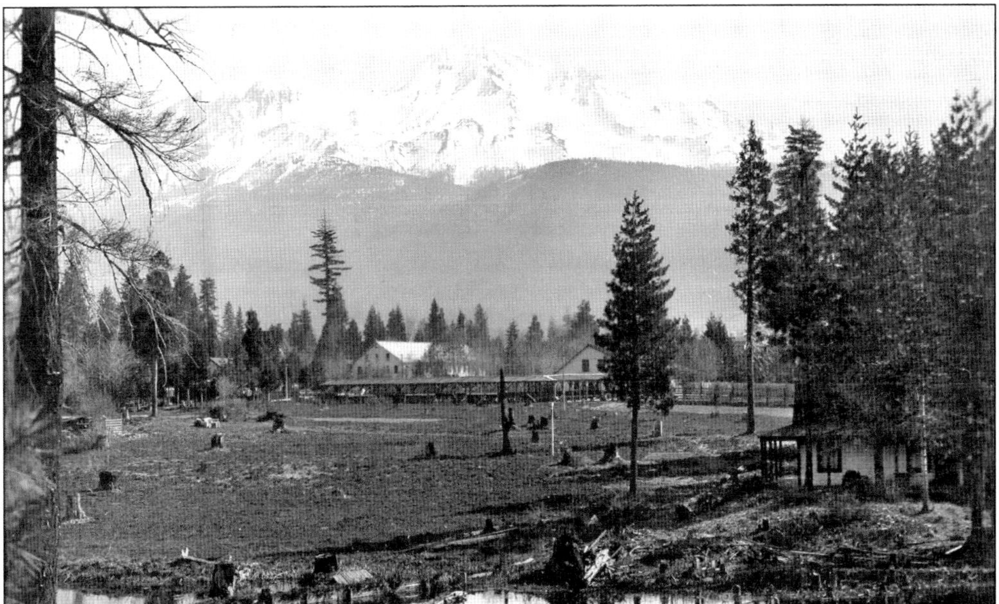

This serene shot of Mount Lassen was taken just two years before the 1914 eruption. Snow packs varied from year to year through the 1800s. In the winter of 1861, settlers noticed that no snow stuck above the halfway mark on Mount Lassen. In the spring of 1862, it was discovered that steam and gasses were escaping through small holes on the top of the volcano's surface.

Alice Olson wrote in her diary that several weeks before the eruption, strong sulfur smells and ground heat were detected, and that "many fish were found dead and floating in Grassy Lake." Her diary notes that she and her sons climbed the peak from the backside and noticed loose rocks tumbling down the grade. Steam could be heard hissing from the summit.

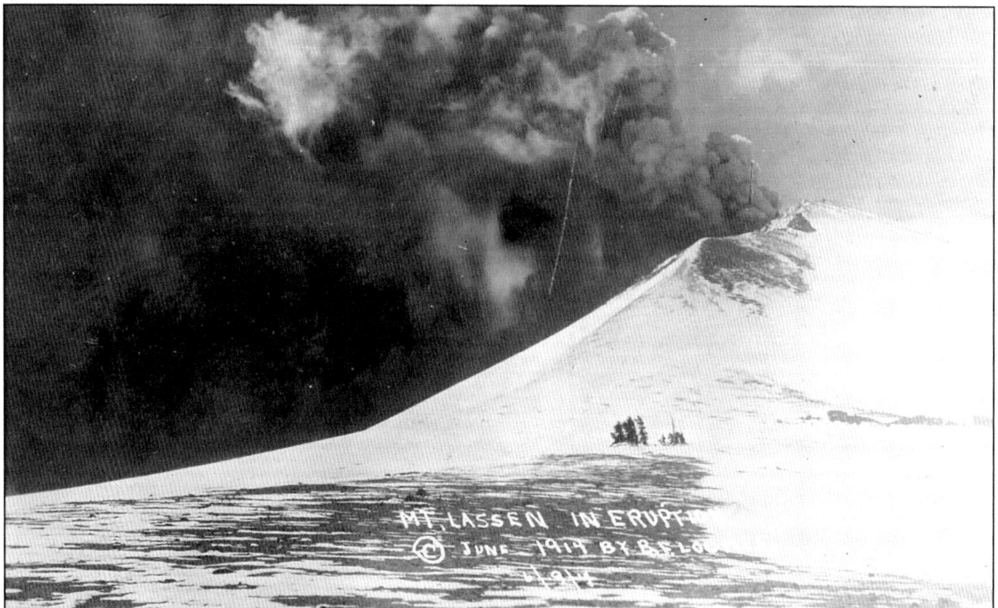

The Charles Avery diary tells of "rocks falling from the sky" in 1862 at night and a "bright glow on the horizon." The next morning, as he surveyed the event, the ground was so hot in some areas, "My horse and I could barely walk across it," Avery wrote. Another eruption is rumored to have happened about 1798 that threw boulders upwards of 50 miles.

This postcard image, taken by B. F. Loomis and dated May 22, 1915, shows the thick black smoke of the mushroom cloud that formed over Mount Lassen. The flow of lava went down the other side of the volcano.

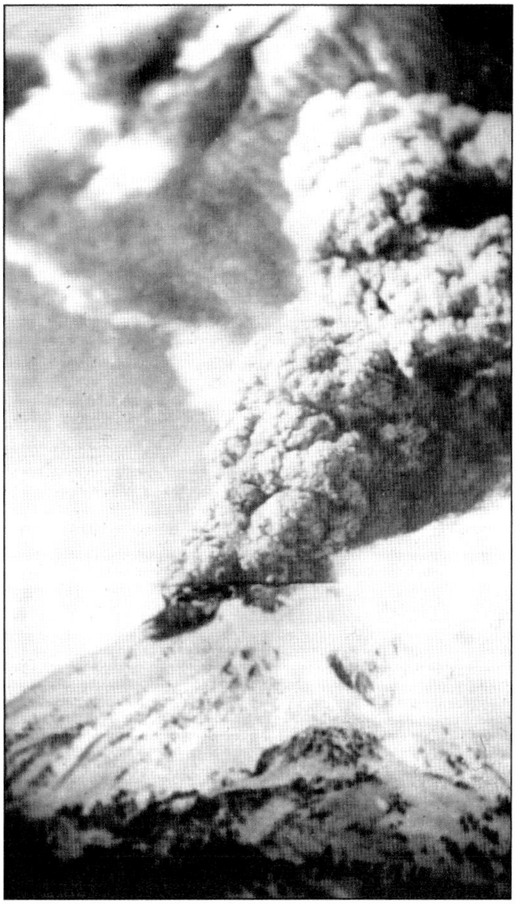

This photograph, taken May 22, 1915, by R .L. Myers, a relative of the Myers Family of Lyonsville, shows the enormous cloud of smoke and ash from a distance of 50 miles away. The wind changed over the course of several days, and a thin layer of ash was spread from Anderson to Redding.

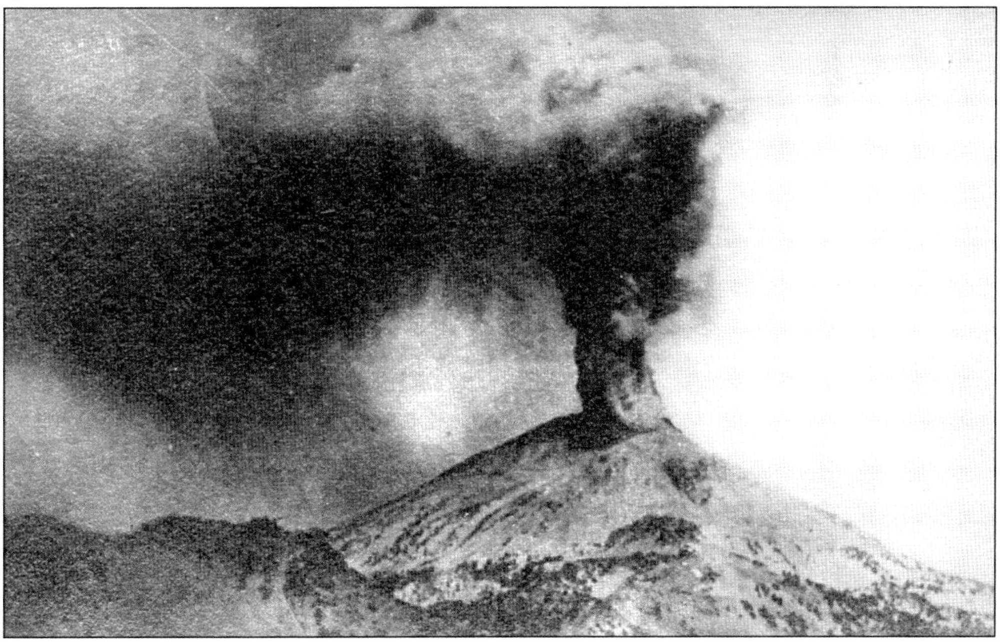

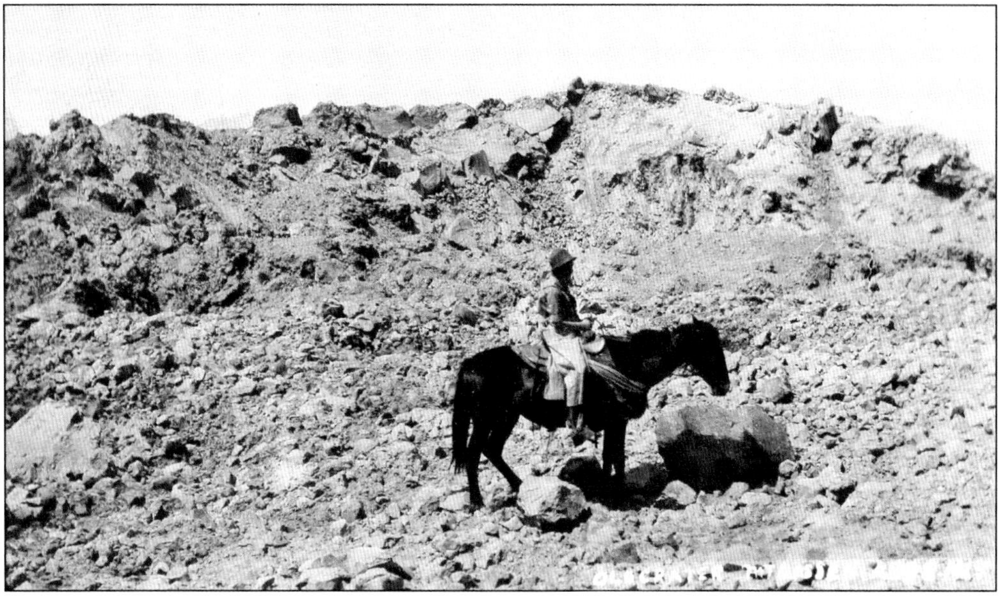

On August 8, 1915, Bert and Hazel Hampton ascended to Lassen crater to take photographs. They camped at Battle Creek and the next day photographed the volcano and surrounding area. The Hamptons sold postcards at their Hamptons Mineral Resort for years after the 1915 eruption; their collection of more than 150 photographs, mostly unpublished, is one of the best depictions of the devastation done by Mount Lassen.

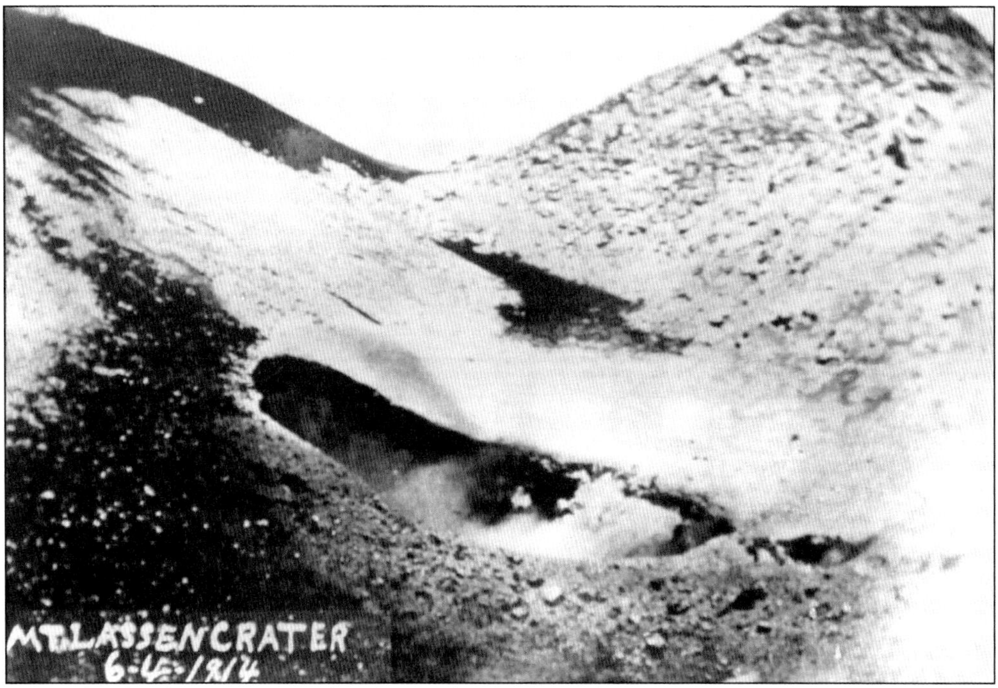

Also taken by the Hamptons, this shot of the depths of the Lassen Crater shows the sulfur and lime deposits at the bottom of the fissure. Bert Hampton was lowered halfway down into the crater by rope, though his wife objected because of the extreme heat.

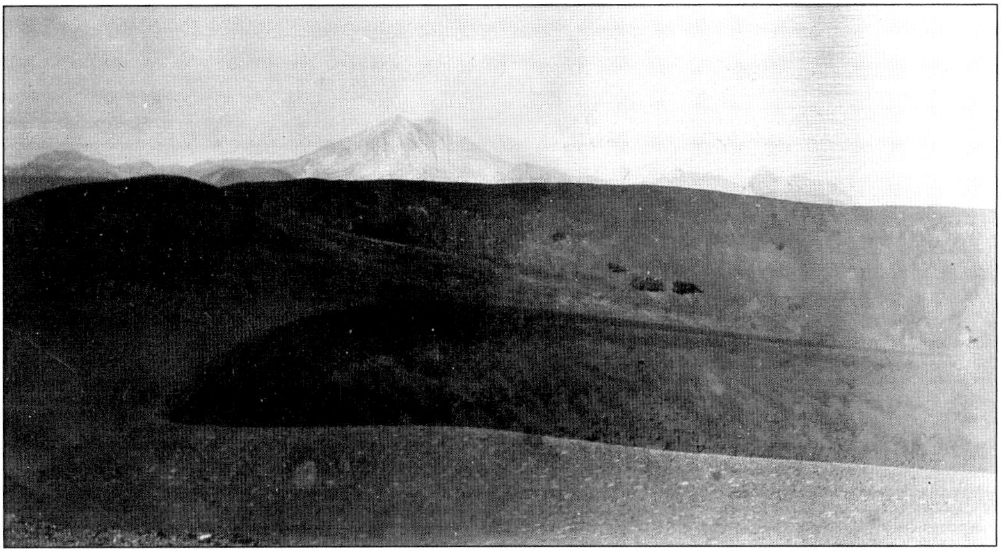

Another view, taken by Hazel Hampton on August 8, 1915, shows the cinder crater hole and Mount Lassen in the background with a heavily covered snowy summit. The Hamptons and the Supan family were mystified by the volcano. Dr. Thomas Supan thought that at one time he could manufacture paint at the sulfur springs. Supan Gulch at the Manton turnoff on Highway 36 is named after him.

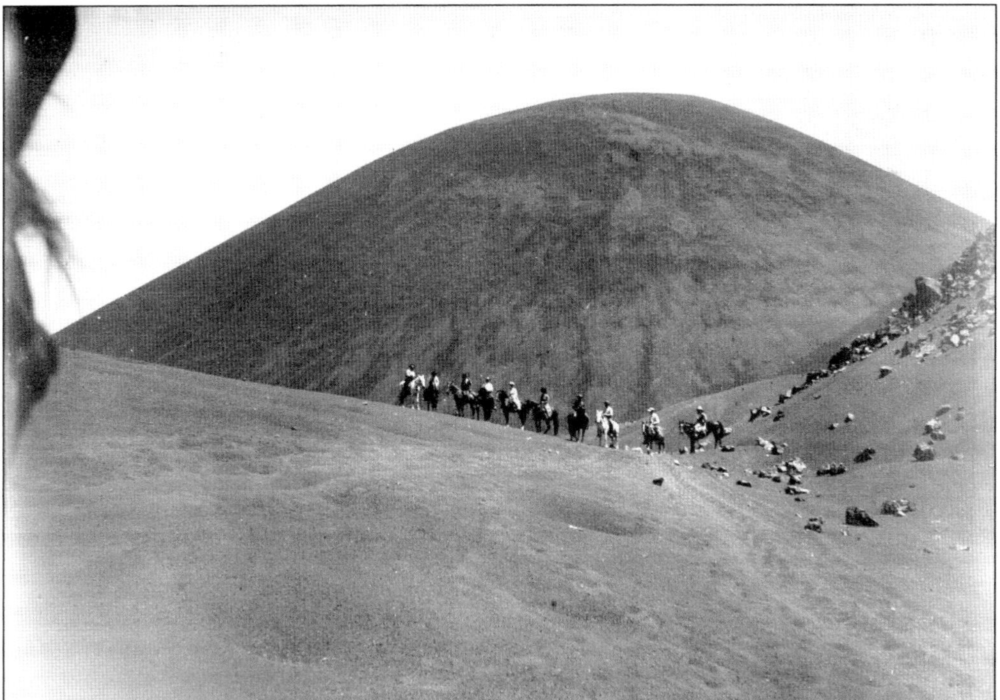

Cinder Cone has been pushed up over many centuries by the miles of extensive lava tubes that lead to the volcano. In this view, a party from Red Bluff heads up the trail to the top. It was said that when Mount Lassen erupted in 1914, there were faint traces of smoke escaping through the cinders, which are very porous, and that Cinder Cone gave off heat.

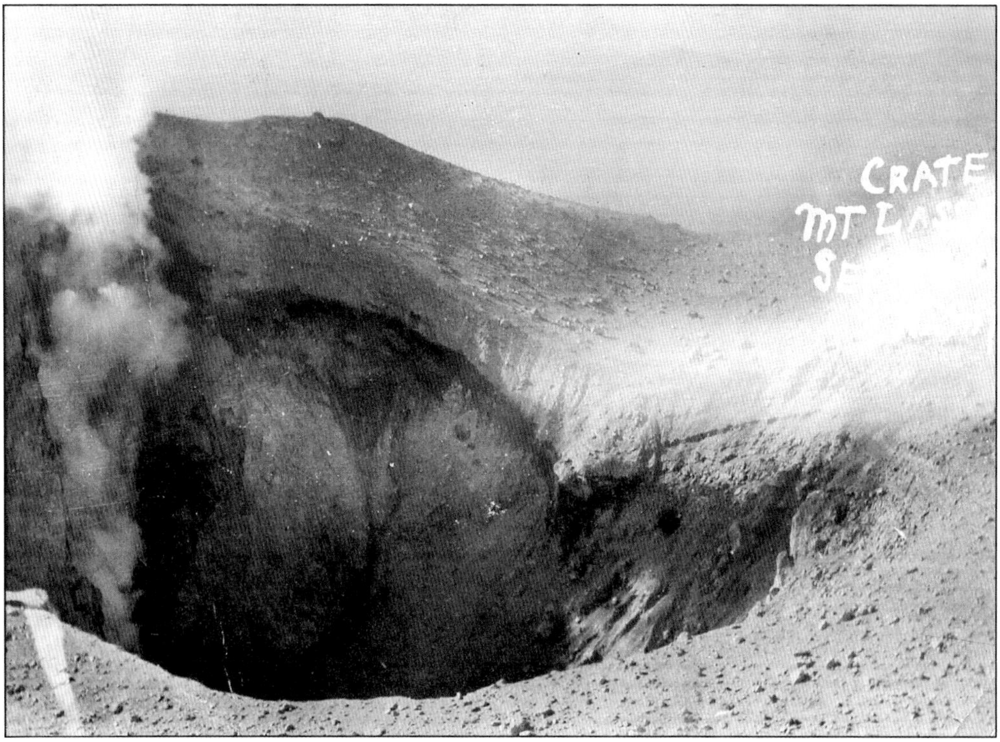

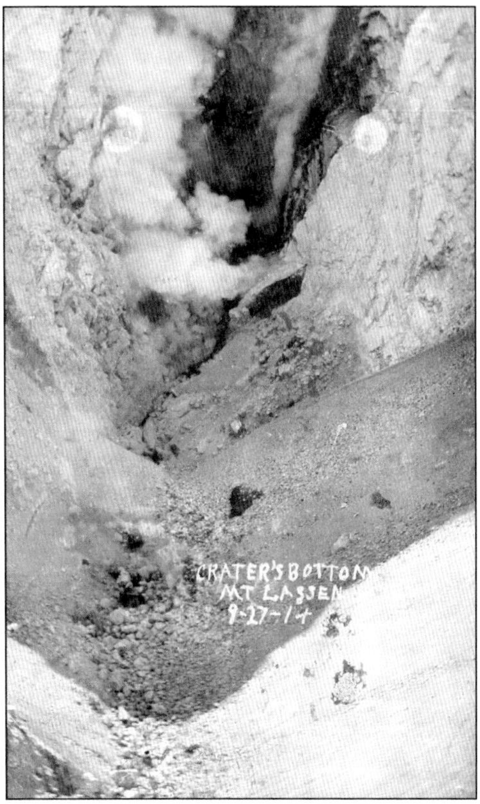

Using an impromptu suspension apparatus, Bert Hampton descended into the crater suspended by a rope secured to his horse's saddle horn, while his wife, Hazel, guided his horse to the rim edge. The two interior crater photographs on this page are the images captured by Hampton with this bold maneuver on September 27, 1915. And even though his wife protested, Hampton worked to capture the most intricate details of the interior of the crater. These actual images were gifts to Alice Olson from Hampton's Resort at Mineral, California.

An interesting contrast to the photograph on page 15, this image was taken several years later of a car caravan at the base of Cinder Cone. As other deposits of cinder were found, it was discovered that when cinder was ground up, the porous stone made excellent paving material for roads. To this day around Mount Lassen, stretches of roadway are paved in red cinder.

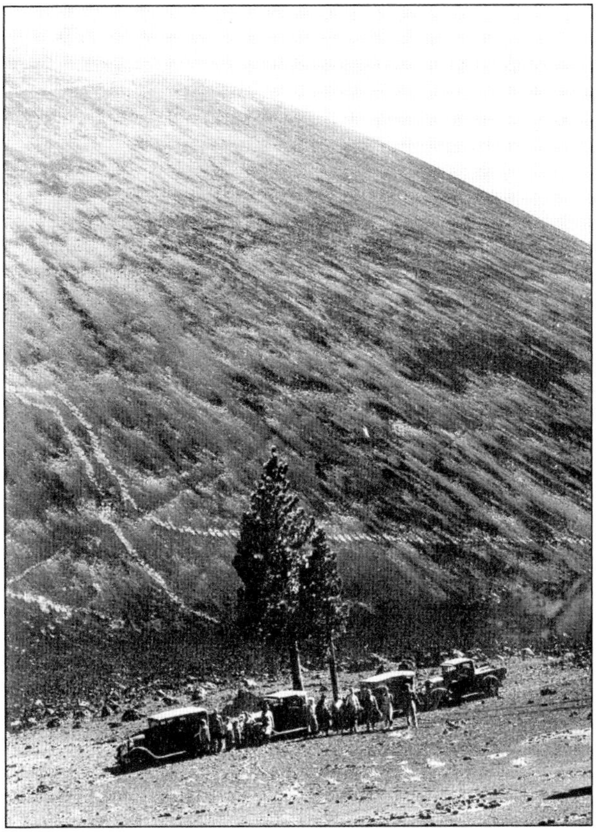

This photograph, taken by Lind Foto around 1930, shows the subterranean caves that spread throughout the Lassen area. Many of the caves are 50 feet wide and 60 feet long. Some of the immediate cave entrances occasionally had ceilings black from smoke soot and discarded tools, evidence that Native Americans used the caves as winter camps. The man on the left in the image is Hobart Moulton.

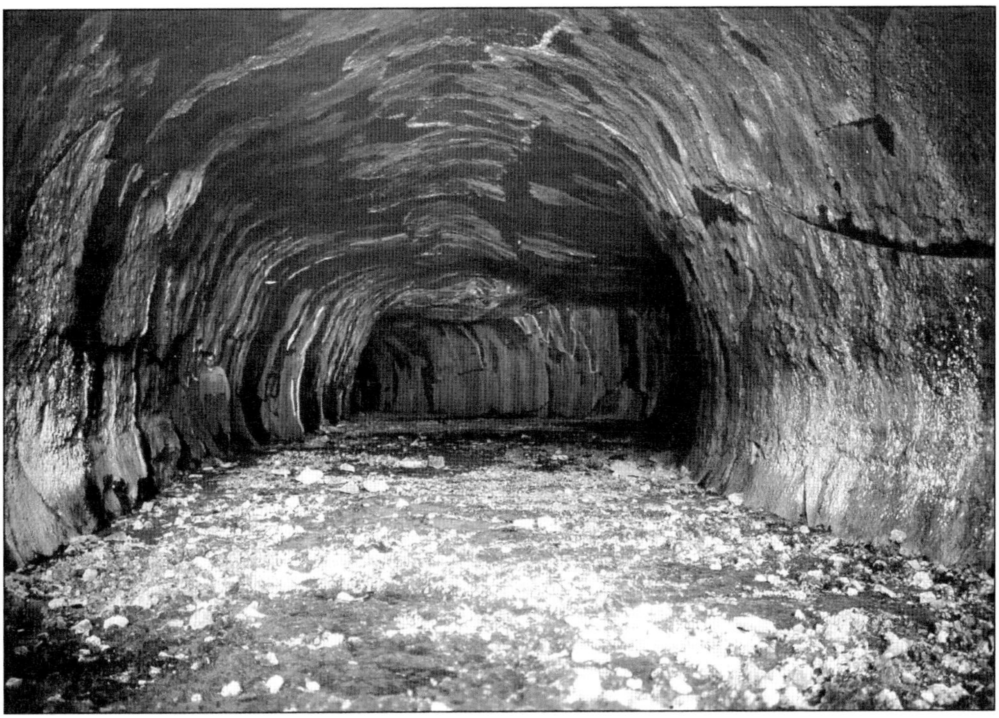

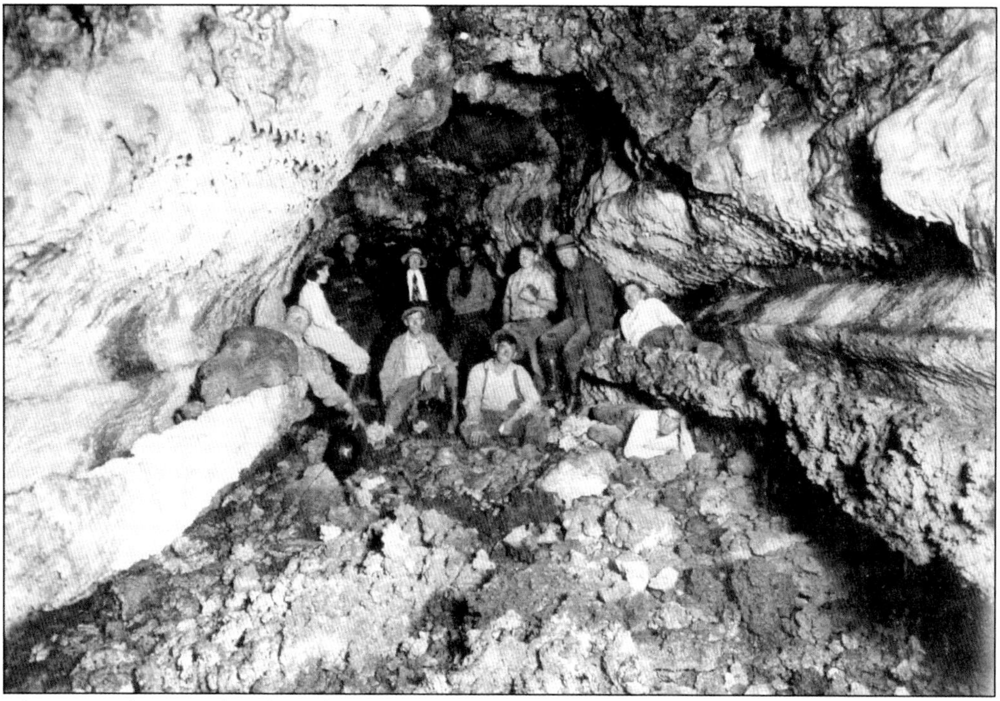

These two photographs, also taken by Lind Foto, show the contrast of how tunnels differ in form and size. However, all of the tunnels seem to have the same troughs on both sides, and in places, there are ledges where a person can walk. Many tunnels are either caved in or are so narrow that it is barely possible to crawl through. Some caves have narrow shafts and vents that might lead to larger unknown chambers, but such exploration is both harrowing and dangerous.

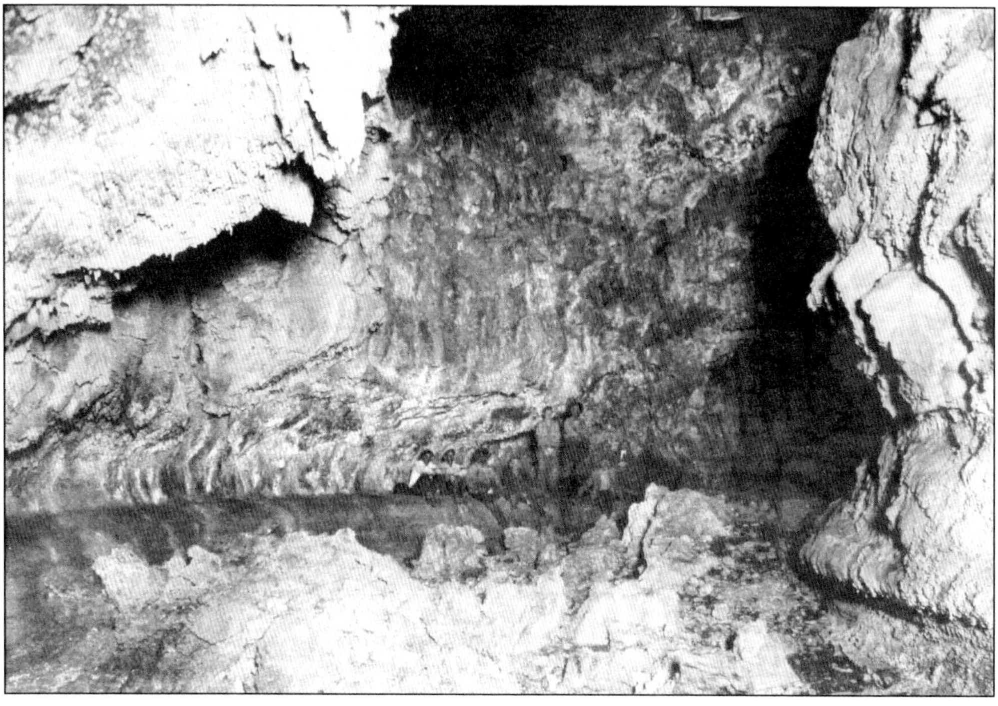

These two views of Lassen Lookout show Mount Lassen's broke-off mountain lookout station as it appeared in 1913 (above) and on March 22, 1915, after the eruption that year (below). The lookout station sat at the second-highest point in Lassen at 9,235 feet. Though the lookout building itself was anchored by heavy cables, the cables were broken as the lookout was inundated with rocks and debris. In a span of two days, the lookout was torn apart and blanketed in ash. The three men are two Lassen rangers and a reporter. The reporter from the *Sacramento Bee* wrote, "The mountain had slept for 65 years." The mountain had erupted in 1850 and 1851 and overlapped from July 1850 into January or February 1851 periodically.

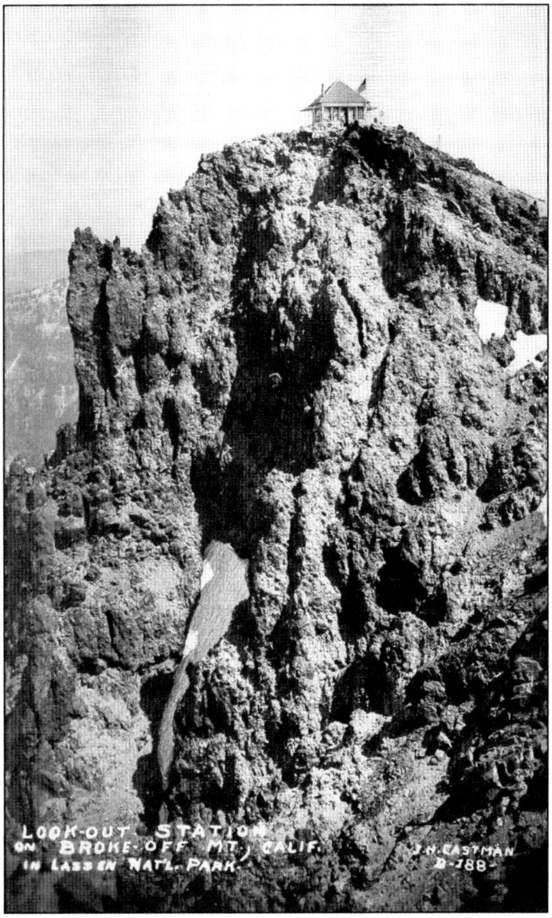

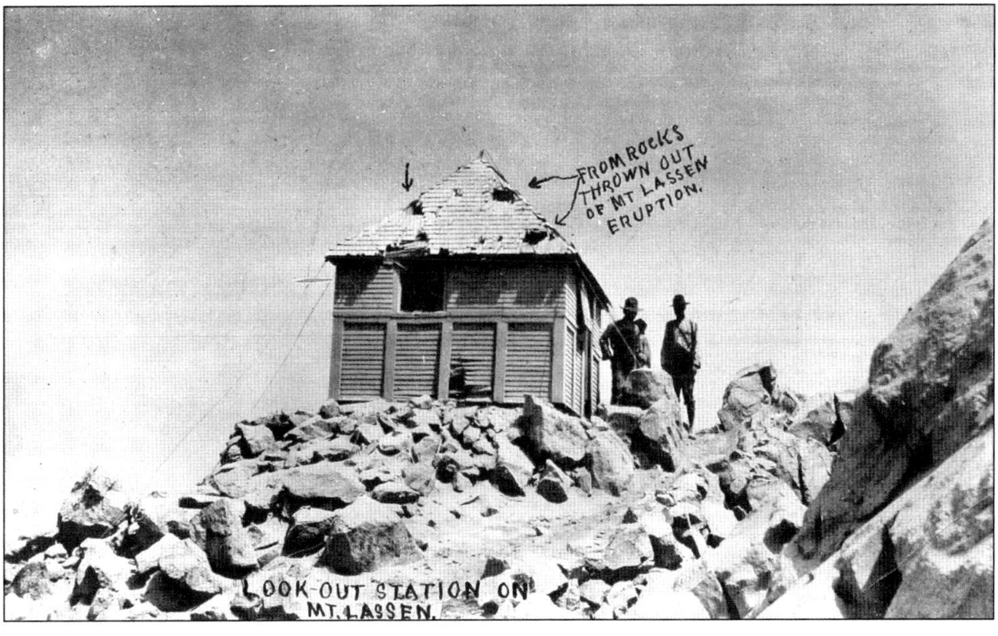

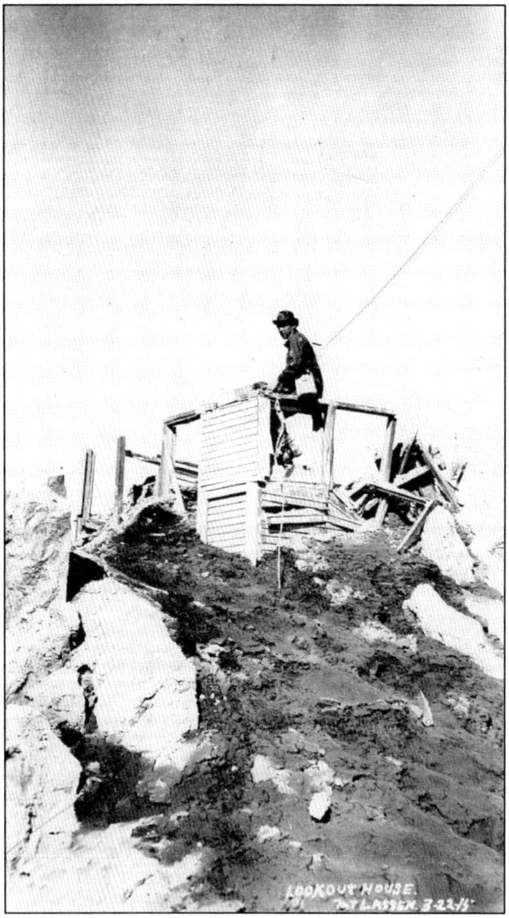

This final photograph of the lookout station was taken a few days after the 1915 photograph on the preceding page and presents the eruption devastation. When Alice Olson returned to the Olson cabin on Grassy (Horseshoe) Lake the following spring, she spotted a hole in the shingled roof, and upon entering the cabin, she found a hole in the kitchen table and a five-pound volcanic stone embedded in the floor.

Bill Gosney brought his camera to Lassen Peak in late 1915 to record views of the flooded and volcanic areas. This photograph, taken by John Gibson, shows the devastated area shortly after the eruption. By then, there were days that the volcano issued no smoke, but there were also days that it was thought it could easily happen again because of the smoke pouring out of the crater.

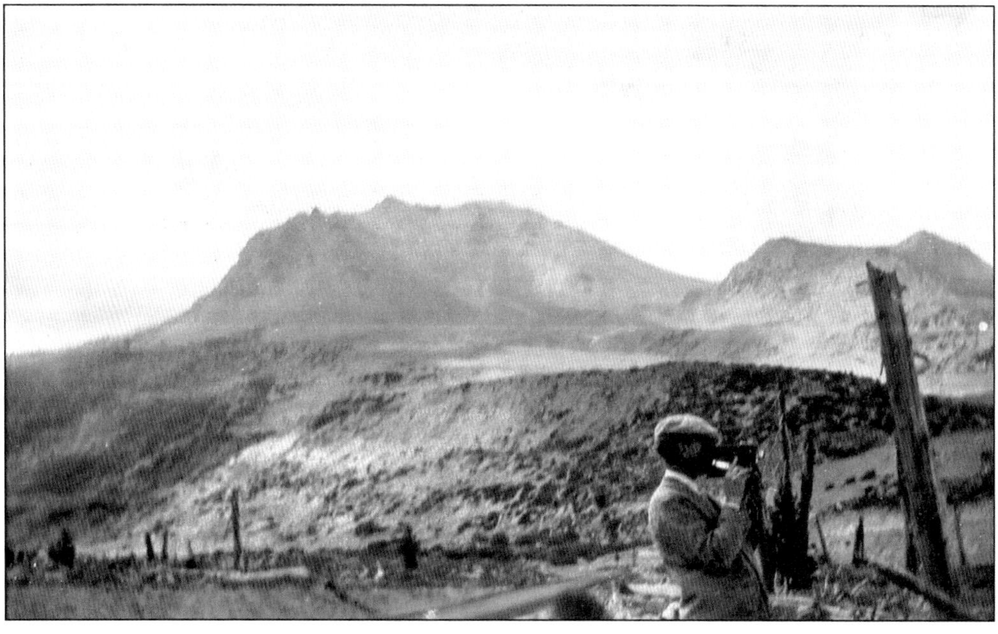

This is one of the earliest photographs of constructing a road through Lassen Park. This is a stretch on Redding Peak at an elevation of approximately 8,000 feet. The steam shovel is powered by a Dolbeer Donkey boiler and engine. This photograph was taken in 1932, and the road was progressing slowly at a rate of 10 to 30 feet a day, depending on the terrain ahead.

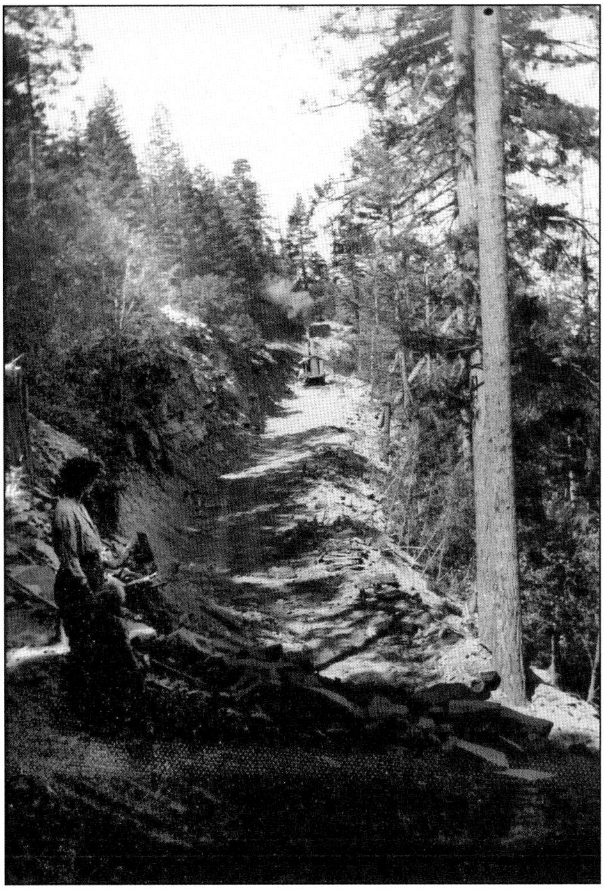

This view of the area was taken in 1926, twelve years after the devastating 1914 flood. It shows the natural reforestation of the area. A combination of mud and water flow and a gas blast had sent an avalanche of thick mud and boulders that decapitated mature trees six to eight feet above the ground.

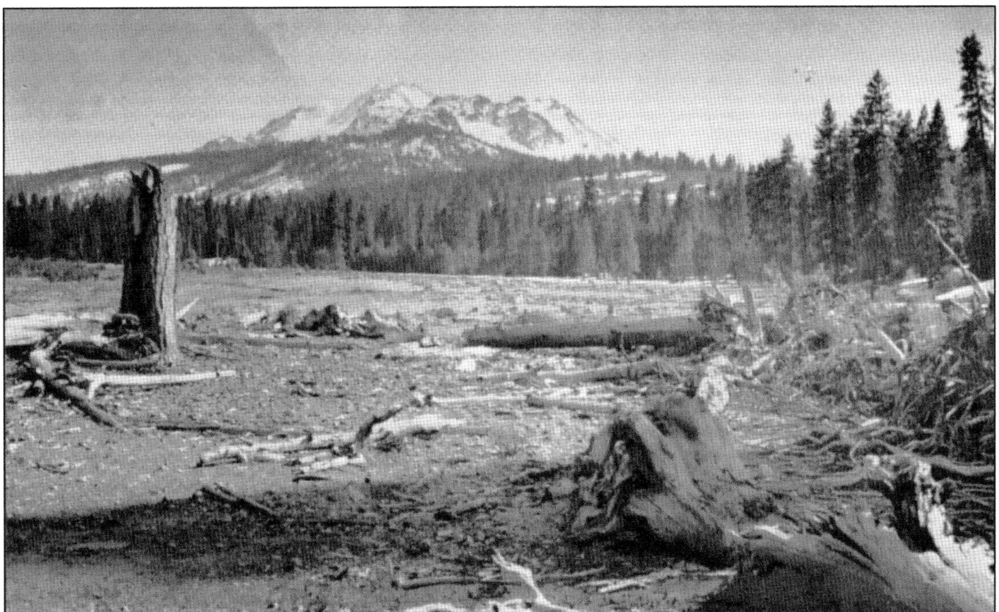

DEVASTATED AREA AND MT. LASSEN IN CALIFORNIA. RESULT OF 1914 FLOOD A-376

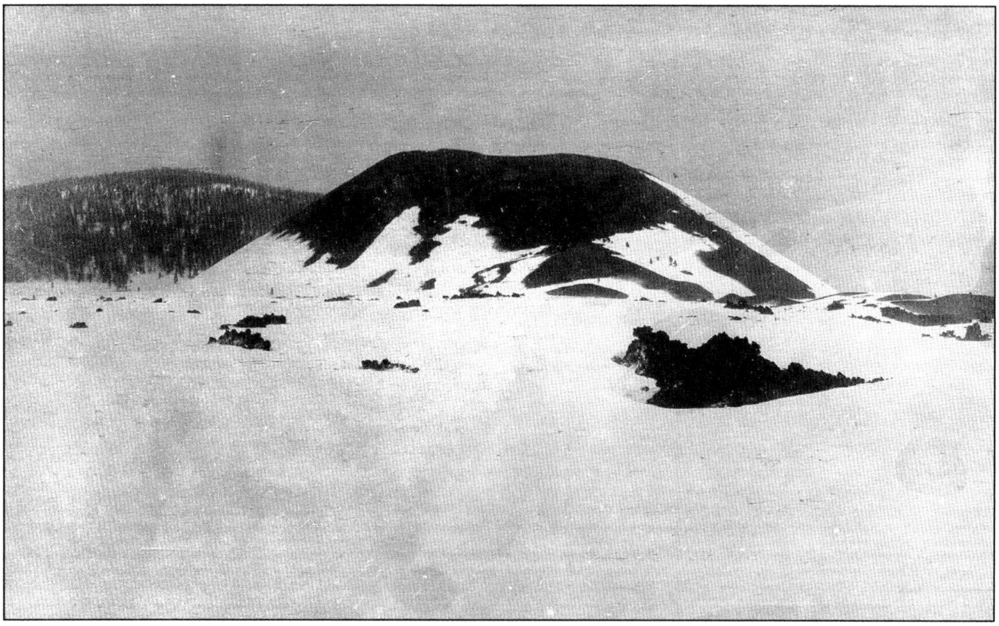

An impressive view of Lassen from atop Cinder Cone was taken by Alice Olson. This photograph was part of a series of images that were taken the same day as the car caravan on page 17. This was the last caravan to Cinder Cone over the Badger Flat Road and was taken by George Simpson of Gerber, California.

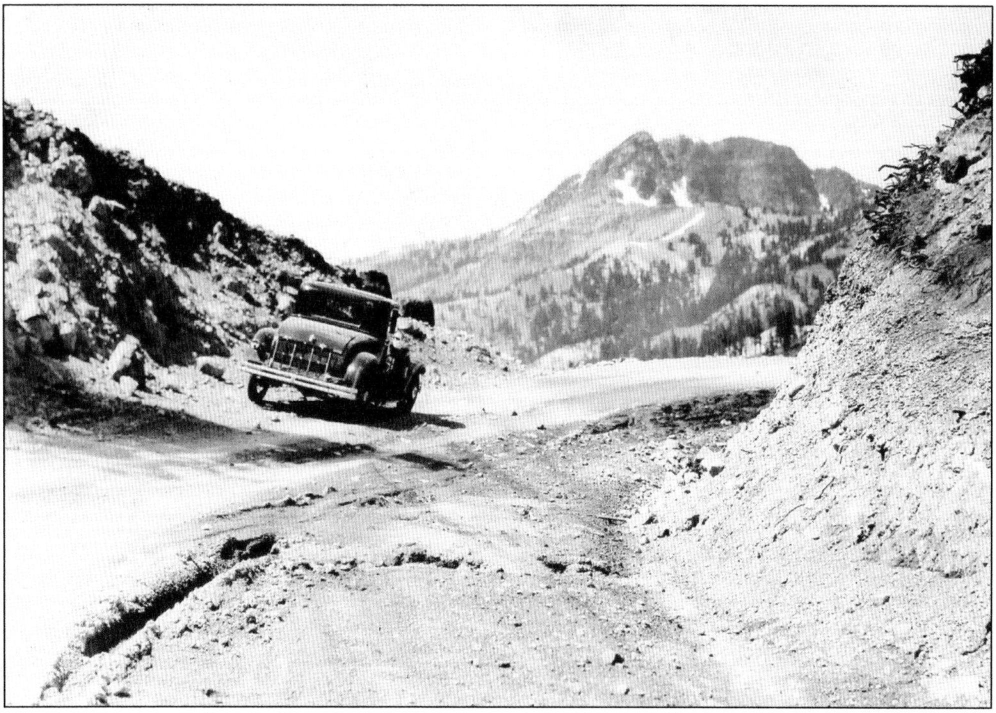

This 1936 image, taken at Windy Point, provides a good view of Lassen Peak. Windy Point is a turn in the road and was also known as "Whistler's Point," because when the wind reached the cut in the mountain made for the roadway and was at a certain angle, it actually whistles loudly.

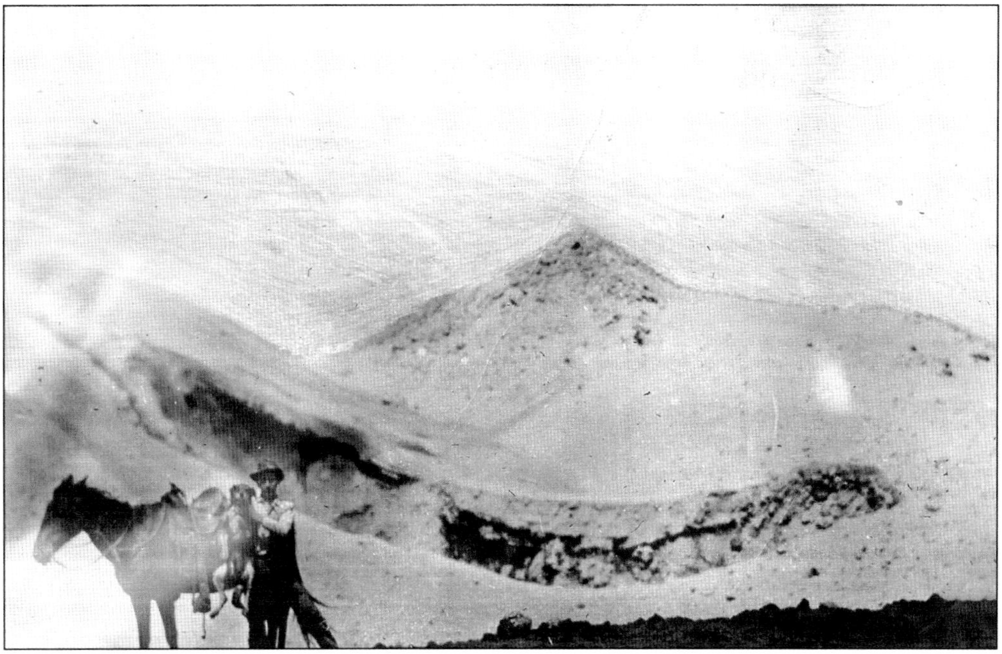

This photograph of Bert Hampton and dog is marked "Old Crater Lassen 1914." It was taken before the massive volcanic eruption. Prior to 1932, the summit was difficult to reach because of loose rocks and steep sides. This did not hamper the many young boys who were avid fishermen and who had discovered the large size of the fish that could be caught in the early settlement of homesteads in what would become Lassen Volcanic National Park.

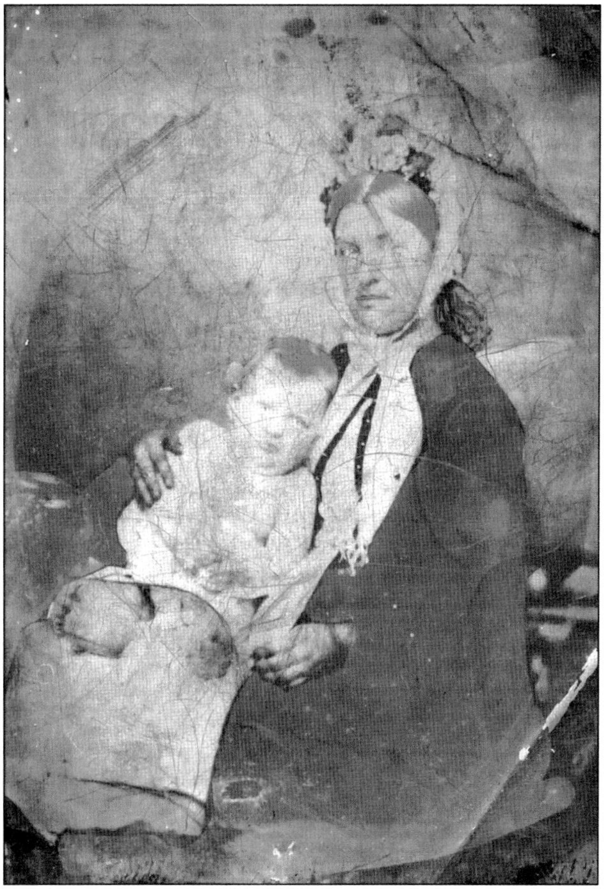

Mary Emily Hayton was born in Illinois on February 28, 1829. She married Samuel Westrope. After crossing the plains, the family arrived in Chico, California, in 1864. The Westropes settled in Battle Creek Meadows, which is now Mineral, in the spring of 1877 and ran a dairy. Mary died at age 48 because of a broken heart over the death of her son, Danny. He was killed in an accident involving a horse. She is buried behind park headquarters at Mineral.

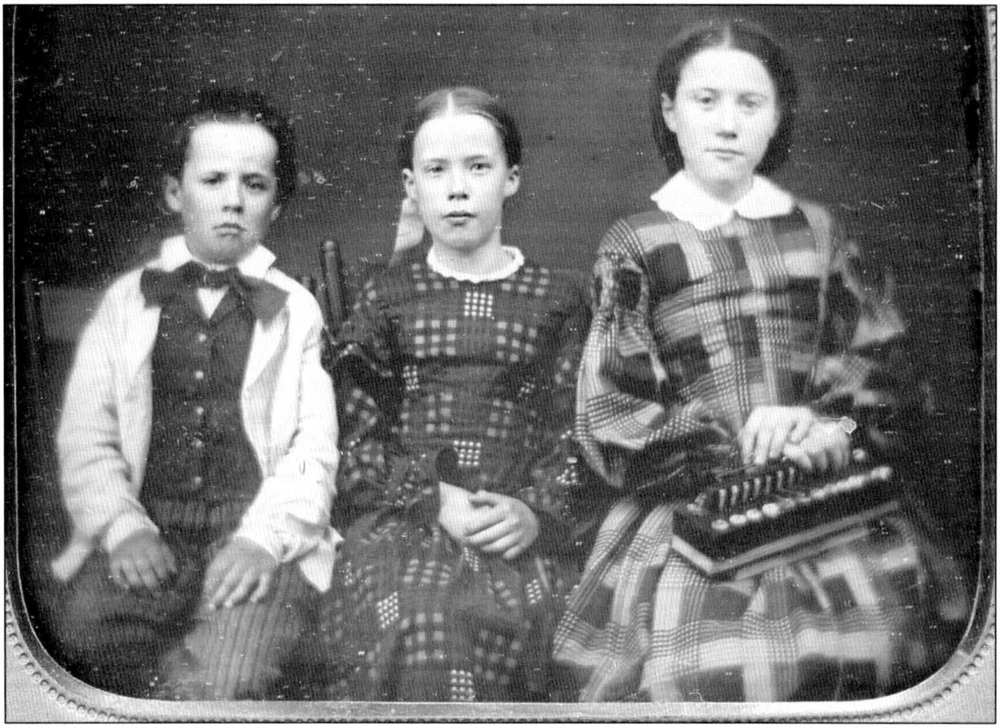

This daguerreotype is of Mary Westrope's two daughters, Annie and Nancy. It was taken around 1876 in Lyonsville, California, by an unknown photographer. Nancy Westrope married John Shelton of Lyonsville on November 5, 1882, and Annie married John's brother, Tom, on November 8, 1882. The girls' brother, Danny, shown, is the child who was killed when his horse bucked him off, which contributed to his mother Mary Hayton Westrope's death. He is buried next to his mother behind park headquarters at Mineral.

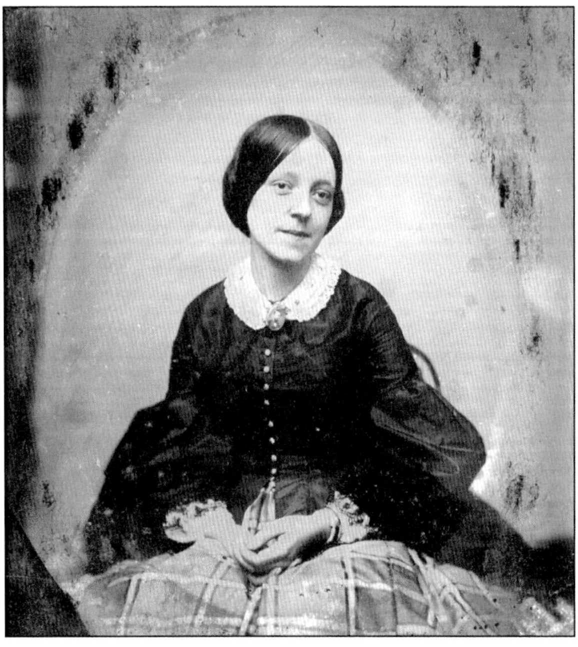

Sarah Cunningham was a half-sister to Mary Hayton Westrope and lived at Battle Creek (now Mineral) from 1860 to 1866. She rests in one of the graves in the park headquarters cemetery. Thelma Cadle Crandall, who died on May 17, 2005, at the age of 109, was one of the other 14 children born to Abraham and Samantha Cunningham at Plateau near Manton. (Courtesy Westrope Bible, *c.* 1843.)

Samuel Westrope was born in Grants Lick, Kentucky, on February 13, 1813, and was a cousin of Daniel Boone. Arriving in Chico, California, in 1864, Daniel did not fit into city life, so he sold the family's home and came to what is now Mineral. This image, taken in Kentucky before the family left for California, is more touch-up than photograph, as early photographers used charcoal to enhance images. It is the only existing one of Samuel.

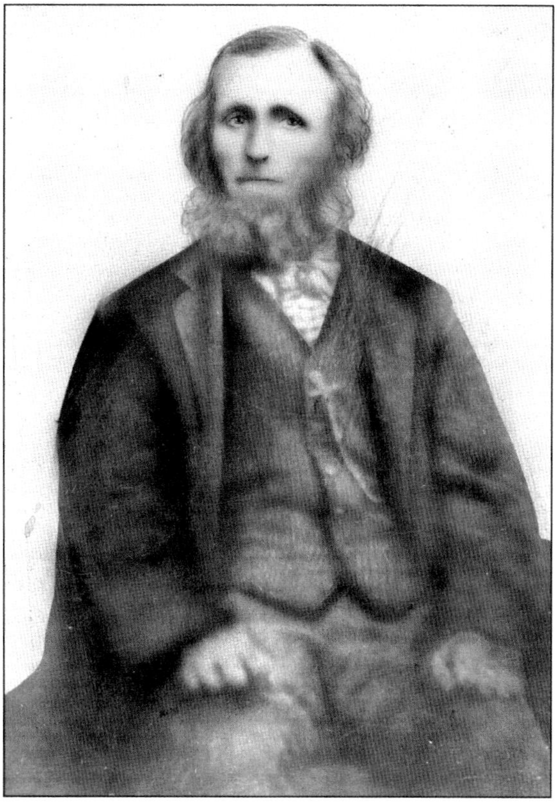

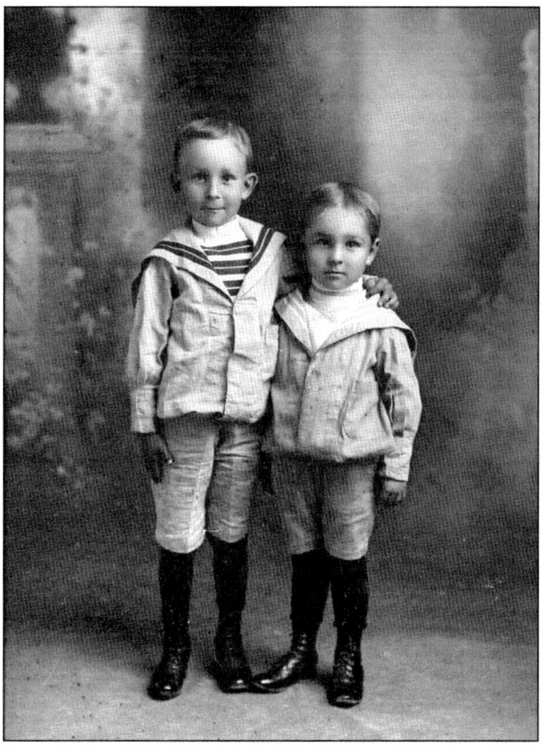

Alvie (left) and Jakie Olson are shown here at seven and four years old. They were lifelong summer residents of the park. They had witnessed the 1914 and 1915 eruptions as children and were hesitant to return to the area. This photograph was taken in 1914. All three of the Olson boys were nephews of the Hayton family from Illinois.

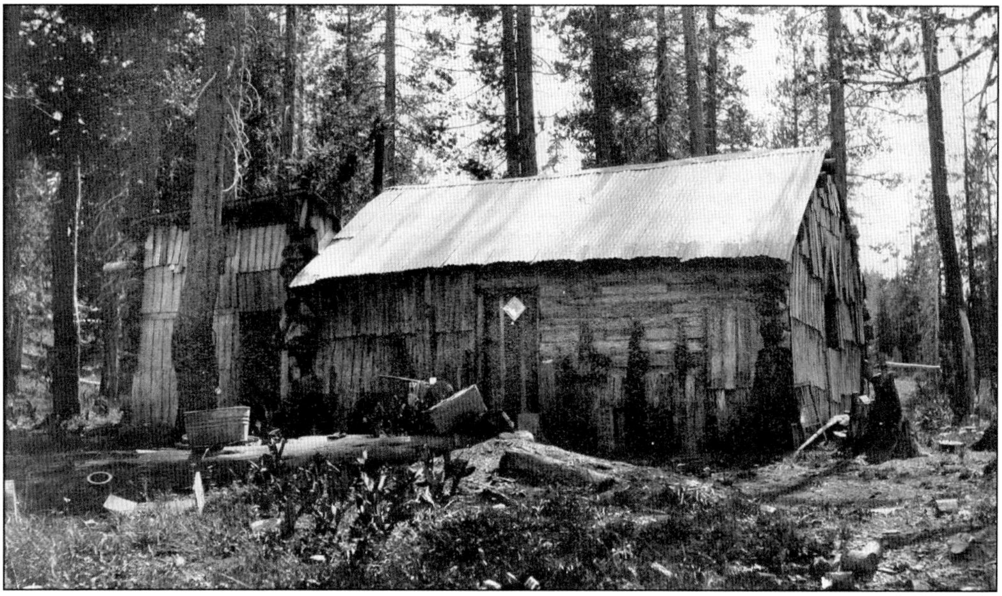

During the 1915 eruption, Alice Olson and neighbors were fishing on Summit Lake. As smoke and ash intensified, they were forced away from their cabins. Crossing a part of the already devastated area, they led their spooked animals and went to Lyonsville, not returning until the following spring. When Alice returned, they found it necessary to put a new roof on the cabin due to damage. The metal roof shown in this photograph was put on that year (1915), just eight months prior to receiving a letter from the Department of the Interior abolishing the homesteads and declaring the area a national park.

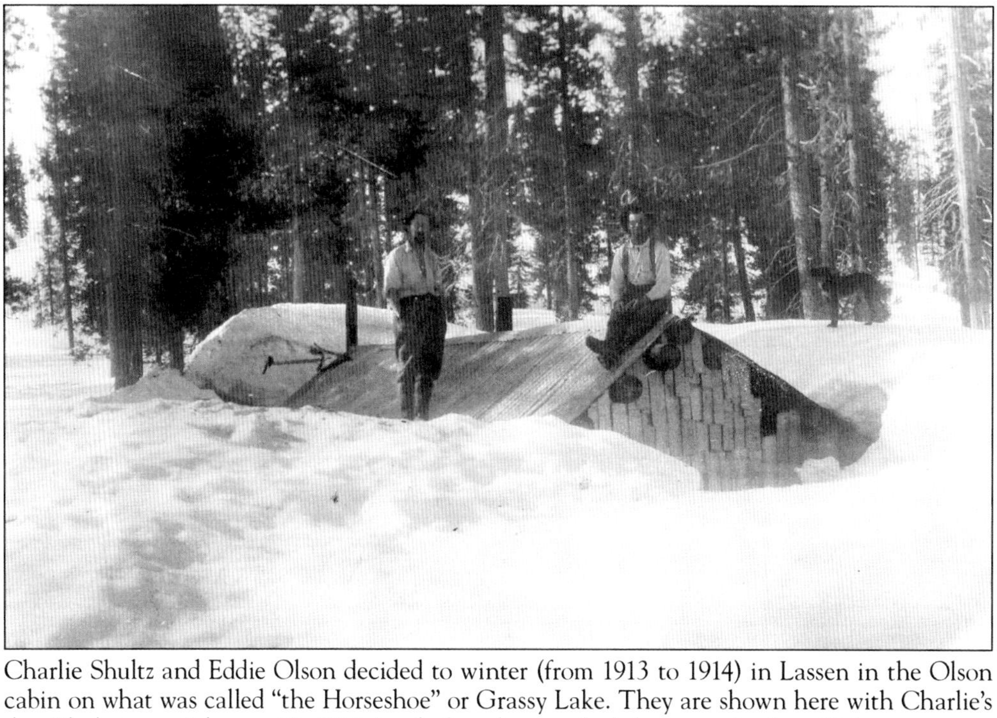

Charlie Shultz and Eddie Olson decided to winter (from 1913 to 1914) in Lassen in the Olson cabin on what was called "the Horseshoe" or Grassy Lake. They are shown here with Charlie's dog, Shultsie, on February 20, 1914, just before they marked the snow depth at 22 feet.

Charlie Shelton is pictured in 1904 with trout he caught in Jakie Lake. The lakes within park limits were full of large fish prior to the eruption. For years, a rumor circulated about a huge fish caught in Lake Helen that emerged from a fissure in the crater that connected to the lake. Supposedly when the fish had surfaced, it had no eyes, armor-plated scales, and was six feet long. It was preserved by taxidermy and was on display at a local business in Mineral; however, when anyone went asking about it, they could never seem to find it.

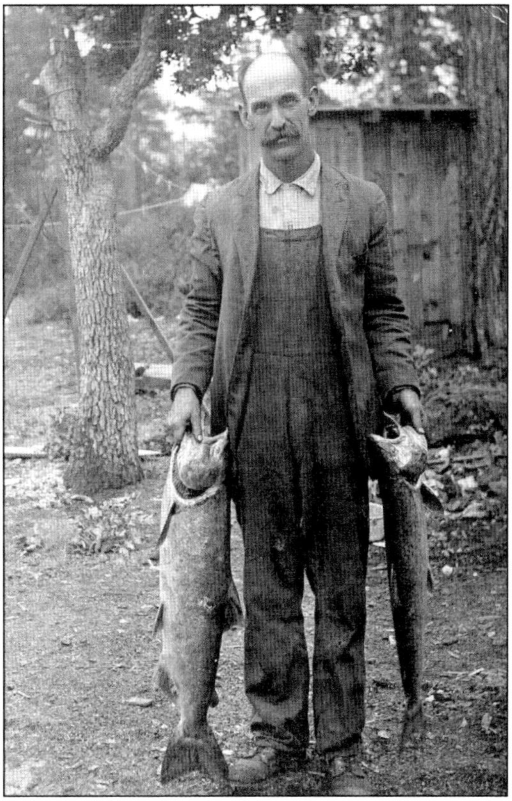

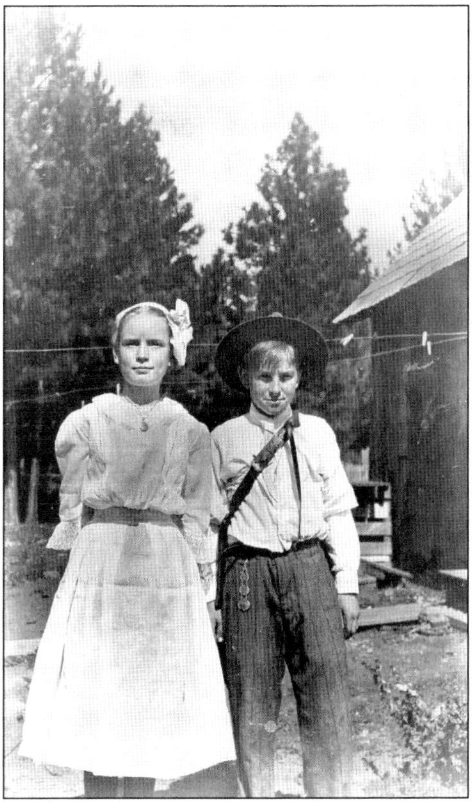

It was a lake near Horseshoe Lake that was first discovered by Daniel Severns and was eventually named for his great grandson, Jakie Olson. Shown here are Vera Severns and Jakie Olson around 1900. The Severns family had also been instrumental in homesteading within the park parameters and had a cabin in what would become Warner Valley.

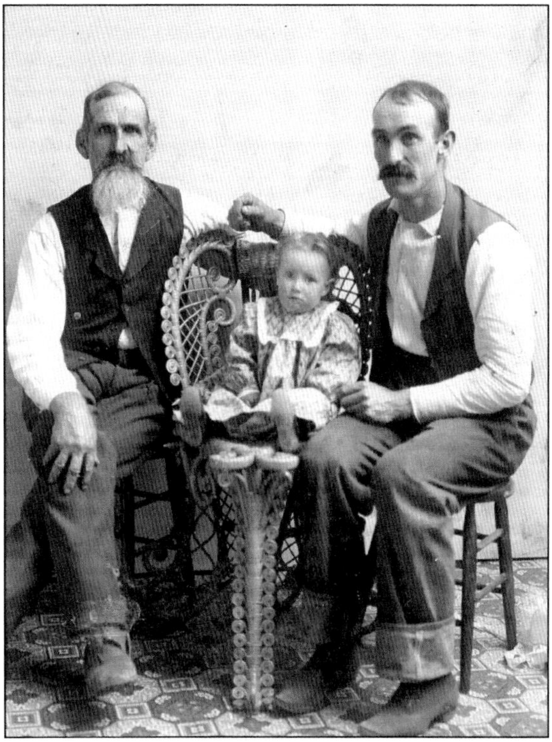

Shown here on the left is "Grandpa" Daniel Severns, who, in the early days of the settling of California, had come west to Truckee Meadows by way of Hastings cutoff. Plagued by Native Americans, he had little patience with them but never lifted a gun to shoot at one. Severns is shown with grandson Charles Shelton and Charles's nephew Alva Olson.

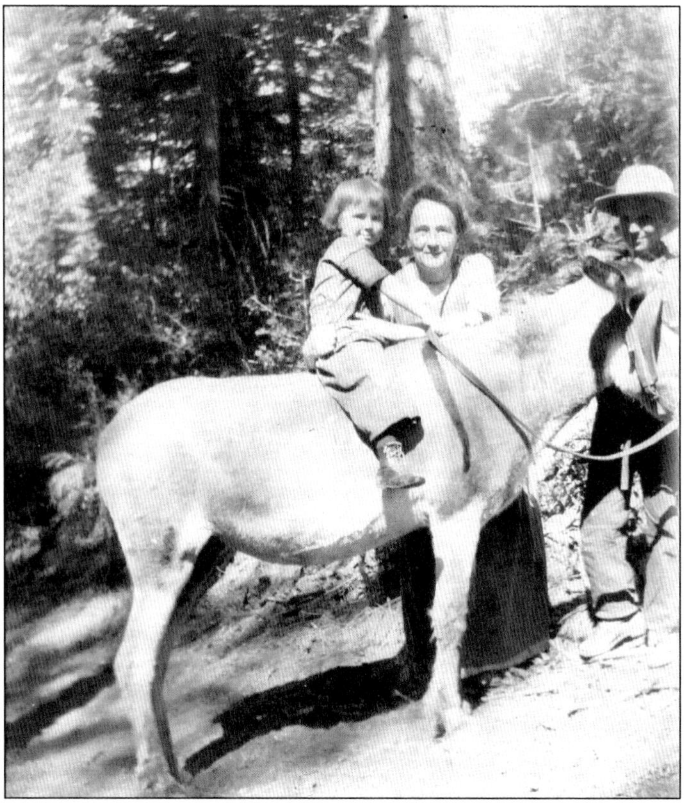

Mary Mae Bandy is pictured with daughter Ila Mae Bandy and son Tom on the steep and rocky trail that led up the slope to Lassen Peak. Mary is using her sister Alice's donkey. The Bandys, along with several other families, had shacks at various places along creeks or on shores of lakes and trails and joined the neighbor's homesteads with the Olsons.

The Spencer family children (pictured from left to right) Gale, Glen, and Glee lived part of the year in Lyonsville and spent summers at Lassen where the family maintained a cabin and ran cattle in pasture near Hidden Lake. Grassy Lake had a trail that led to the Olson homestead. Some Spencer graves are in the Belle Mill Cemetery at Lyonsville.

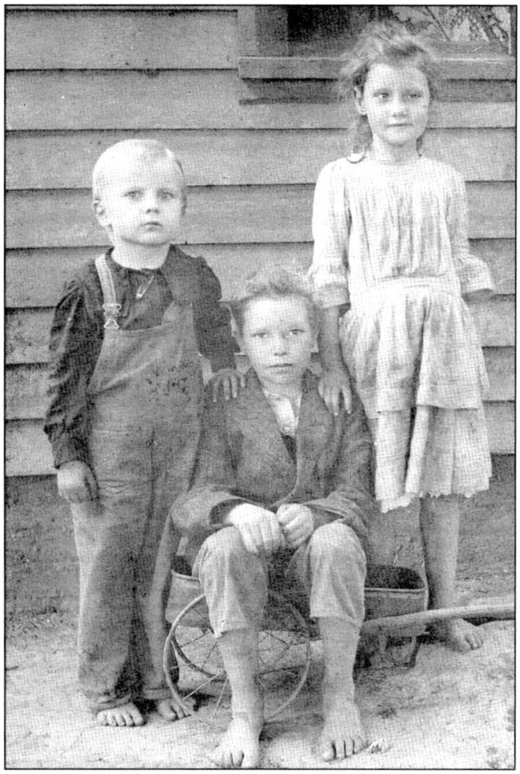

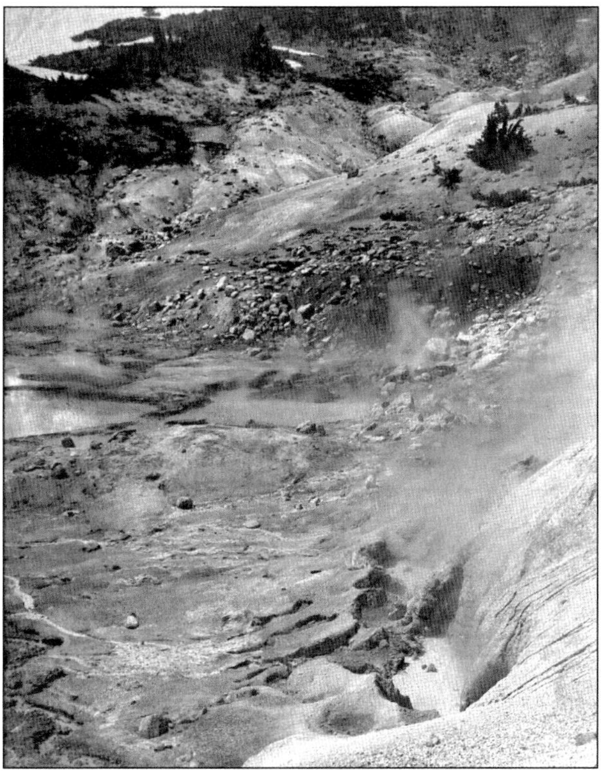

When this photograph was taken from the Bumpas Hell area, Mount Lassen was smoking in full force and, as can be seen, white ash was pushed up by the hot gases and flowed down over the lip of the crater like an avalanche. The mountain began a seven-year cycle, culminating in violent eruption. There were no lava flows, but intense heat triggered a mud flow and flood.

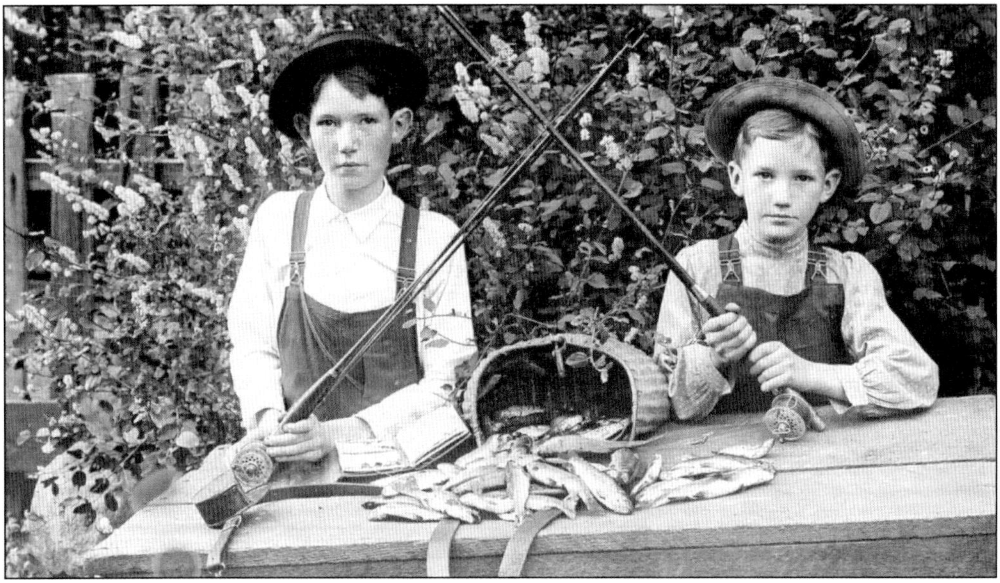

In 1915, fishing within the perimeters of Mount Lassen was unsuccessful. Shown with their catch of the day at Grassy Lake and not looking very happy are John and Walt Shelton. They are using a six-sided split bamboo pole made by several families in a shop at Lyonsville. The book by the creel, which John is proudly showing off, is actually a fly pouch with hand-tied flies made by his family.

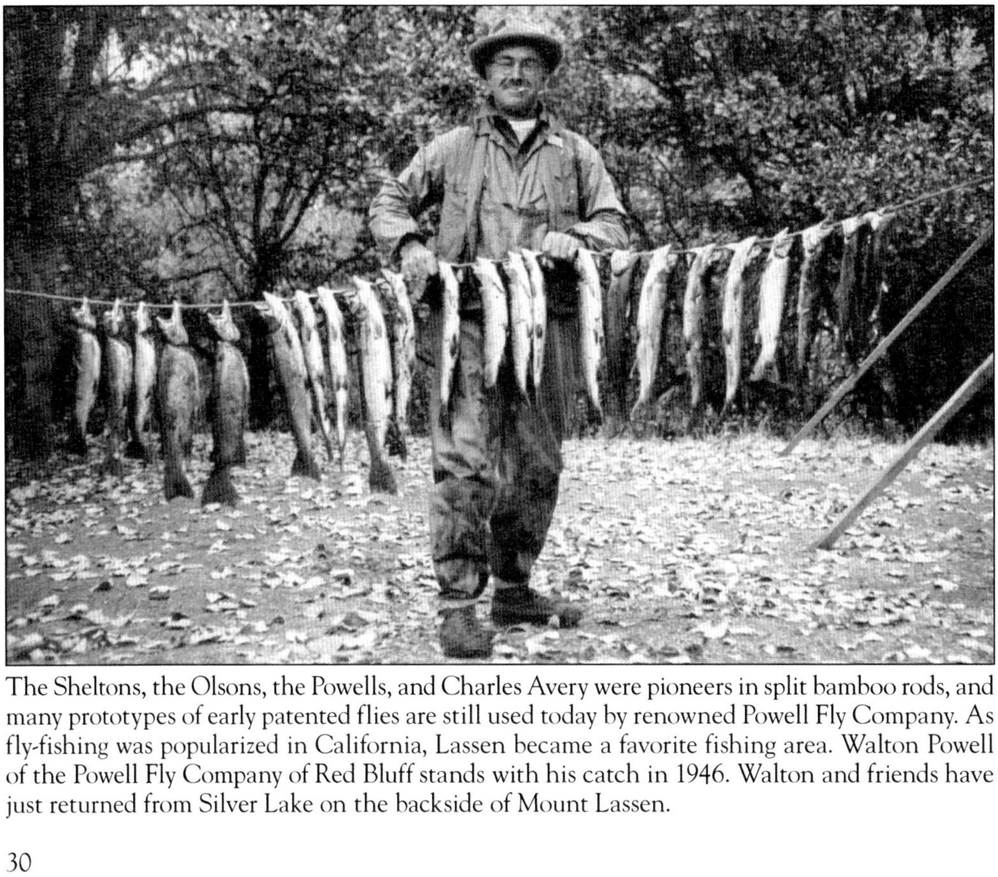

The Sheltons, the Olsons, the Powells, and Charles Avery were pioneers in split bamboo rods, and many prototypes of early patented flies are still used today by renowned Powell Fly Company. As fly-fishing was popularized in California, Lassen became a favorite fishing area. Walton Powell of the Powell Fly Company of Red Bluff stands with his catch in 1946. Walton and friends have just returned from Silver Lake on the backside of Mount Lassen.

Two

SETTLING OF THE HOGSBACK

FATCHS ROCK PILE

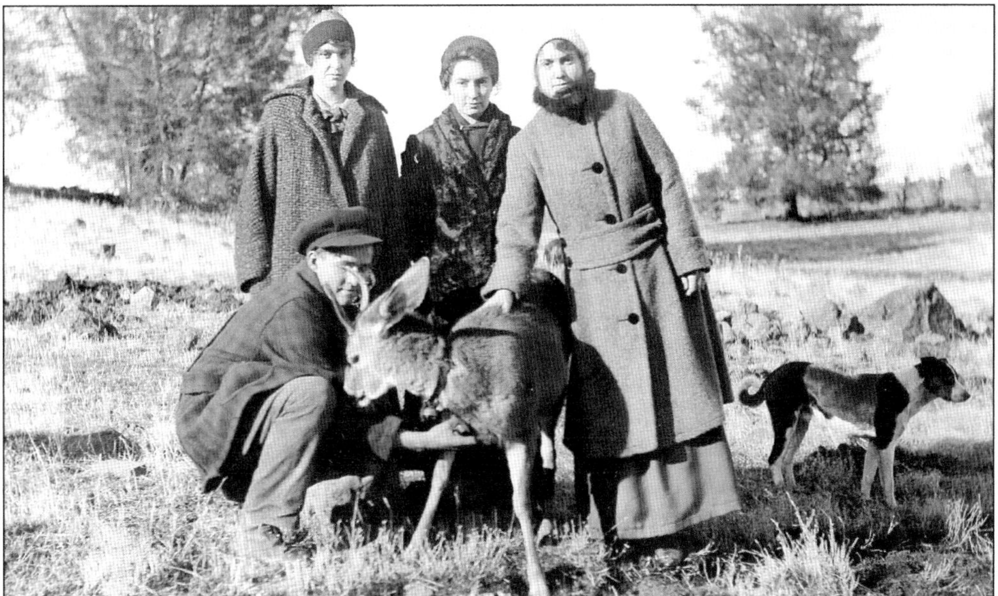

Fatchs Rock Pile was on the Hogsback Road a mile or two above Hog Lake and afforded the only water on the ridge from the Fatch home to Shakehouse Ravine, though only a spring and marshy area. Early on, the Fatch children were set to work stacking the rocks into circular piles that were used to secure fence posts. Travelers on the road gave early accounts of seeing the tattered and dirty children by the roadside stacking rocks for several years. The spelling of the families name varies on records, deeds varies, sometimes it is Facht or Fatch.

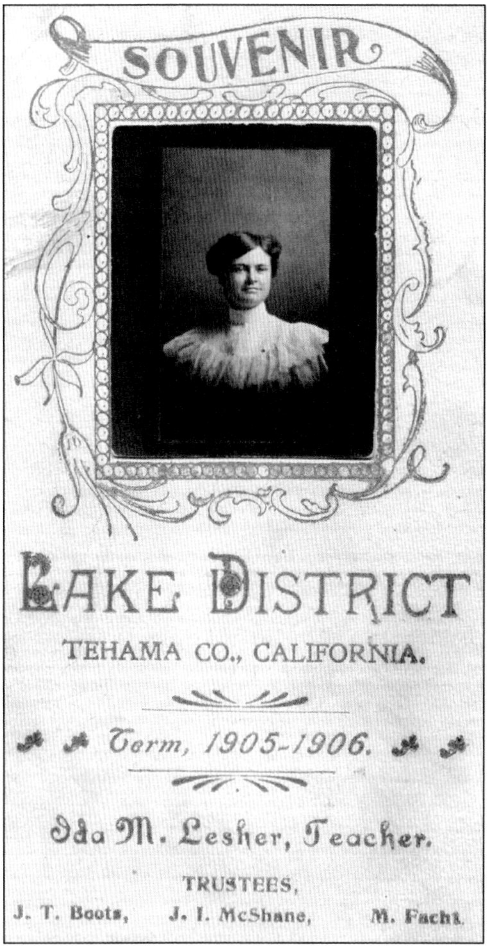

The Lake District of Tehama County hired Ida M. Lesher for the upper and lower grades in 1905–1906. School was rotated from Fachts to Halfway House to Finley Lake. The teacher generally boarded with a family in the vicinity of the nearest school. Parents served as the trustees for the schools. This souvenir card was issued at Fatchs School and belonged to Vera Fatch. Shown below are "Slim" and Ida Fatch.

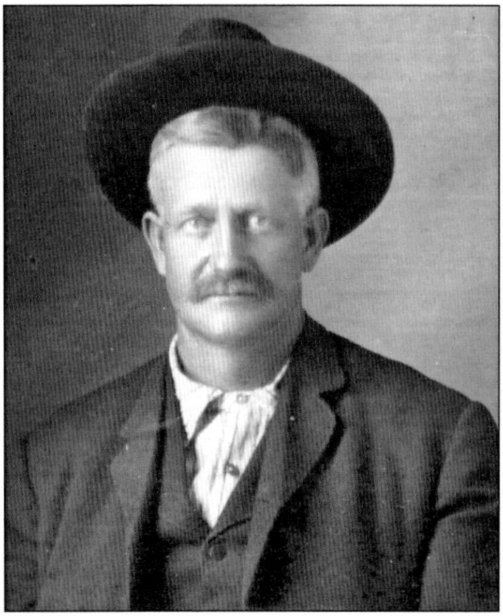

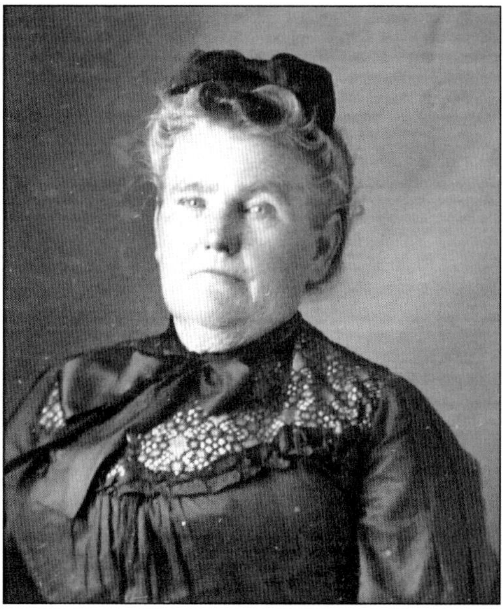

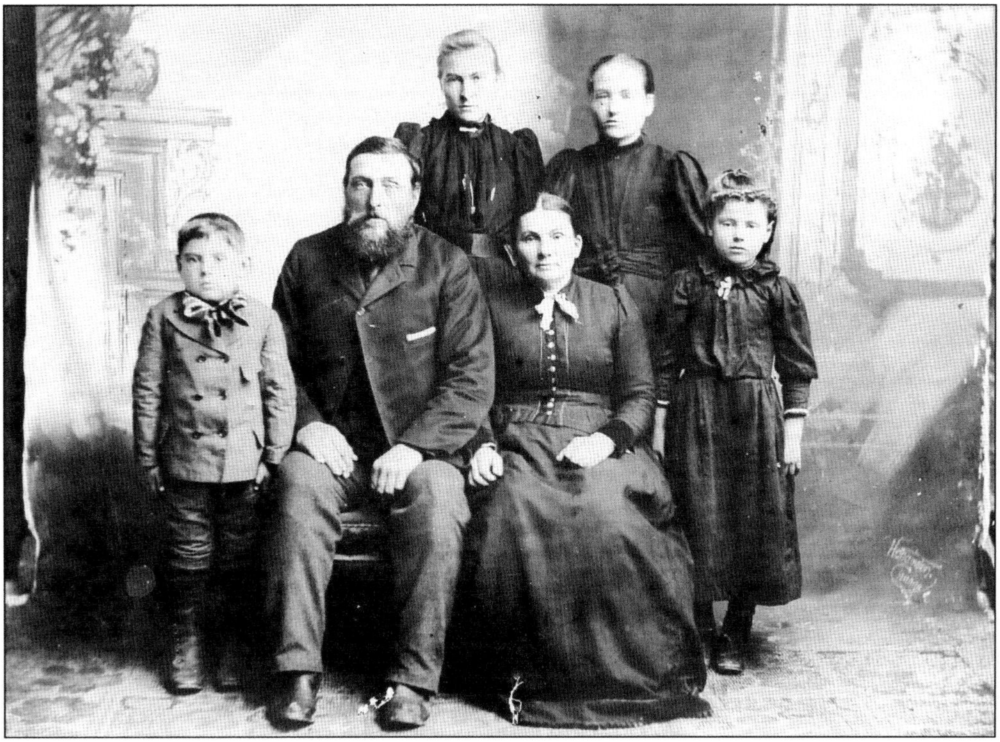

This photograph is of the Fatch family a few years after they settled the Rock Pile in 1903. Both of the Fatch parents served as trustees on the Lake District School Board.

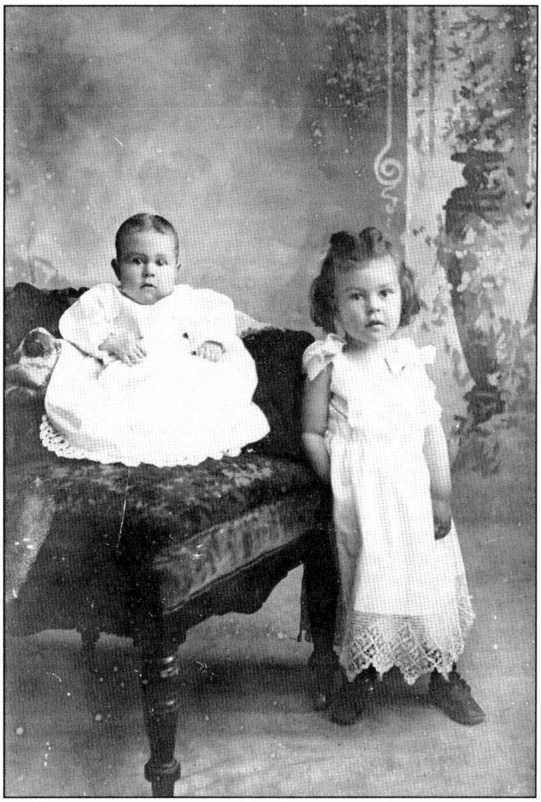

This photograph of the two oldest Fatch children, Tom and Vera, was taken by Reinhart Gallery of Red Bluff.

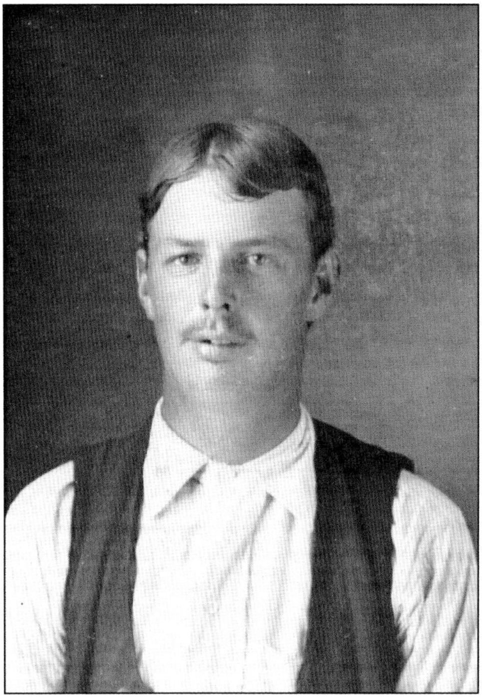

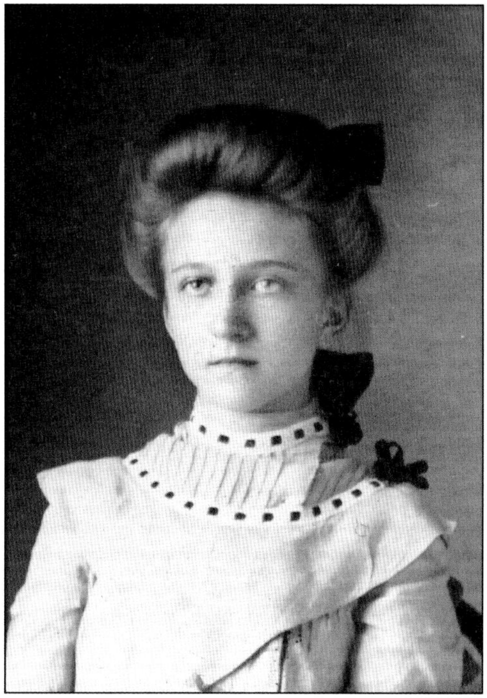

The Fatch family homesteaded at the Rock Pile in 1884 and possibly before. The family endured hardships because the scarcity of water and the hard, untillable soil. They remained on the Hogsback for 24 years. Seen above are Mike (left) and Eula Fatch. Pictured below are Emily (left) and Vera Fatch, taken in 1886.

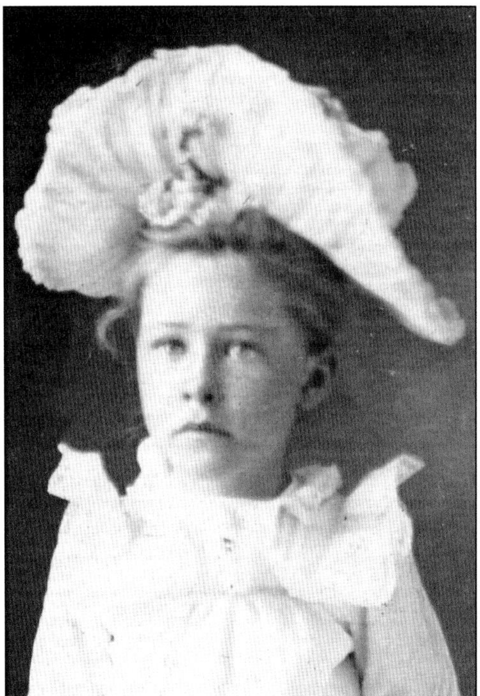

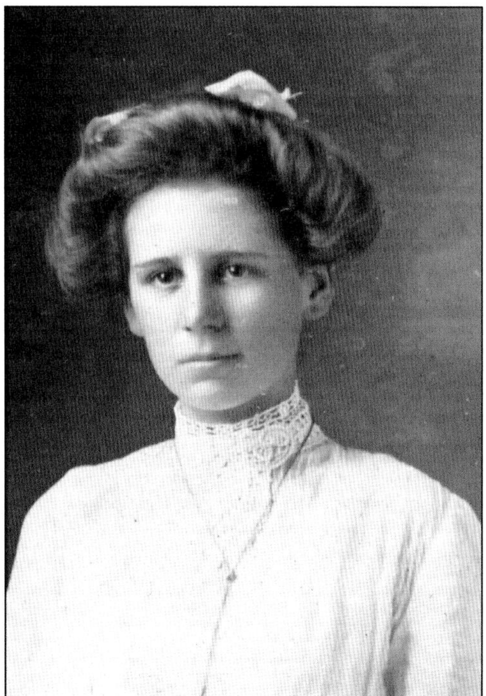

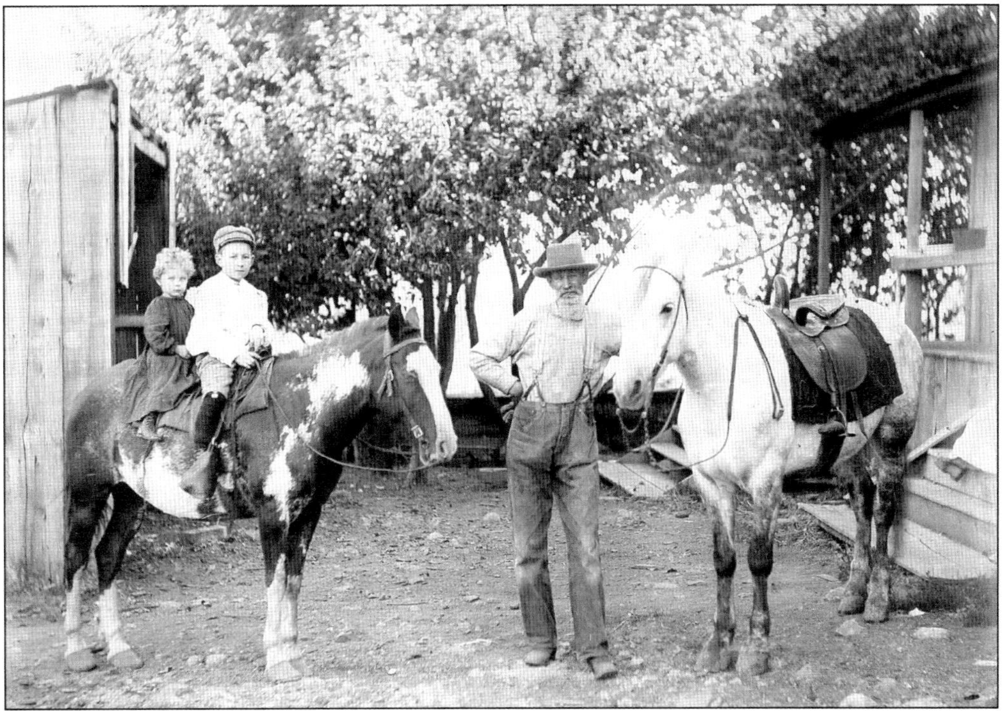

Halfway between Red Bluff and Lyonsville, a way station was built by Adolf and Alice Olson and was later run by Leander Myers. Here Jakie Olson (on horse) is being led by his grandfather James Emory Gray in the corral that attached to the way station.

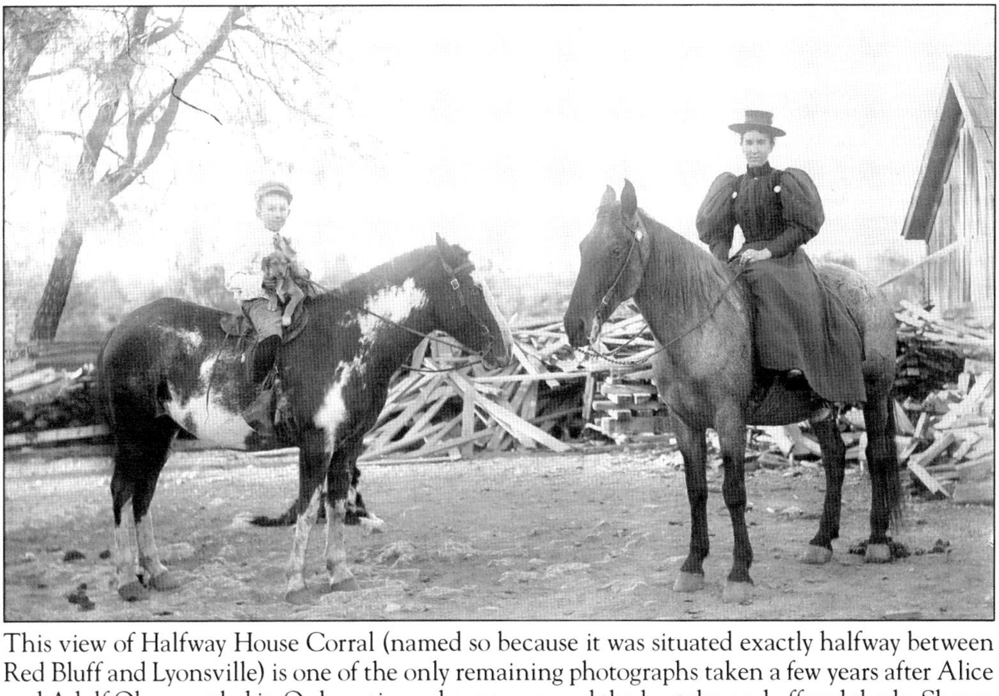

This view of Halfway House Corral (named so because it was situated exactly halfway between Red Bluff and Lyonsville) is one of the only remaining photographs taken a few years after Alice and Adolf Olson settled it. Only native oaks grew around the hostelry and offered shade. Shown here are Eddie Olson (with dog) and Alice Olson.

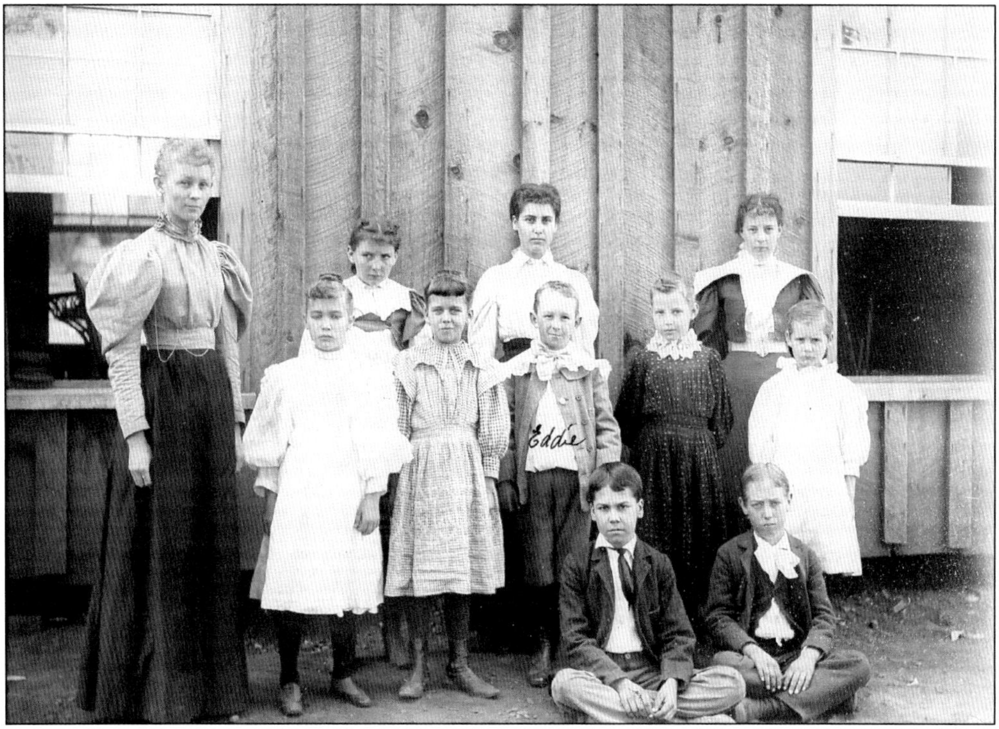

The school at the Halfway House was an afterthought, built three years after the way station. A town was never planned because water had to be hauled in most of the year. Some water was piped from the flume at night. It served the 12 students Alice Olson and Florence Tolley taught.

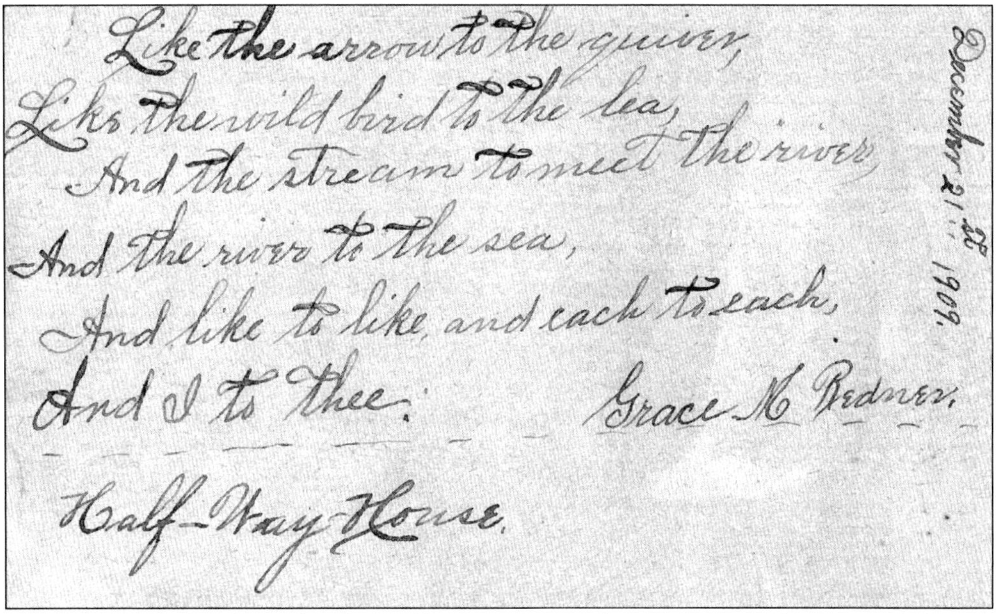

Like the arrow to the quiver,
Like the wild bird to the sea,
And the stream to meet the river,
And the river to the sea,
And like to like, and each to each,
And I to thee. Grace M Redner.

Half-Way House.

December 21st 1909.

Many people lived and stayed at the Halfway House over the years it existed. A guest book, kept by Alice Olson, eventually burned with the building, but many autograph albums survived that were kept mostly by children. This page is from the album of Grace Redner and was written by Angie Shelton of Lyonsville.

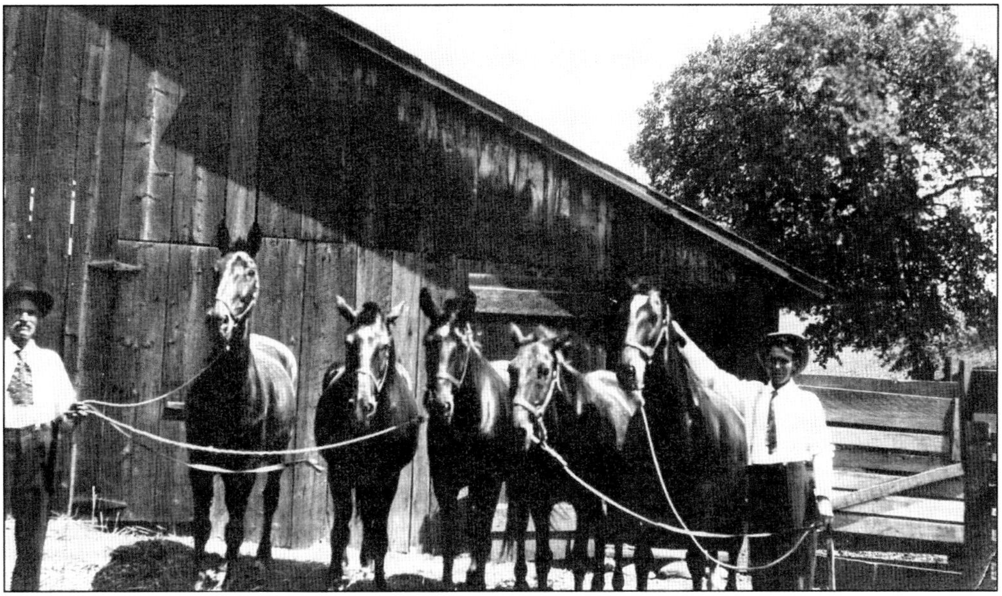

The livery barn at the Halfway House was very large and could hold an entire stagecoach complete with horses. The barn sat across the road from the house and in wet weather afforded passengers a dry place to unload.

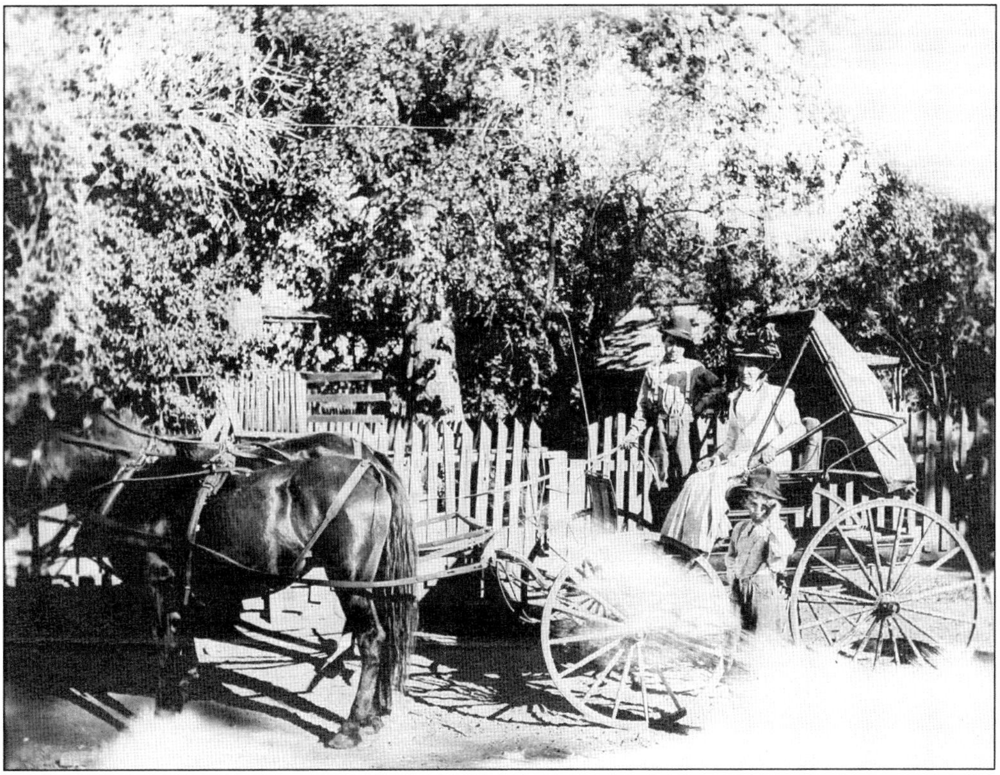

The Halfway House, originally built in 1886 before the town of Lyonsville to aid travelers on the road to Big Meadows, was constructed by Adolf and Alice Olson. Shown here from left to right are Alva, Jakie, and Alice.

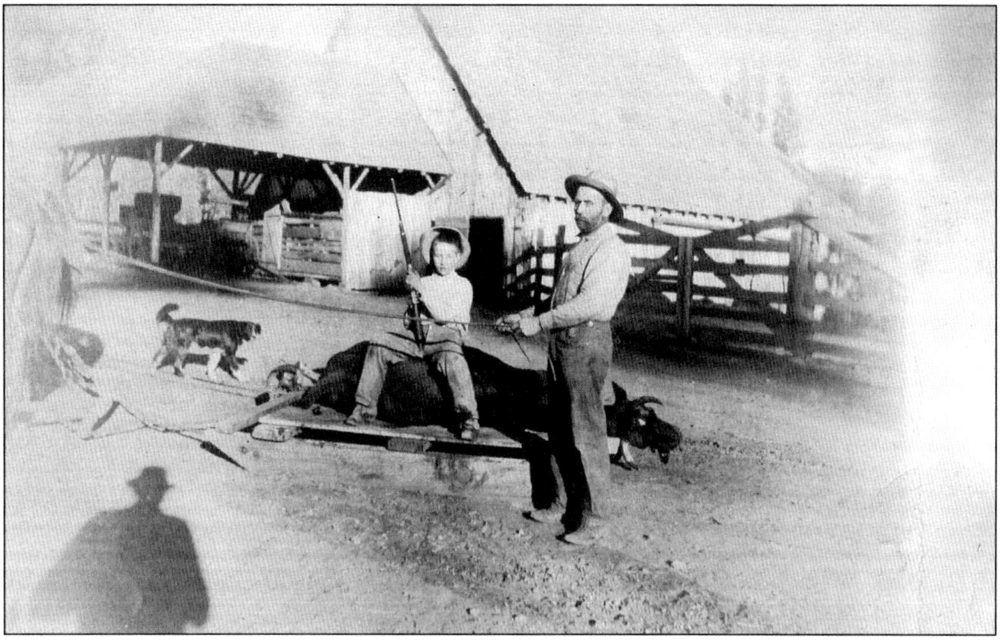

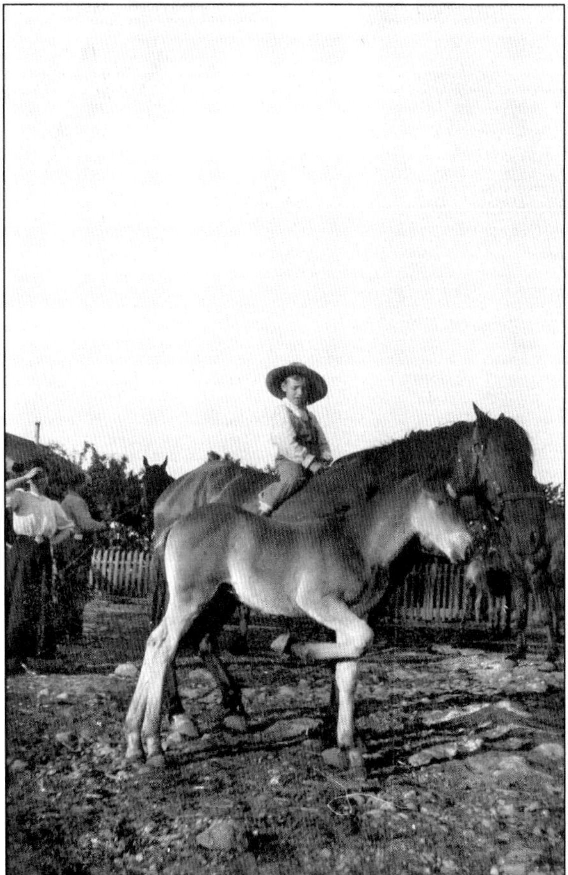

Adolf and Eddie Olson are pictured in the barnyard at the Halfway House with the slaughterhouse in the background. The Olson's raised all their own meat for guests and family. They also maintained a sheep herd at Finley Lake and a corral at Lyonsville.

Mike Fatch is pictured on horseback at Halfway House with Mr. and Mrs. Fatch at left. Mr. Fatch periodically drove stages and is hitching a fresh team up in the background. Also shown is Eddie Olson's pet colt.

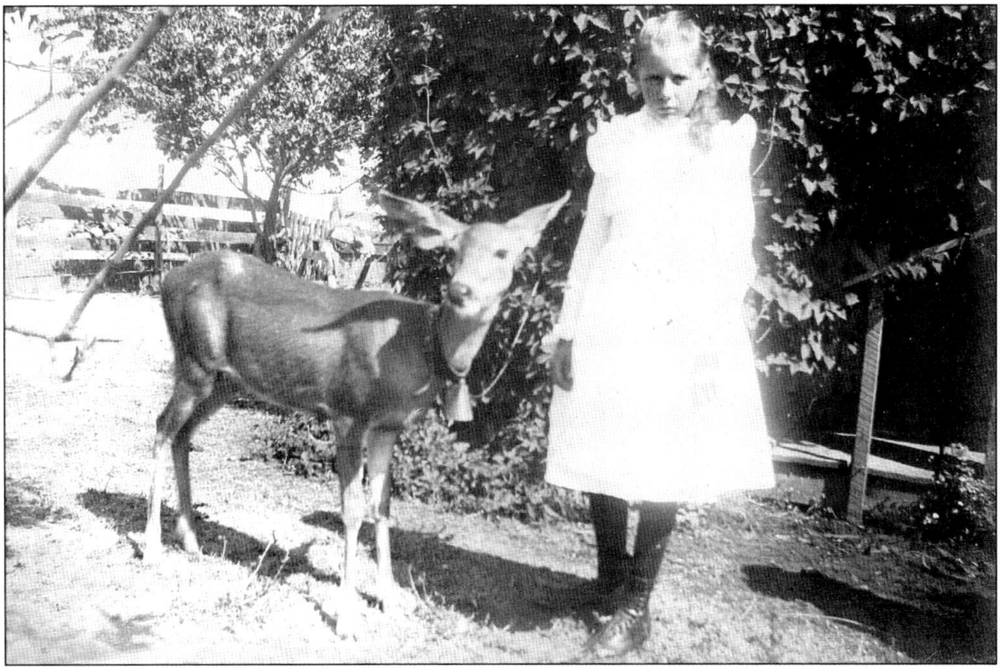

Vera Fatch is shown with Alice Olsen's pet deer at the Halfway House in 1892. This is in the side yard nearest Red Bluff. No matter how desolate and rocky, Alice Olson always maintained a patch of lawn, garden, and hops for Adolf's Swedish beer.

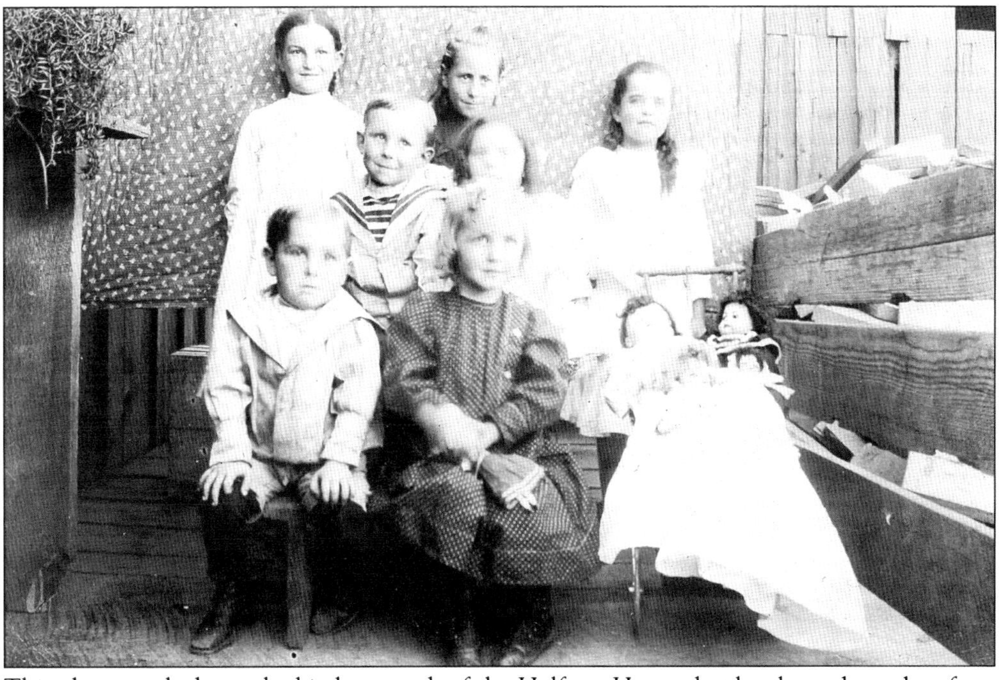

This photograph shows the kitchen porch of the Halfway House that has been dressed up for a children's photograph. Pictured from left to right are (first row) Jakie Olson and Edith Engebretsen; (second row) Alva Olson and Annie Engebretsen; (third row) Vera Severn, Vera Fatch, and Grace Redner.

> Word was received here about 2 o'clock Friday afternoon that the Half Way House, situated on the Lyonsville road, nineteen miles from this place, had been burned between the hours of 12 and 1 that day.
>
> The fire is reported to have been started by the explosion of a coal oil lamp which a lady friend of Mrs. Olson had lighted and left burning in a room while she went out for a short time.
>
> The burning embers from the house were blown by the strong wind into the dry grass north of the house and in a short time a raging grass and brush fire was raging and burning rapidly towards Paynes creek.
>
> – Daily News, July 14, 1901

The Halfway House fire caused a great loss to many travelers. While the station was rebuilt, visitors lingered in tents in the shade. The Myers family, cousins of the Olsons, oversaw the reconstruction. The Olson's relocated their business to Lyonsville.

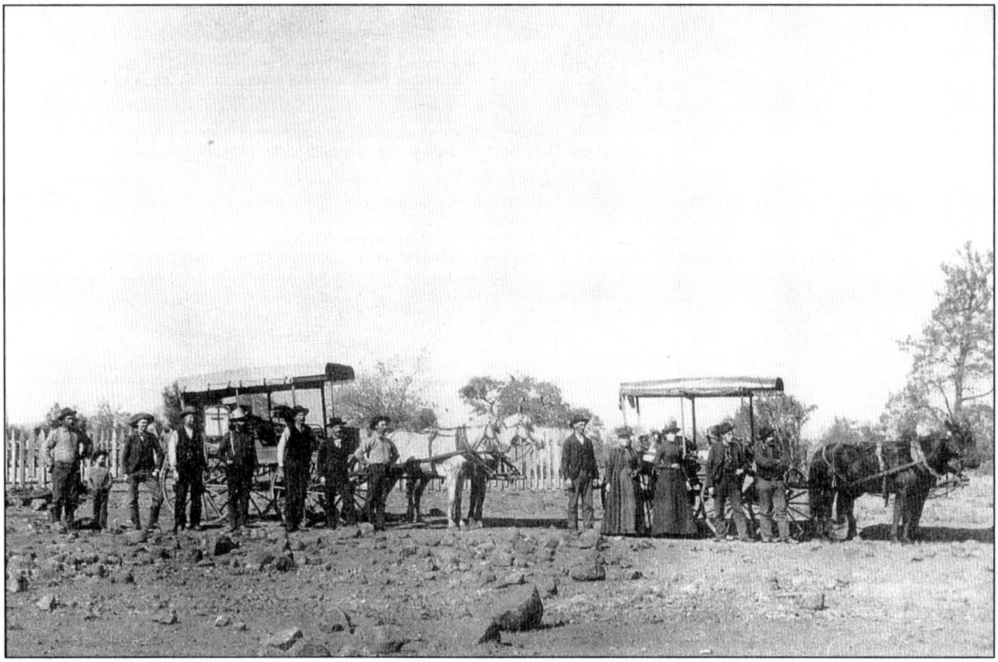

The Halfway House was a way station set up by Alice Olson to serve travelers en route to Lyonsville and points north. It offered hot meals, rooms, and cold evening showers with water from the Sierra Lumber Company's flume. Here travelers unload from stages. (Photograph courtesy of Opal Mendenhall.)

KNAUSS RANCH

Sara Jane Knauss and family built a homestead on the Hogsback around 1900, but the family maintained a home in Lyonsville also. They first intended to flume water and raise produce to sell, but after a small patch of land was cleared of many rocks for an orchard, it was abandoned along with the building, which was dismantled and rebuilt as a barn at the Halfway House. Shown here is Sara Jane with grandson Tom Gosney.

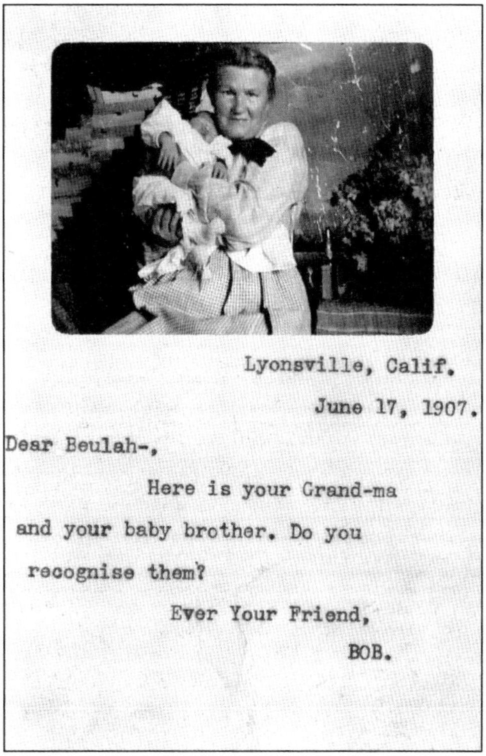

Lyonsville, Calif.
June 17, 1907.

Dear Beulah-,

Here is your Grand-ma and your baby brother. Do you recognise them?

Ever Your Friend,

BOB.

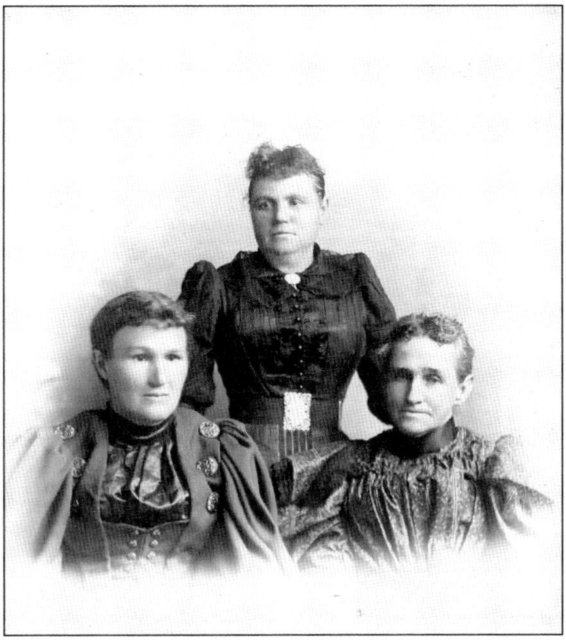

The Knauss family figured prominently in the founding of the town of Lyonsville. Many early maps of Tehama County show sections of land owned by the Knauss family. Sara Jane was younger than her husband, and when Mr. John Knauss died, she became a shrewd property manager. Sara Knauss is shown here with Jane Barbar (back) and Letha Jane Shelton.

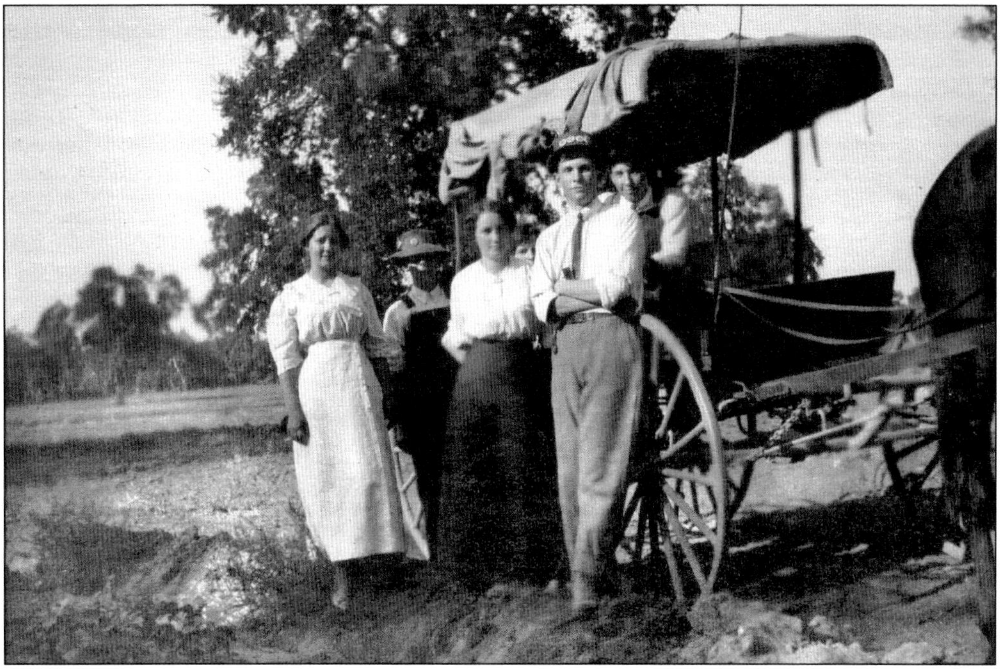

This is the stage at the Knauss's ranch on the Hogsback. The July 8, 1906, view shows, from left to right, Eula Fatch, Jakie Olson, Vera Fatch, Tom Fatch, and Alva Olson (the person in rear is unknown). Stages ran twice daily for many years up the Hogsback Road with passengers and mail.

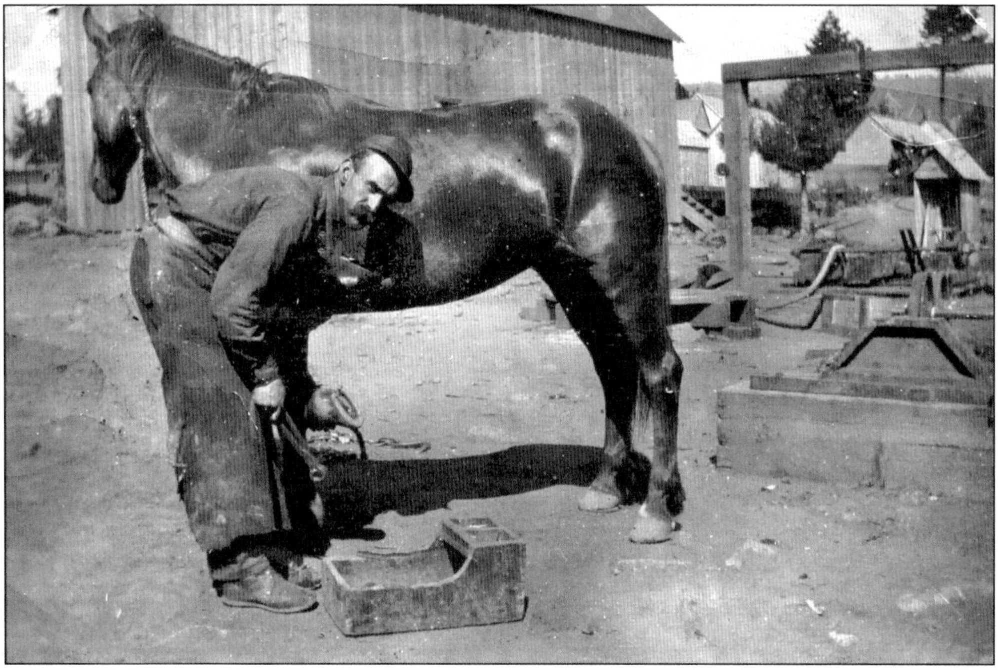

Charles Shelton was head blacksmith for the town of Lyonsville and surrounding homesteads and ranches. Shown at Champion Mill "Charlie," as Shelton was affectionately called, was the blacksmith for the Knauss Ranch. The blacksmith was one of the most important members of the community and figuratively held the town and the mill together with spit and bailing wire.

Three

Shakehouse Ravine and Surrounding Area

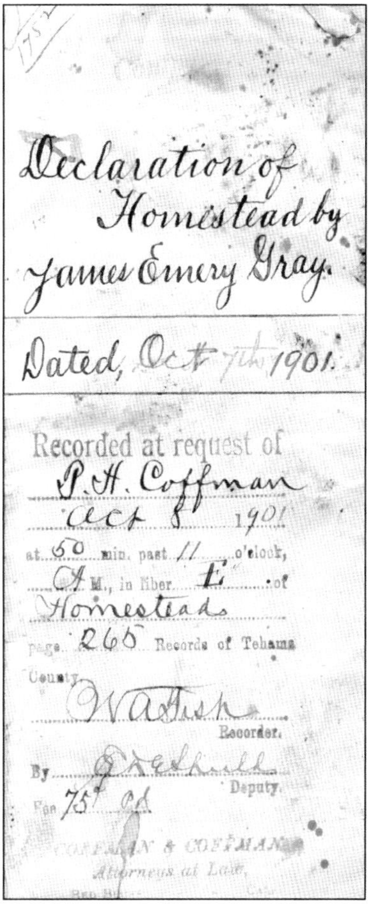
Declaration of Homestead by James Emery Gray.
Dated, Oct 7th 1901.
Recorded at request of P. H. Coffman Oct 8 1901 at 50 min. past 11 o'clock, A M., in liber E of Homesteads page 265 Records of Tehama County.
W A Fish Recorder.
By Deputy.
Fee 75 cts
Coffman & Coffman Attorneys at Law.

From the Halfway House, the trail proceeded slowly up the slope of the Hogsback and flattened out just above Shakehouse Ravine. Homesteading here in 1901 after living on the property for 20 years prior, James and Hannah Gray were often plagued by plundering Native Americans. The first frame building (the Gray House) was built in 1886 and replaced a log cabin that sat in the ravine itself. A present-day Christmas tree farm occupies the land, and the second Gray House was built where the original Native American trail from Black Rock crossed the ridge. The new Gray House, built in 1903 with water tower and outbuildings, still exists today on the site. An old abandoned Pelton wheel was removed from the creek long ago. James Gray had originally covered his log cabin with hand-split sugar pine shakes in 1880, and the name Shakehouse Ravine was given.

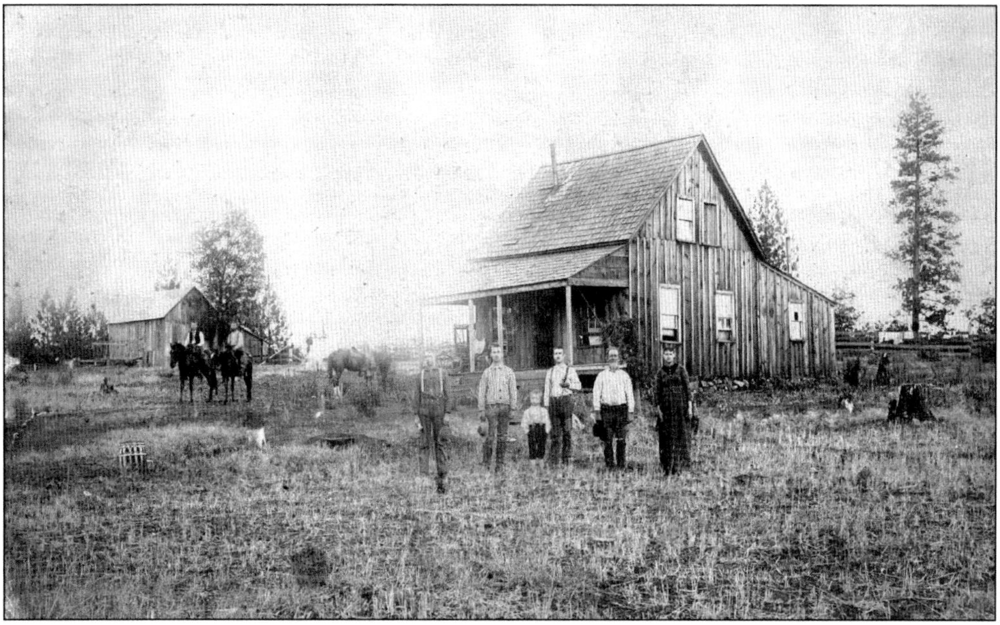

Shakehouse Ravine, which was the cut-off to Mill Creek and Black Rock (also called Jackrabbit Ridge), was the homestead of James Emory Gray. Shown are the Apperson boys with James and Hannah Gray. James had built the rude cabin in 1896 over the previous Bryan family cabin site and declared homestead in 1901. James met his death by Native American arrows near the Turner Ranch and is buried in Lyonsville Cemetery.

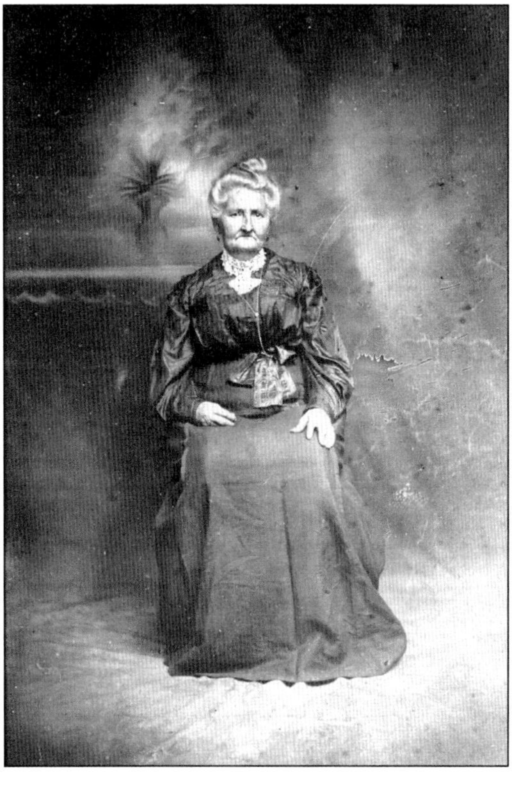

Years later, James and Hannah built a new house and water tower. When Hannah saw this print taken by traveling photographer Valentine the Rambler, she was so appalled she spit tobacco on it and threw it on the floor. Deathly afraid of Native Americans after being abducted at a young age, her shotgun was never far away. Hannah was the daughter of William Gurnsey and Miranda Parsons.

Though she claimed not to have a surname prior to marrying Madison V. Shelton, Emma Redwing was the daughter of Hannah Gurnsey Gray. Hannah had been abducted and held hostage for a year by Native Americans before escaping by gaining her captors's trust. Emma Redwing divorced Shelton in 1909 and returned to live for many years in Mill and Deer Creek Canyons.

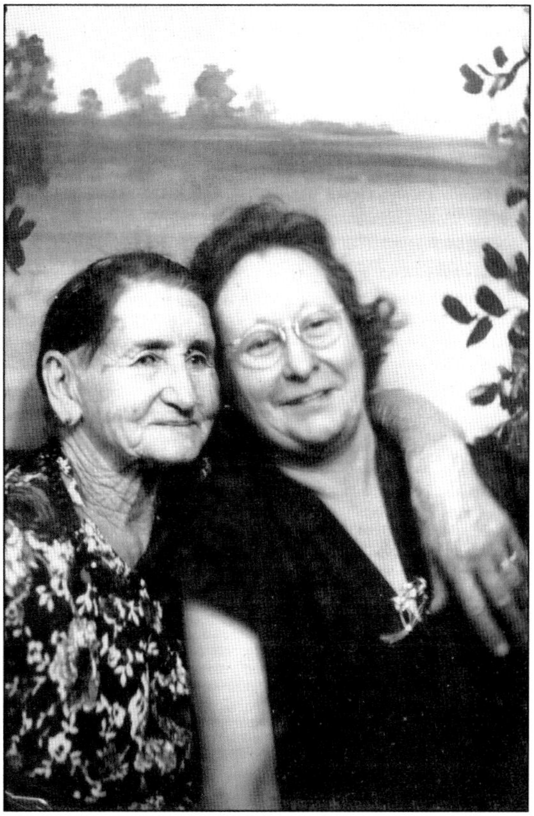

The original Gump place sat in the gulch where today's California State Department of Forestry Correctional Facility is located. Mr. Gump worked in Lyonsville as a sawyer at the Champion Mill. The John Gumps were friends of William and Miranda Gurnsey and the James Grays.

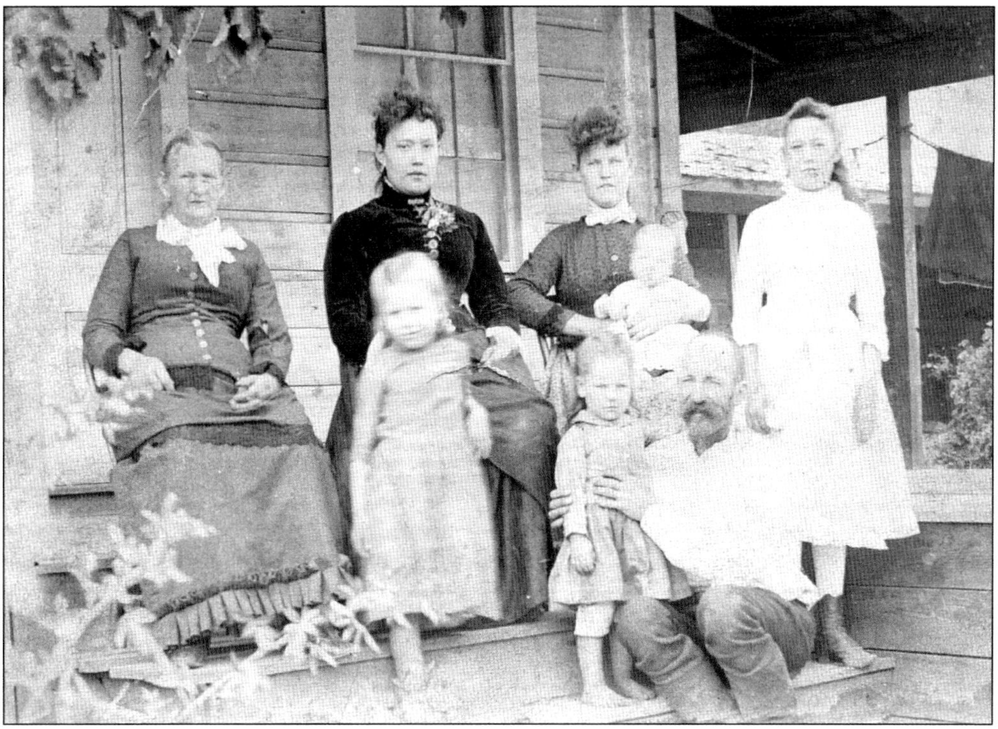

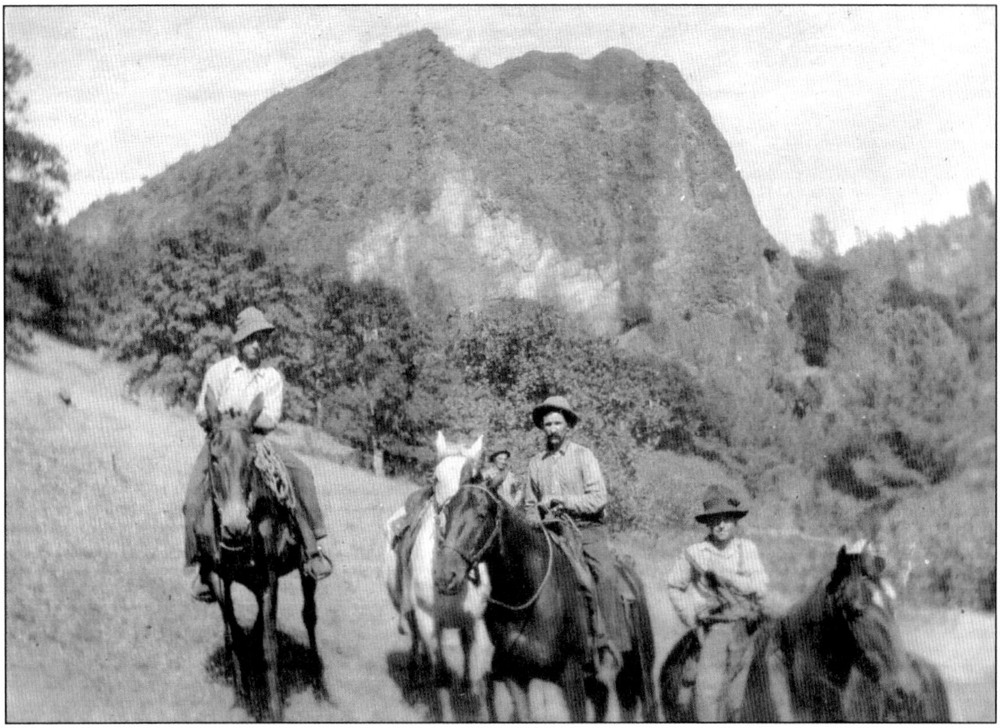

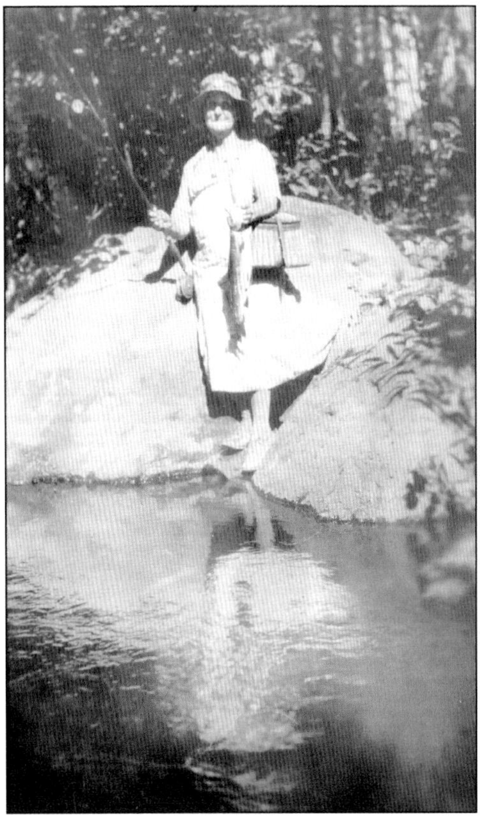

The famous pinnacle of Mill Creek, Black Rock, appears in the background. Here the Apperson boys and the Olsons have broken camp and returned to Deer Creek. A long-lost notebook found under a staircase in a crate at the University of California, Berkeley, attests to many more facts of the Ishi Expedition than had been known before.

The trout-rich waters of Mill Creek were called *wasadula* by the Native Americans, meaning "wild waters." Here Alice Olson poses with a fish she caught in 1935. She was an early fly tier, and fishing until she was in her 90s, Alice maintained a round pond in her backyard in Red Bluff stocked with trout and covered by a buggy wheel lined with chicken wire to keep the raccoons out.

Avid fishermen, the Olsons were lifelong anglers of Mill, Deer, and Antelope Creeks. Here Jakie Olson fishes the lower south fork of Antelope Creek in 1912. Long evenings were spent tying flies by kerosene lamp at Charles Avery's cabin in Mill Creek Canyon. The Sheltons, Powells, and Averys also fashioned 12-foot Bamboo and split-Bamboo rods, which were the forerunners of today's famous bamboos.

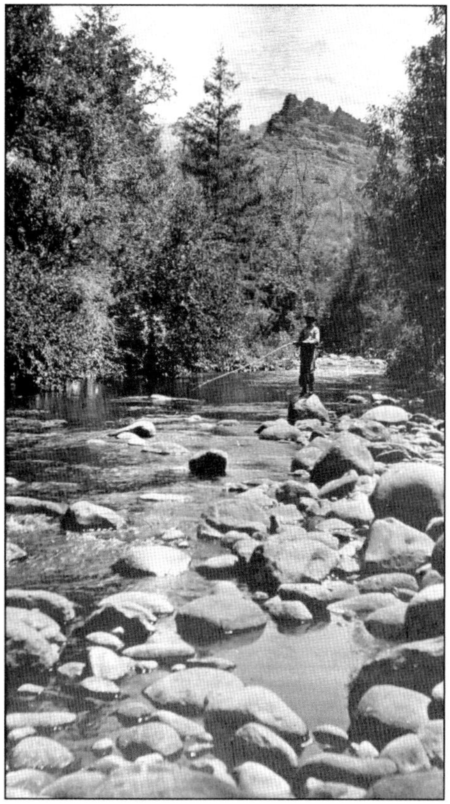

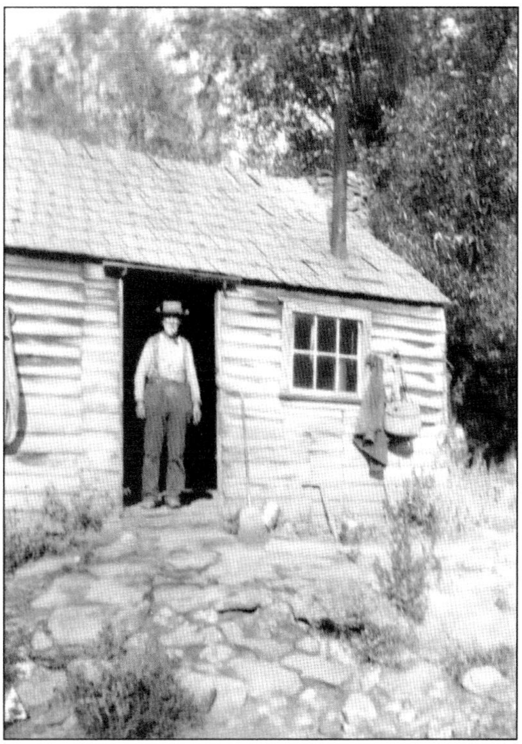

Charles H. Avery, a doctor, lived in Pine Flat in Mill Creek Canyon, but also maintained a home in Red Bluff. Charles never had a wife, but did have a son, Charles Jr. Charles Sr. was a cousin to the Shelton family, and after his death in his cabin, his certificate and license to practice medicine, tattered and yellowed, was found in a trunk.

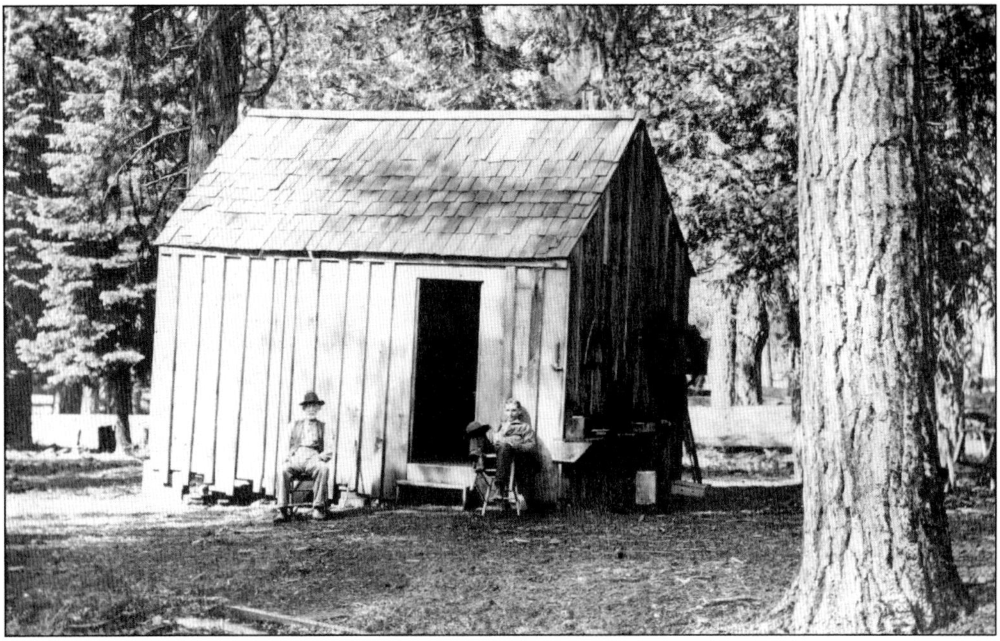

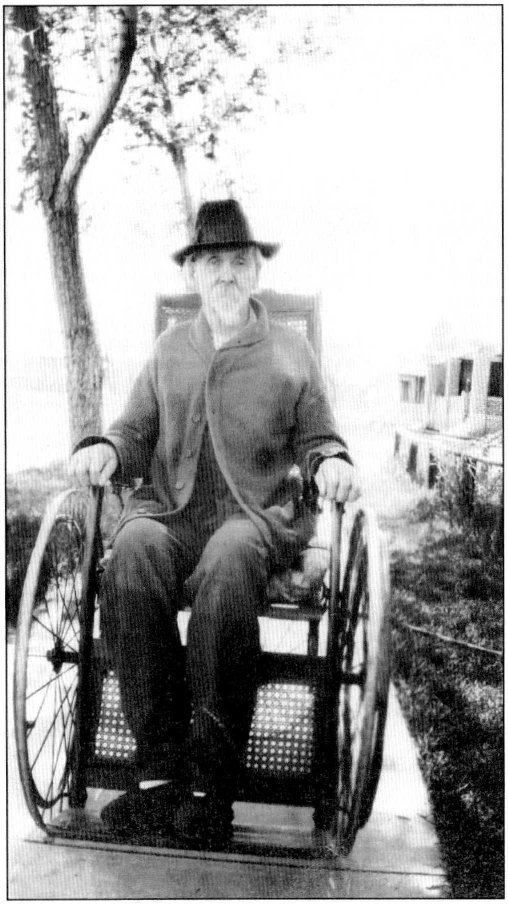

Charles Avery Sr. and Charles Jr. enjoy a relaxing day in front of their other cabin in Deer Creek Canyon. Often plundered while he was away, remnants of his cabin still remain today but are rotting away rapidly. It was located near upper Deer Creek Flats and was near the Cunningham cabin.

Elijah "Lije" Graham, shown in Red Bluff, lived more than half a century in Mill Creek Canyon. Disgusted by Native Americans looting his cabin, Graham left poisoned flour and tainted whiskey for thieves. Graham is buried only a few feet from his beloved cabin, although his gravestone disappeared in 1950. A saw filer and welder, when Frank's leg was amputated, he took his welding torch and fashioned a new peg leg.

Plagued by Native Americans, Lije Graham would often leave his cabin by night and spend the entire night and next day on a steep rim of the canyon far above, constantly on the watch. It is unknown whether he had ever killed a Native American; he constantly hoped to get a shot at them. Shown here is the old Graham cabin after Native Americans had supposedly destroyed it.

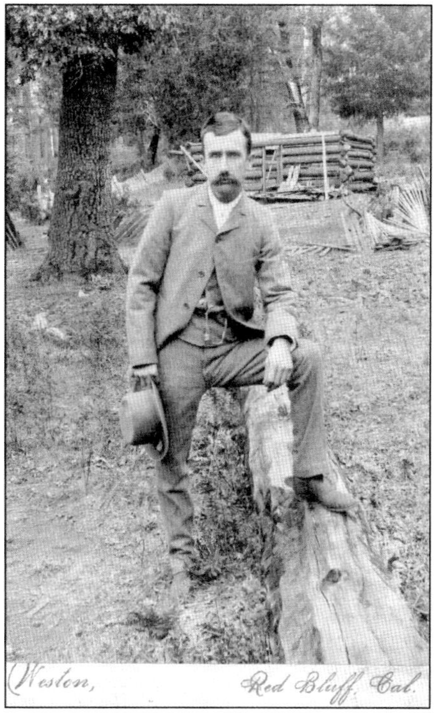

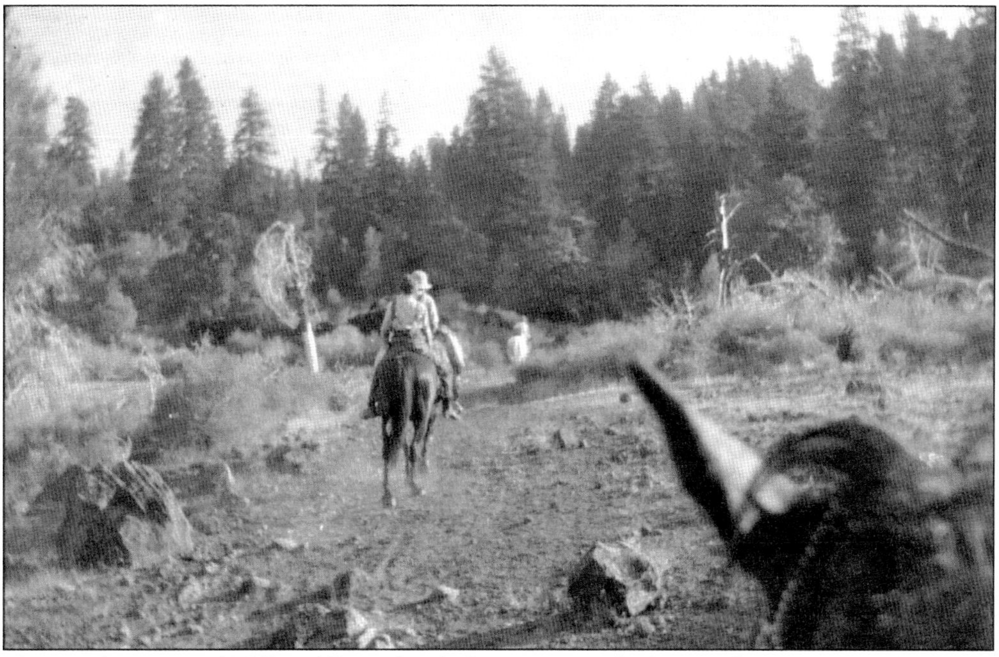

The rough terrain of Mill and Deer Creek Canyons was the home of many Native American tribelets as it had been for centuries. Shown here in 1911 is Alice Olson (in the distance) and Jakie and Beulah Olson traveling by horse to fish at Charles Avery's cabin in Mill Creek. The photograph was taken by Charles Avery Jr. Even in 1911, people were fearful of Native Americans, and with the discovery of Ishi, the last Native American to live within a purely tribal culture, this fear was intensified.

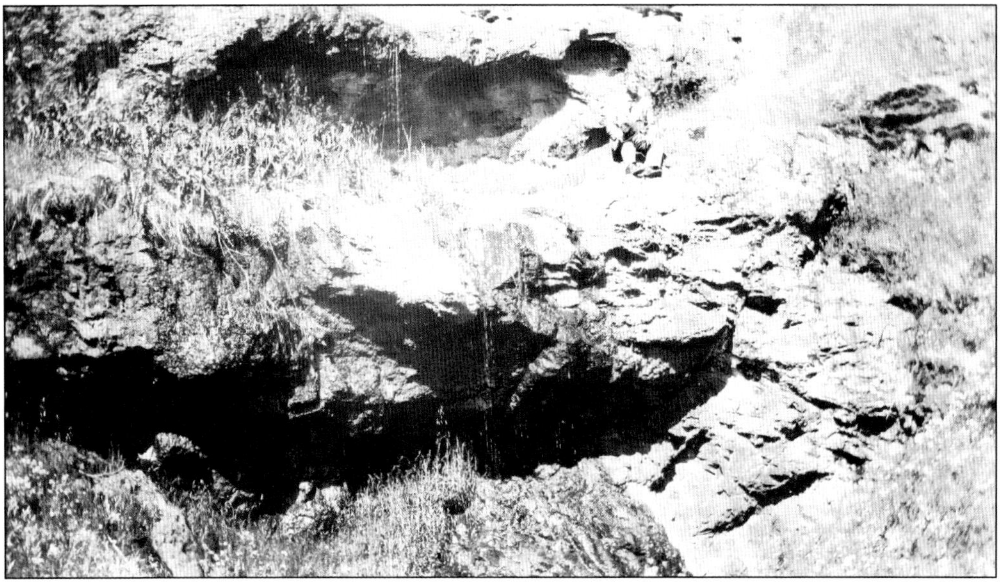

These two photographs were taken more than 78 years ago. The man seated in the upper photograph is Joe Martin. This cave, located somewhere between Deer and Mill Creeks, was mortared shut by the Native Americans prior to 1900 with mud and dozens of stone mortar bowls to conceal it. Known as the "Cave of the Spirits," the cave contains a large, flat stone etched with the tracks of Mill and Deer Creeks and *Waganupa* (Mount Lassen). Around the stone is a thick layer of ash in which are buried the bones of the warriors of Lano Seco—the last battle of the Mill Creeks. As late as 1957, the Cave of Spirits still had the pine poles in the ground to mark the location of the graves. Today six hewn stone steps are concealed with thick moss from the spring that runs over the face of the cave as well as thick brush.

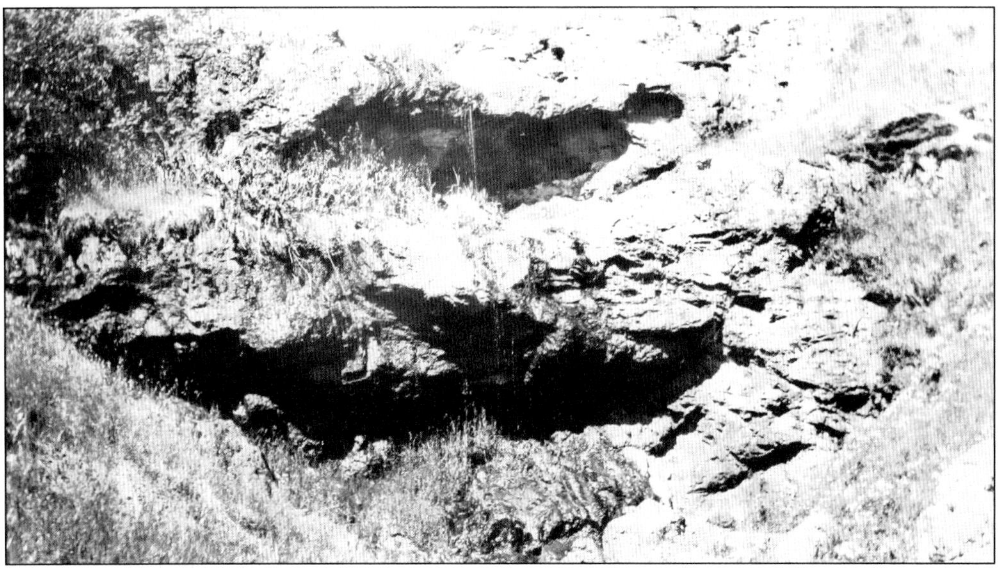

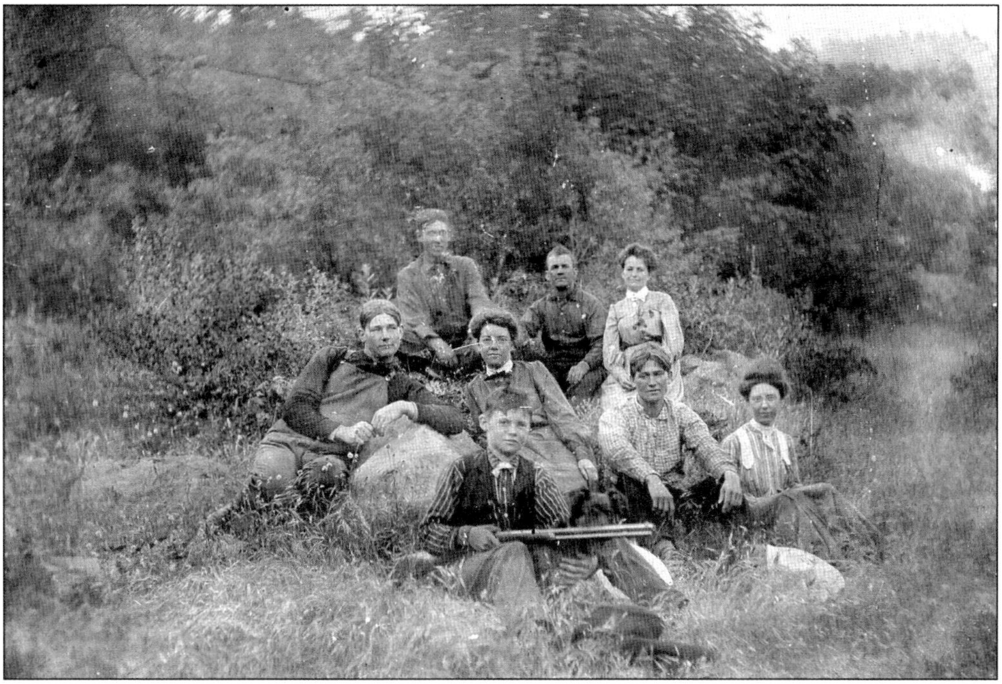

When Lyonsville was in its heyday, picnic parties were encouraged to travel in groups and warned not to wander unaccompanied. This August 18, 1898, photograph was taken on the Mill Creek rim. Shown from left to right are (first row) T. J. Shelton and his dog; (second row) John Lucas, Eva Clough, Tom Lucas, and Patty Lucas; (third row) John Jensen, Ed Shelton, and Eva Jensen.

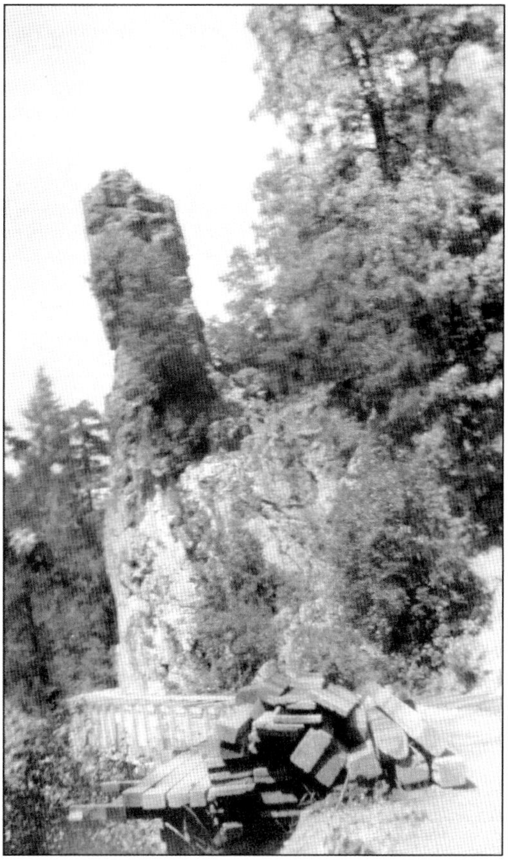

The flume of Antelope Canyon traverses the Pinnacles, a formation of many giant, sharp posts, some of which rise 100 feet. Like black rock itself, some pinnacles were used by Native Americans as promontories from which to observe comings and goings by the *saldu* (white men).

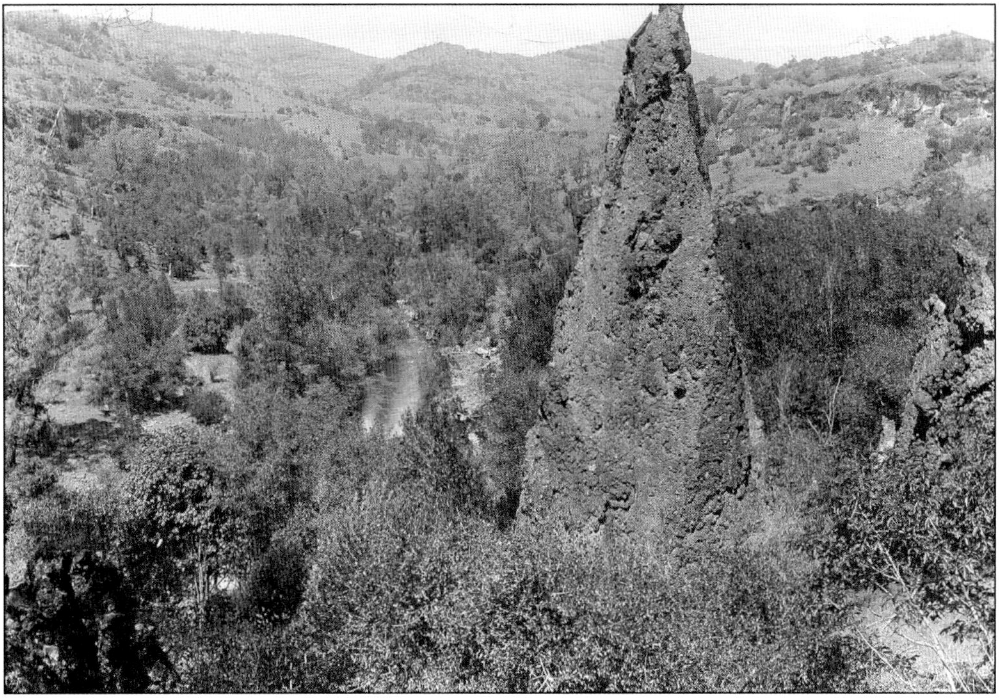

This fabulous view of Antelope Canyon was taken by Alice E. S. Olson in 1942 and the caption on the back states, "This is a picture where we always crossed Antelope Creek above the Lucas home. It was always a happy visit for us to go there." Antelope Flats, seen below, had been the early day site of a killing of a family named Williams.

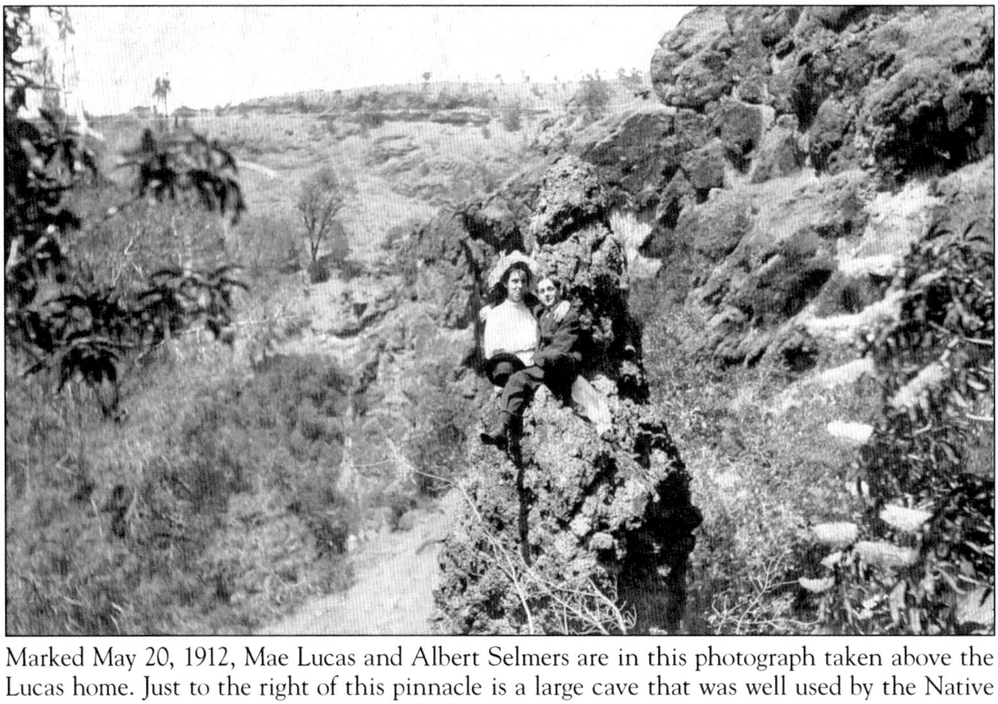

Marked May 20, 1912, Mae Lucas and Albert Selmers are in this photograph taken above the Lucas home. Just to the right of this pinnacle is a large cave that was well used by the Native Americans and contains many eight-inch-deep mortars.

Cragston Rock exists today above Mill Creek and is adjacent to Black Rock, high above the creek. It was a popular picnic spot on Sunday afternoons because of the narrow trail that led from Mill Creek. Presumed to be a Native American trail and a vantage point, it commands a full view of the entire canyon clear to the valley. Shown is a group from Lyonsville on July 23, 1904. From left to right are (first row) Alice Olson, Mary Betts, and Tom Betts; (second row) James Jensen; (third row) Janie Knauss and Edy Clough; (fourth row) Mary Westrope.

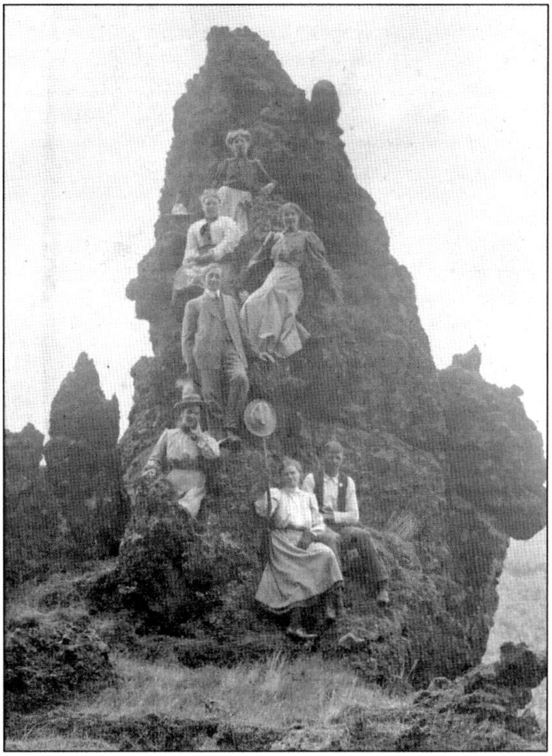

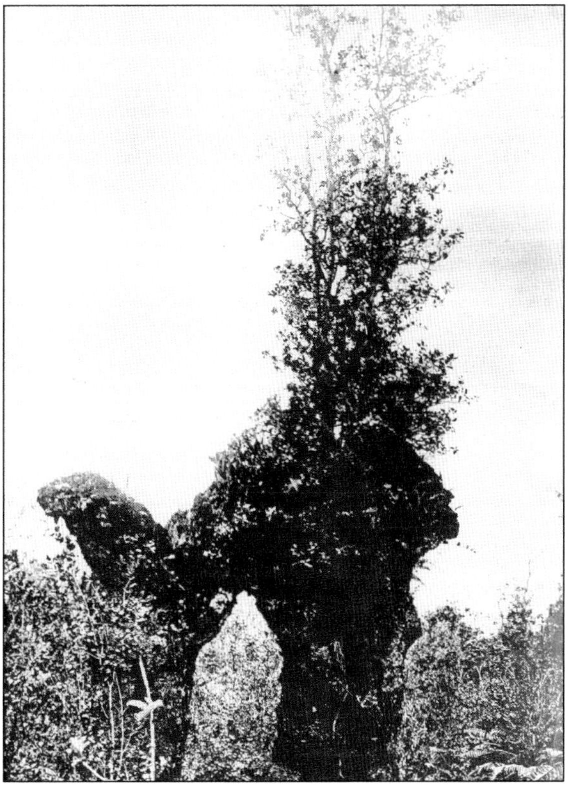

Camel Rock has been vandalized because of recently published maps to the location in addition to bus field trips to Native American sites in the area. Though thick brush covers it, the head shows signs of being knocked off with a sledge hammer. It was first discovered in the 1850s or 1860s, when wagons were hacking their way through the brush, trying to discover an easier route to the valley floor.

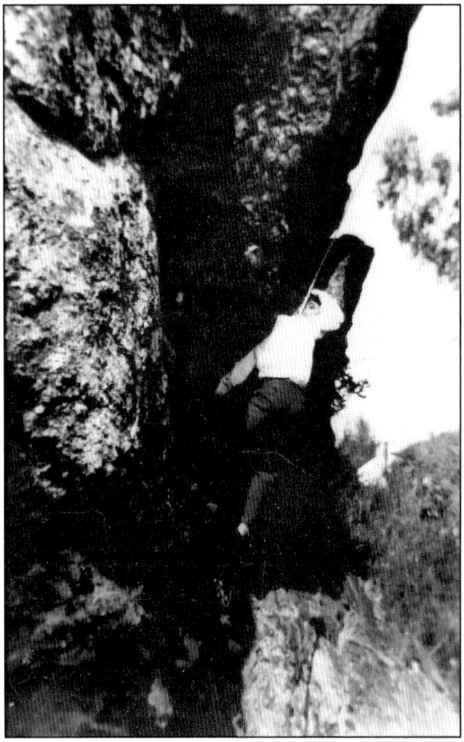

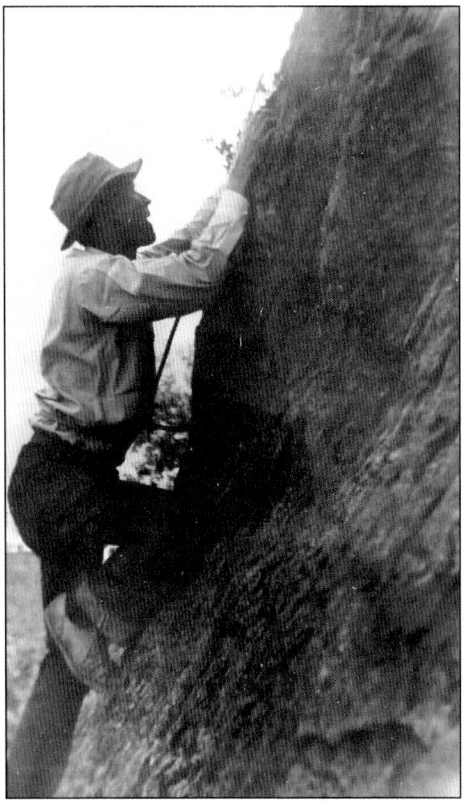

During and after the survey crew had climbed the ridge that fateful day in 1912, many souvenir hunters came to Mill and Deer Creek Canyons. Many artifacts were either plundered or destroyed. The caves of Mill Creek Canyon had held a wealth of artifacts as well as cultural evidences. After the final massacres of the Mill Creeks, every remaining possession of the Maidu was taken either for sale or for exhibit. Shown above, a later expedition climbs the rim rocks above "Grizzle Bear's hiding place." It was rumored that vast amounts of gold coin lay buried in inaccessible caves, just out of reach, and so ropes were employed to traverse the canyon walls. Shown below in the 1920s, Eddie Olson is hoisted into one of the caves by his lifelong friend Earl Kelley.

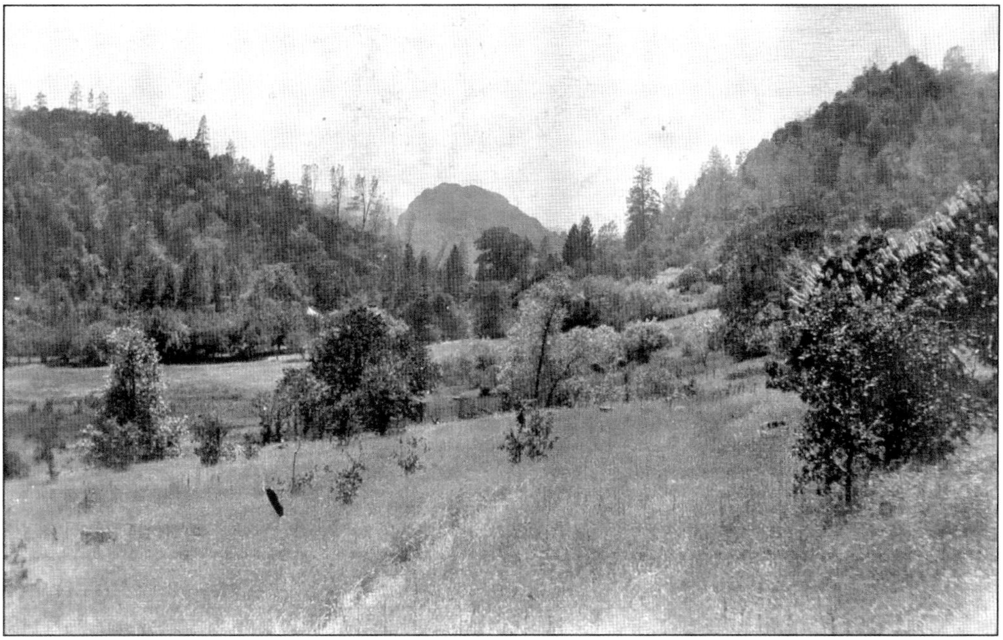

Three Knolls Village was the scene of the final battles in Mill Creek Canyon. People often search for the village site by looking for three mounds in the meadow, when in fact they form a line along the ridge. In the 1950s, the barrel of a hexagon rifle, as well as other artifacts, were found buried in the central meadow where the main massacre of the Three Knolls took place.

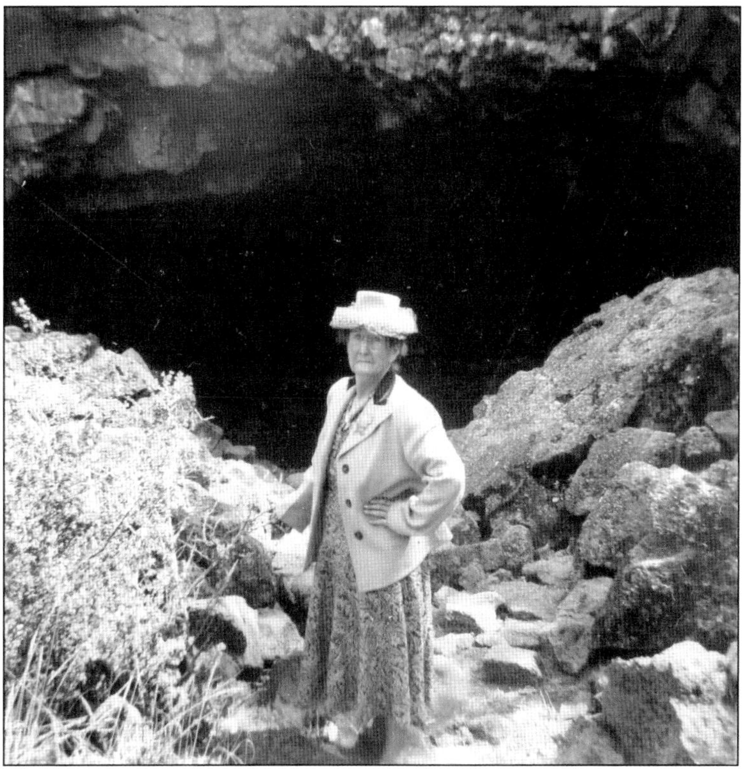

In 1948, Alice Olson Pitts and former sister-in-law Emma Redwing took a trip from Red Bluff into Mill and Deer Creek Canyons. Appalled by the desecration of caves and sacred sites by university archaeologists and amateurs, they found only two caves that had not been sifted. These caves, sealed by the Native Americans and considered sacred, are still undisturbed today. Alice captioned this photograph of herself on the back, "Alice in Wonderland."

Finley Lake

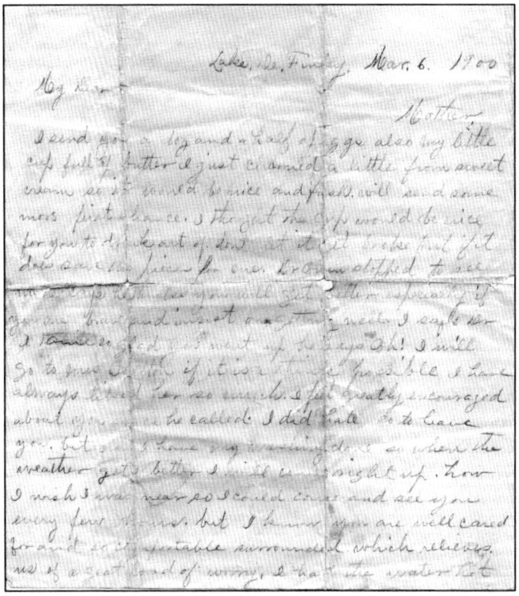

Lake, Co. Finley, Mar. 6. 1900

My Dear

Mother

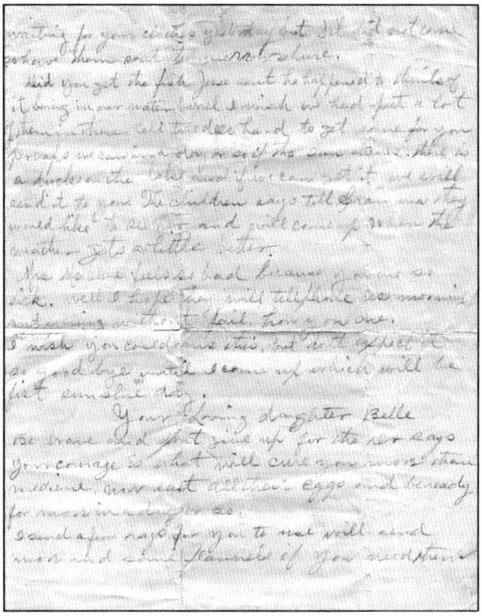

Your Loving daughter Belle

This letter, dated March 6, 1900, was sent to Letha Shelton in Lyonsville by her daughter Sophrona Belle. The letter states, "There is a duck on the lake and if we can get it will send it to you." Finley Lake was built to supply the water for fluming lumber to Red Bluff and provided water on the typically dry Hogsback Ridge. Alice Olson's dog can be seen in the bottom of the photograph retrieving the aforementioned duck.

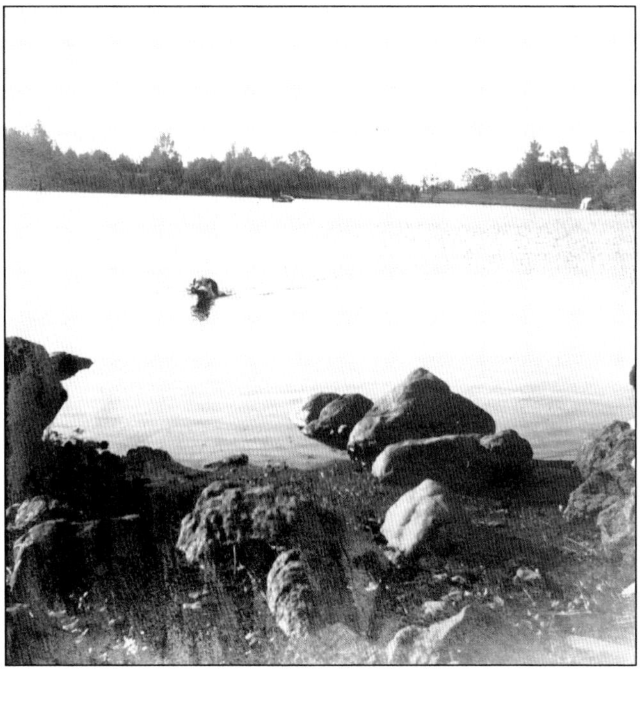

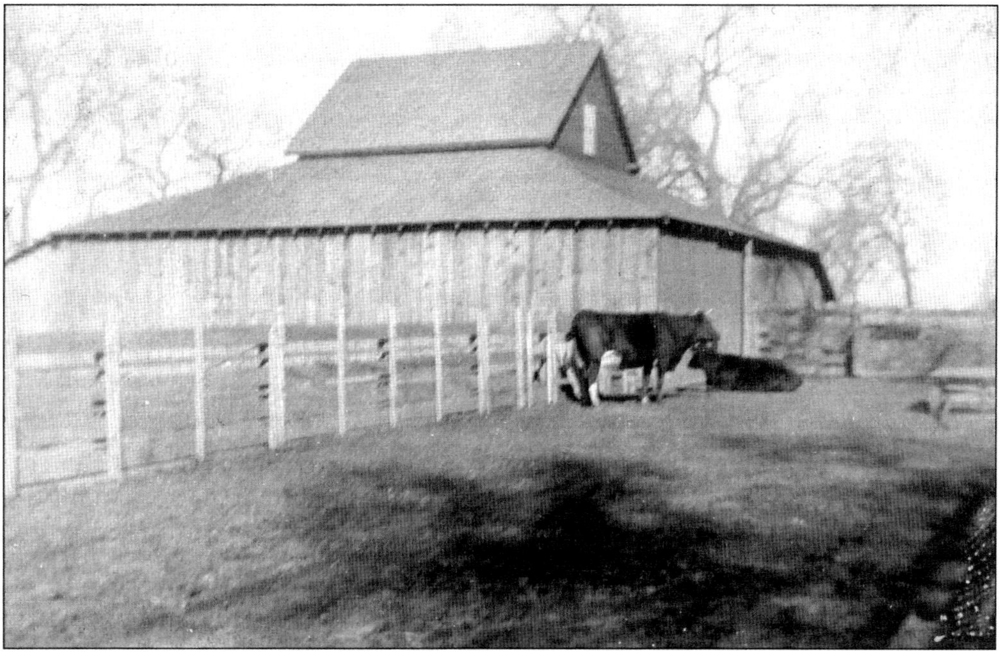

Often referred to by locals as "Lake De Finley," Finley Lake was primarily a sheep and cattle camp to supply fresh meat for the town of Lyonsville and the camps of the Sierra Lumber Company. At its peak, Finley Lake had 600 sheep and just as many cattle. The Finley home, barn, and outbuildings sat on the southwest shore. A small cemetery still can be seen near the house, just past the barn shown here.

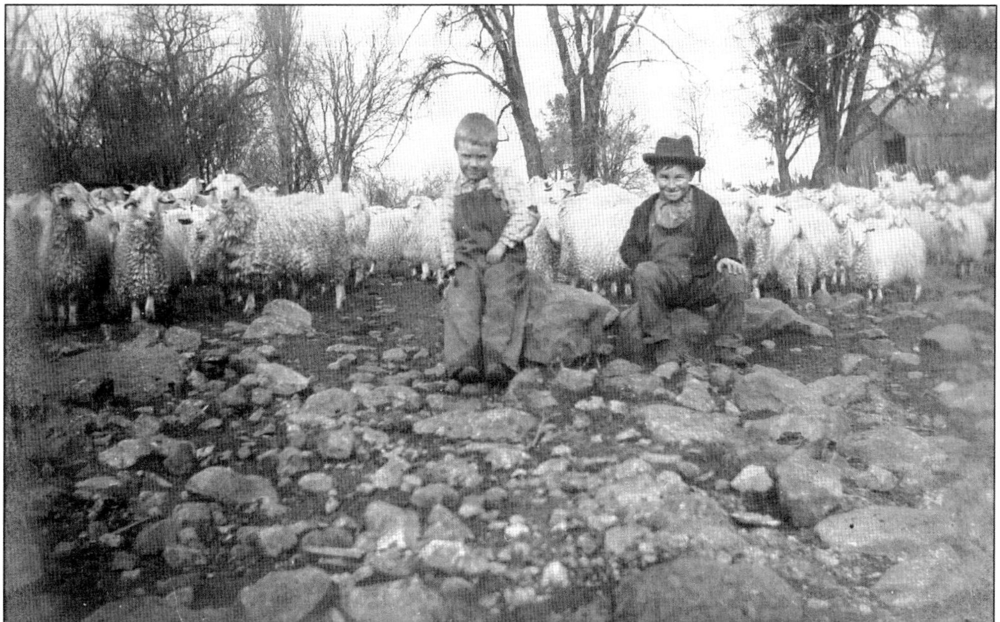

This photograph, also taken by Alice Olson, shows some of the Finley sheep herd. Sheep were often looked down upon by cattle people as scavengers that stripped good grazing land. Sheep provided wool and mutton for the homes of Lyonsville and the camps.

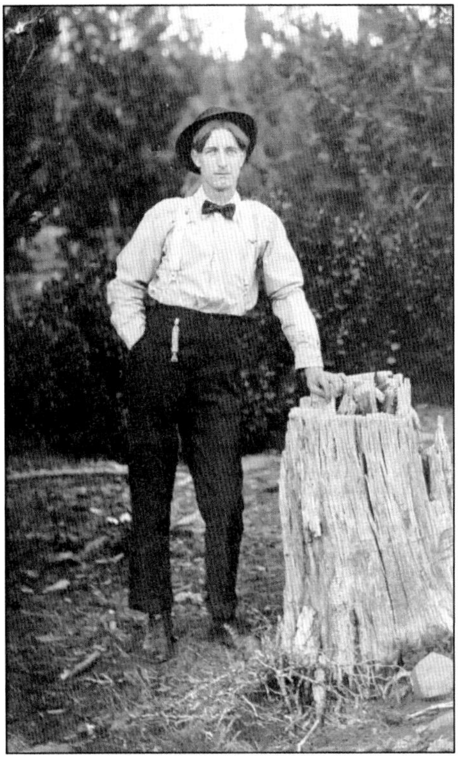

Albert Finley lived more than 20 years at Finley Lake. He worked for the Sierra Lumber Company, but on weekends, when he returned to Lyonsville, he drove sheep and cattle for slaughter. The building of the high trestle, the Belle Mill Flume, and permission to use water from the flume at night made settlement possible. The high trestle was 96 feet tall. Water from this flume was the sole source for six settlements.

This image of the high trestle at Finley Lake, taken in 1901, shows Jakie Olson and his mother's black-and-white sheep dog at the base. The highest trestle in the area, it was the most susceptible to winds, and in 1912, more than 50 feet of the flume and trestle collapsed. It was never rebuilt and was finally scrapped for the lumber.

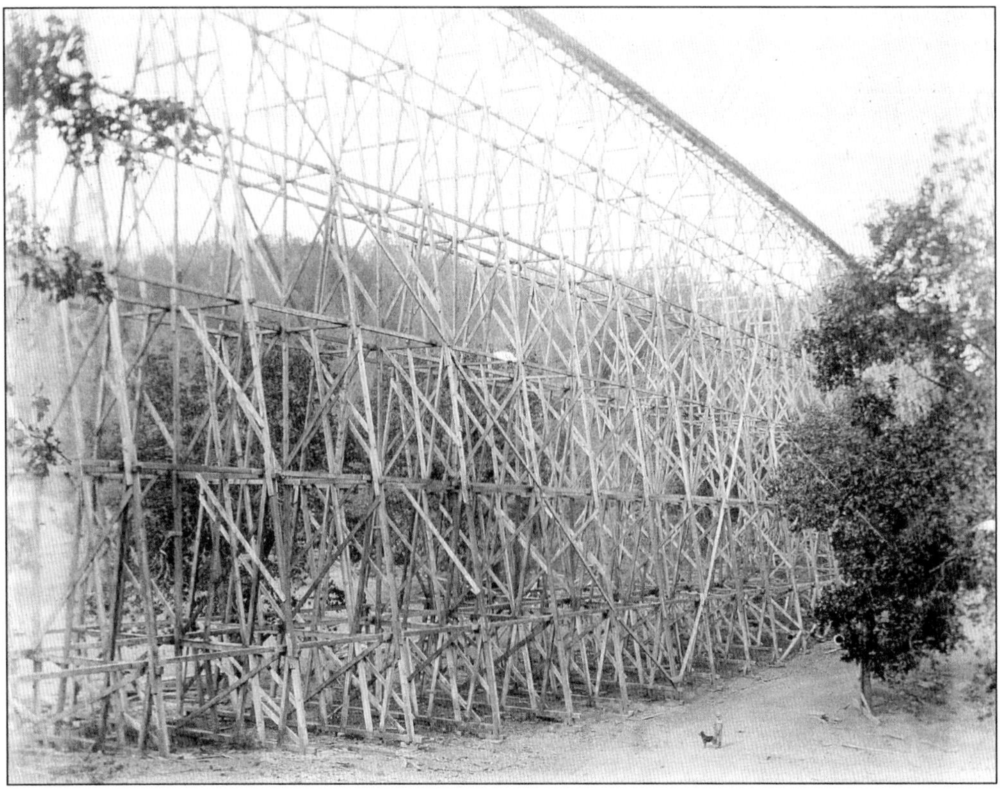

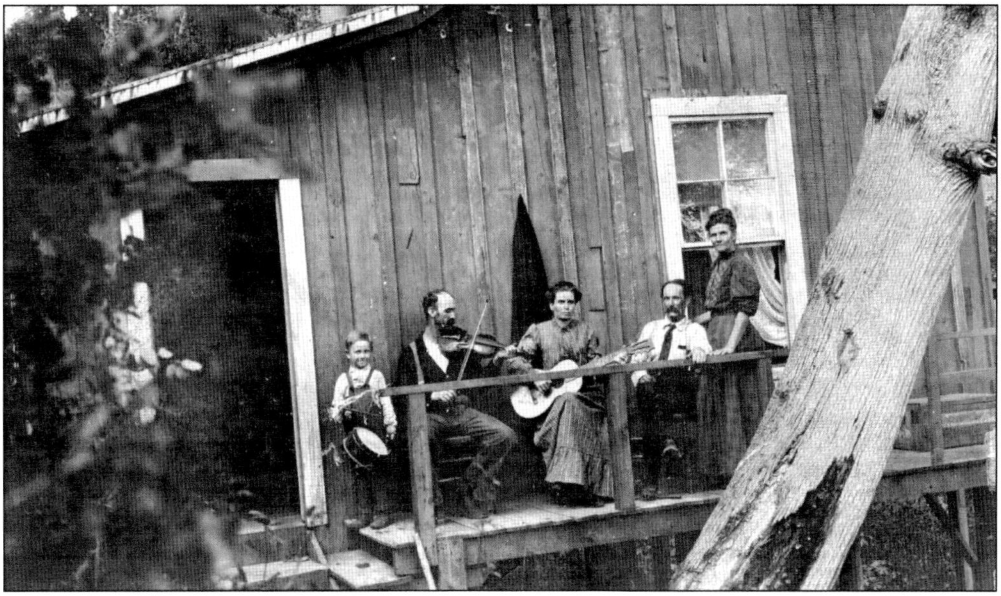

The Finley family was musically gifted, and it was widely known that every member of the family could play multiple instruments. The Finleys had a large plank dance platform that connected to their house and people from the many camps and towns would "flume down" or ride the flume boats down for entertainment and catch the stage back up on Sundays.

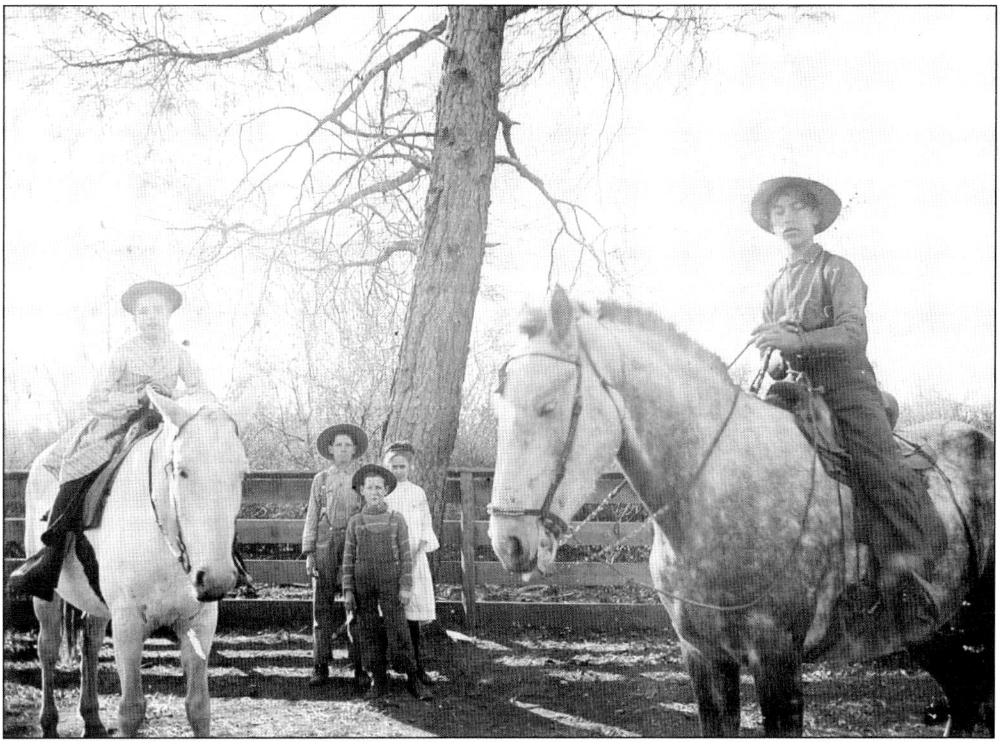

The Finley Lake corral could easily accommodate several hundred animals. Shown here from left to right are Sadie Myers, Tom Shelton, John Shelton, Angie Shelton, and Albert Finley. Every child had his or her own pony or horse and learned to ride at an early age.

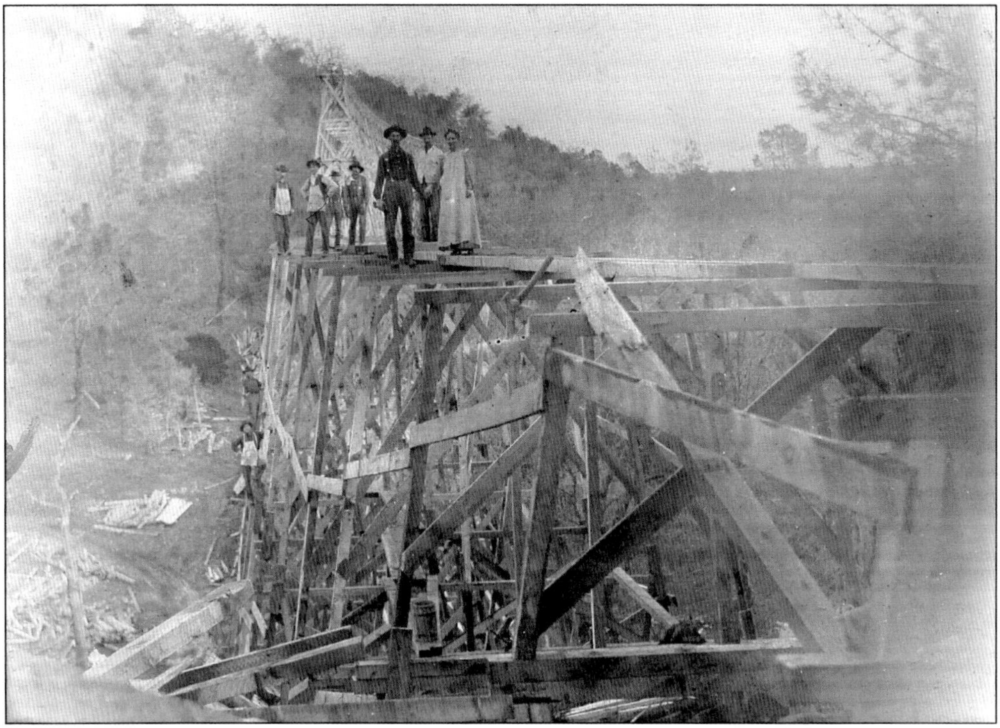

This image shows the building of the Belle Mill trestle in 1902. The Belle Mill was named for Belle Shelton, who was 1 of 11 children of T. J. and Letha Shelton. The Belle Mill flume was 84 feet high at its highest point and transported water from Battle Creek. It ran near Lyman Springs, and a branch supplied water to the Adolf Engebretsen Mill, house, and Engebretsen town. Finally abandoned when no longer needed, it eventually rotted away into the ground, leaving a trail of rusty nails.

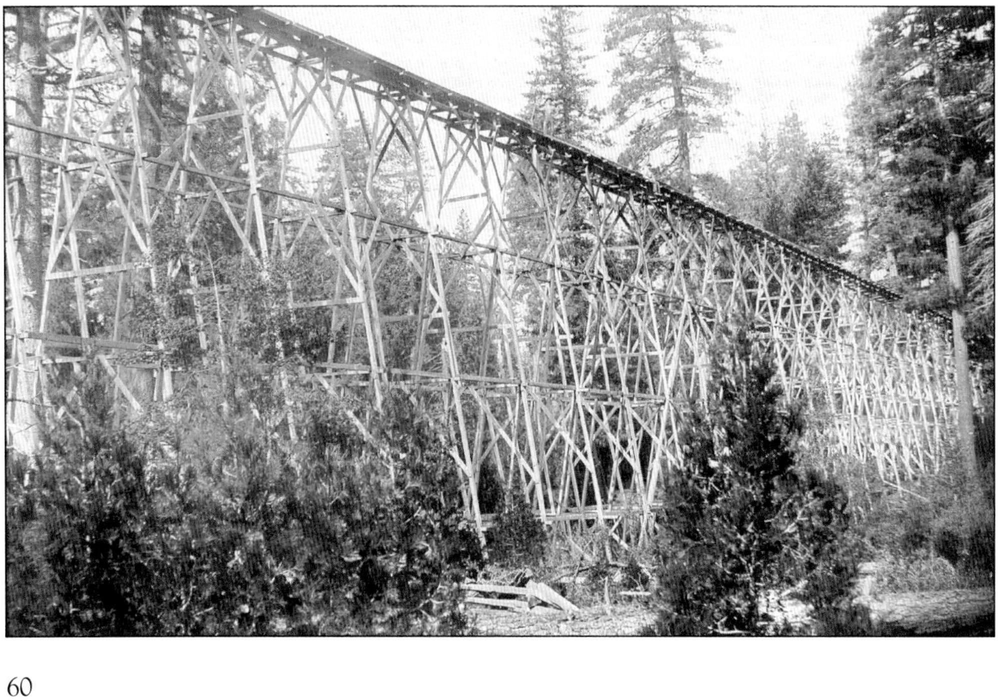

ENGEBRESTEN TOWN

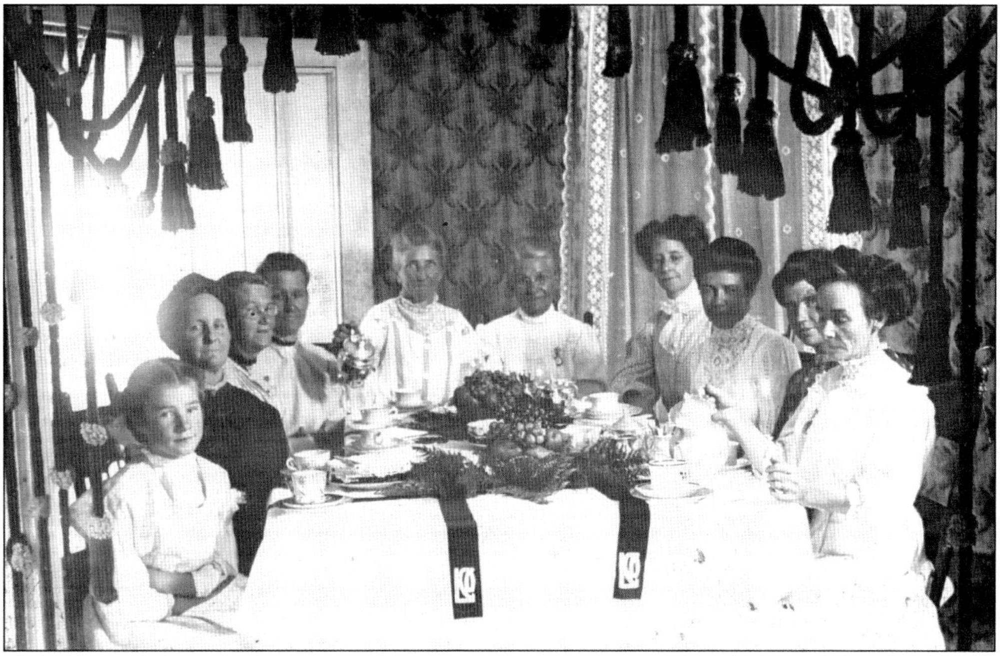

The Ladies Auxiliary Club of Lyonsville is meeting here at the Engebretsen home in May 1906. This club later collected funds for the victims of the San Francisco earthquake and firestorm. Shown from left to right are Grace Redner, Alice Olson, Sara Knauss, Mary Knauss, Annie W. Shelton, Edna Saygrover, Mrs. Engebretsen, Carrie Heibner, Amanda Heibner, and Belle Shelton Moulton.

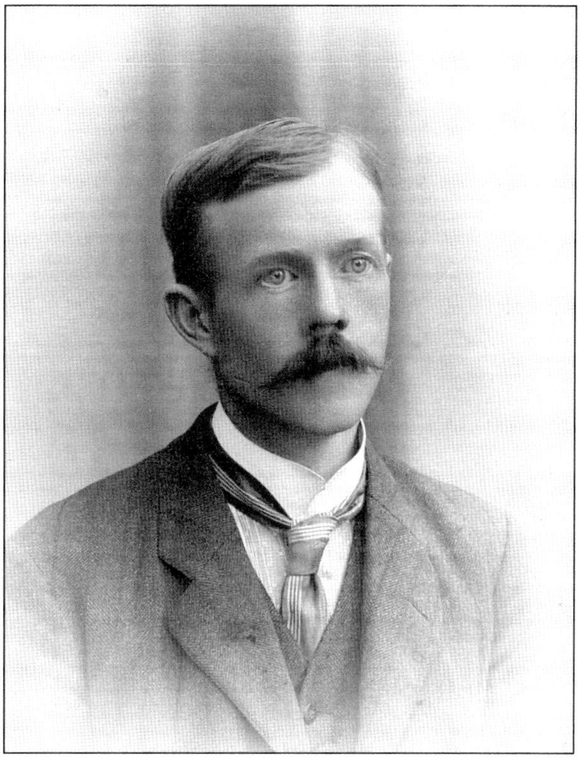

Coming from Sweden in 1860 with his cousin Jonas Jensen, Adolf Engebretsen settled first near Red Bluff and then at a place he called "Swedes Flat," later known as Lyman Springs. Adolf built a large home, barns, and a mill as well as a private railroad siding to transport his lumber.

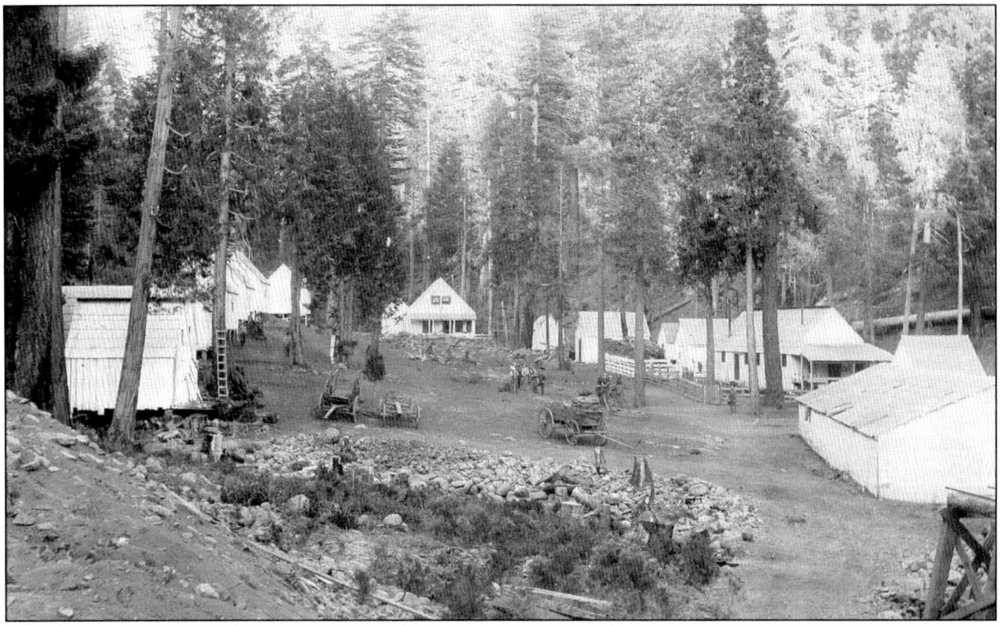

"Engebretsen Town," as it was called, sat just around the bend from Adolf Engebretsen's Victorian house, whitewashed to the last fence post as a reminder of Adolf's native-born town in Sweden. The town housed the Engebretsen crew, which numbered 30 to 40, and was a great comfort to Mrs. Engebretsen and her children who periodically spotted Native Americans in the area.

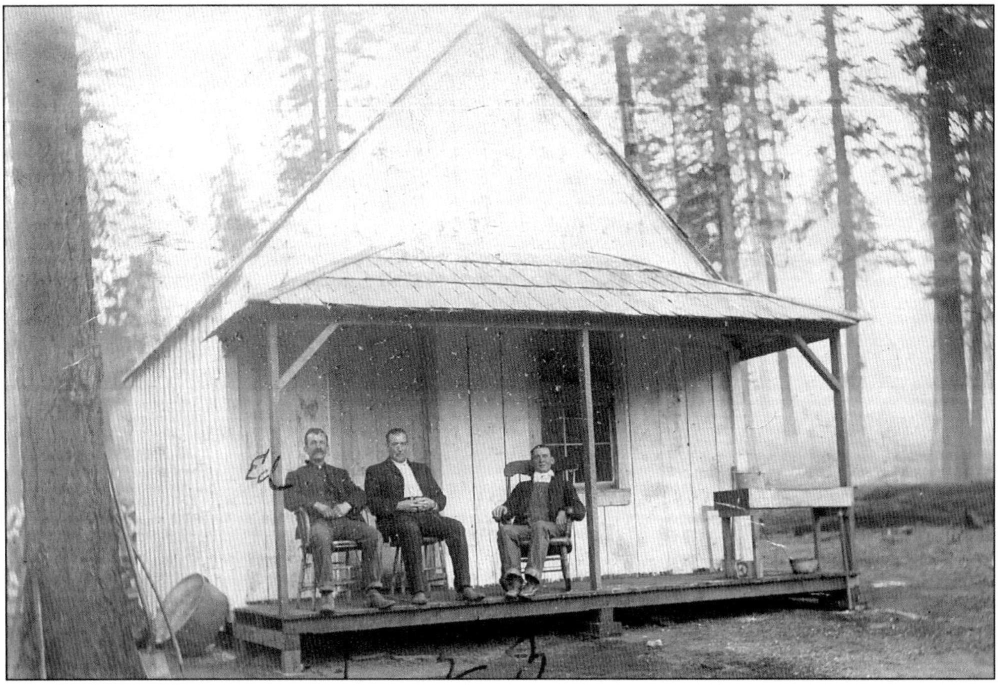

Built in a meadow just around the bend from Engebretsen, the town, which was constructed of lumber from the mill and square nails from a blacksmith shop on the premises, was supplied water from the original Lyman Spring, which still runs to this day. Shown here on the Ed Shelton Cabin porch are, from left to right, Ed Shelton, Walter Gusney, and Ed Cameron.

The Adolf Engebretsen house, built in 1868, sat on the hillside above the mill, flume, and pond at a vantage point so that the whole operation could be watched from the house. The elevated flume carried water to the mill and also supplied water to the house. Early on, the Engebretsens had been attacked by Native Americans, so the house was built on the steep hillside with a security lookout point.

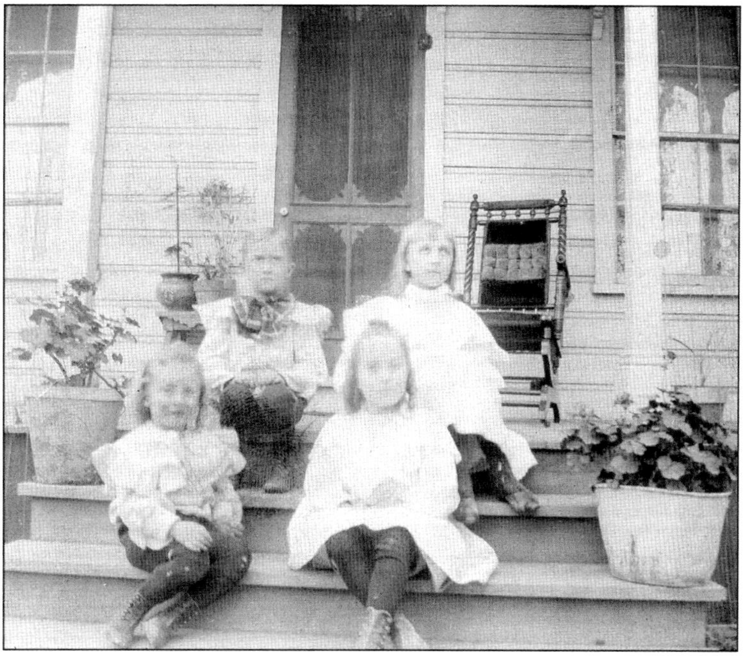

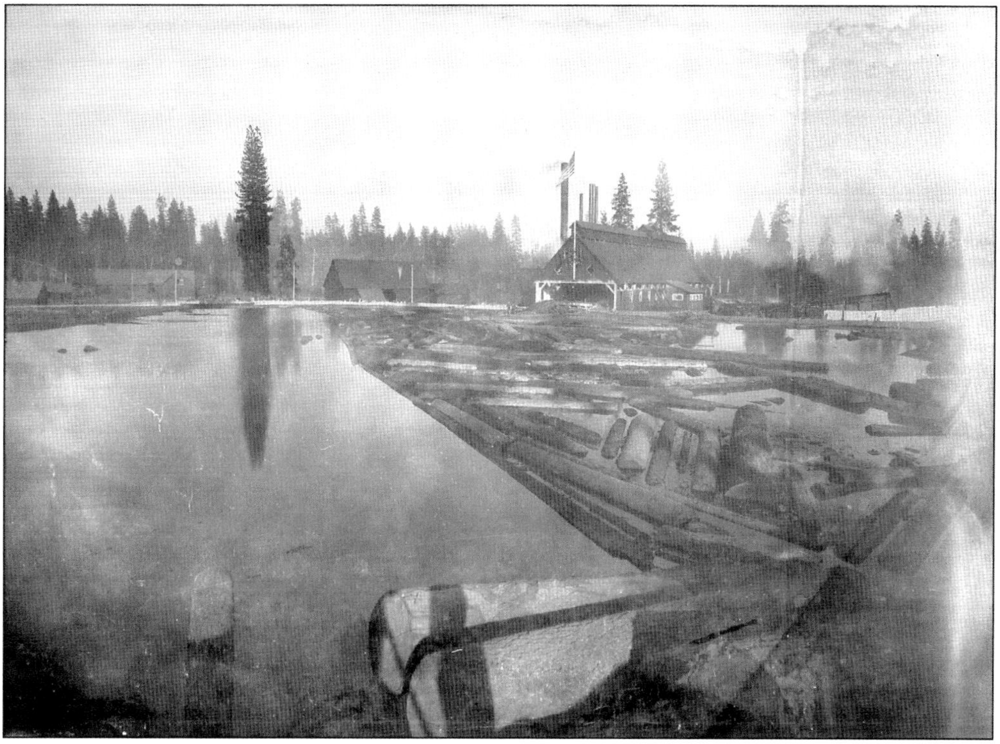

The millpond at Engebretsens, where present-day Lyman Springs is, could hold hundreds of oxen-hauled logs and was operated by men called "river pigs" who maneuvered the logs with "can't" hooks while riding on the floating logs. On the hillside above the pond site today stands an apple tree planted by Adolf Engebretsen. This new mill with an expanded pond replaced the original mill on the same site.

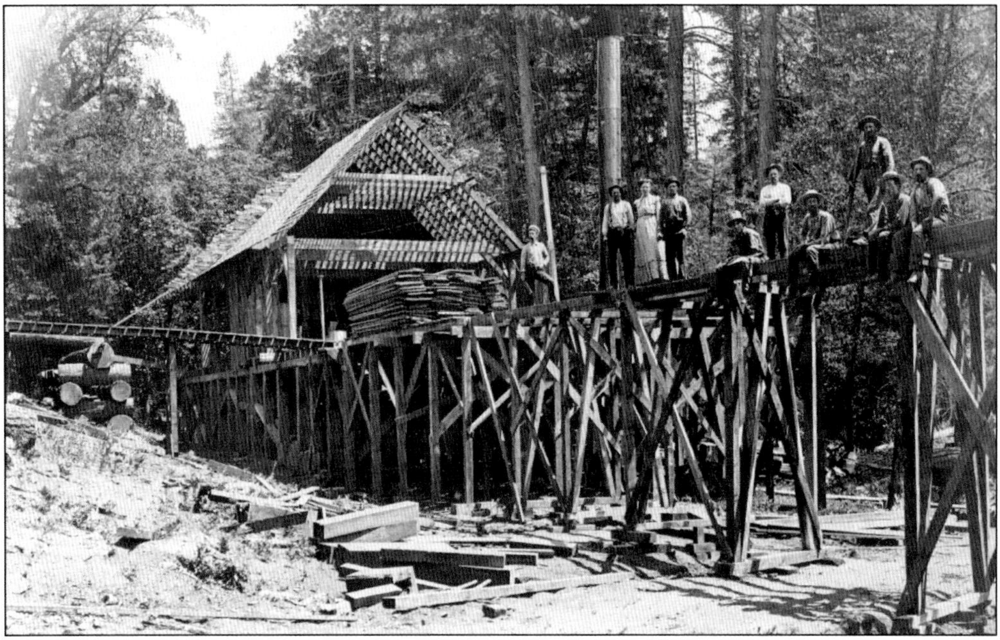

The foundations for the walkways and gangways were large stones reinforced with concrete. The crisscrossed logs supported the mill floor. A portable mill had supplied lumber for the original mill shown here. It was built first, followed by the house. The flume and rail spur came a few years later.

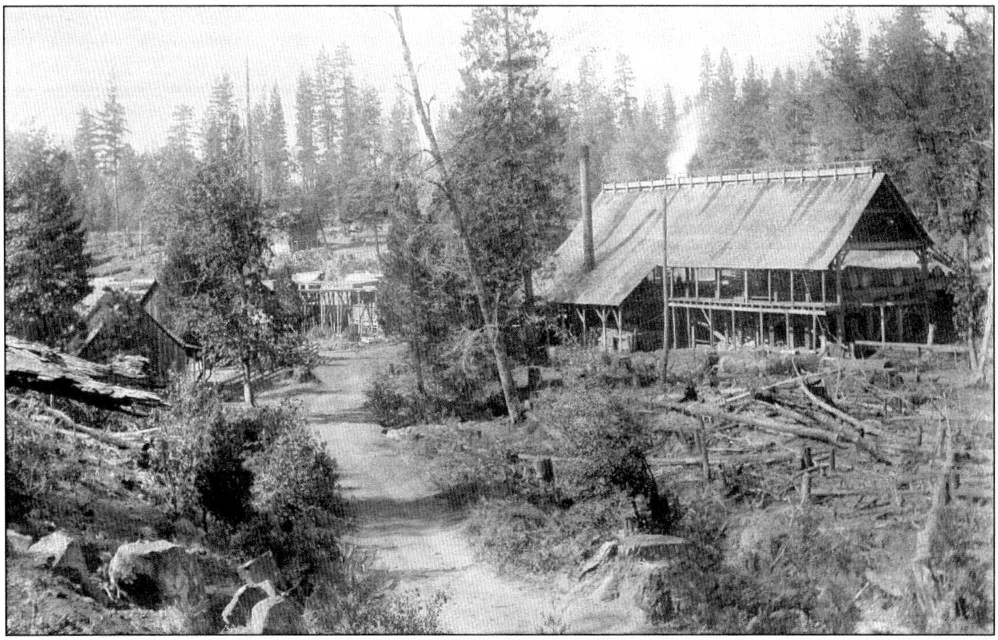

Adolf Engebretsen's steam sawmill was equipped with all the latest amenities—large, circular saw blades and a flume atop the mill for fire protection with gates that could be raised to flood the roof at intervals. Wooden-wheeled oxen trucks and three rail spurs brought logs to the mill while the winding V flume floated cured or dried lumber to Red Bluff. This photograph was taken from the porch of Adolf's house.

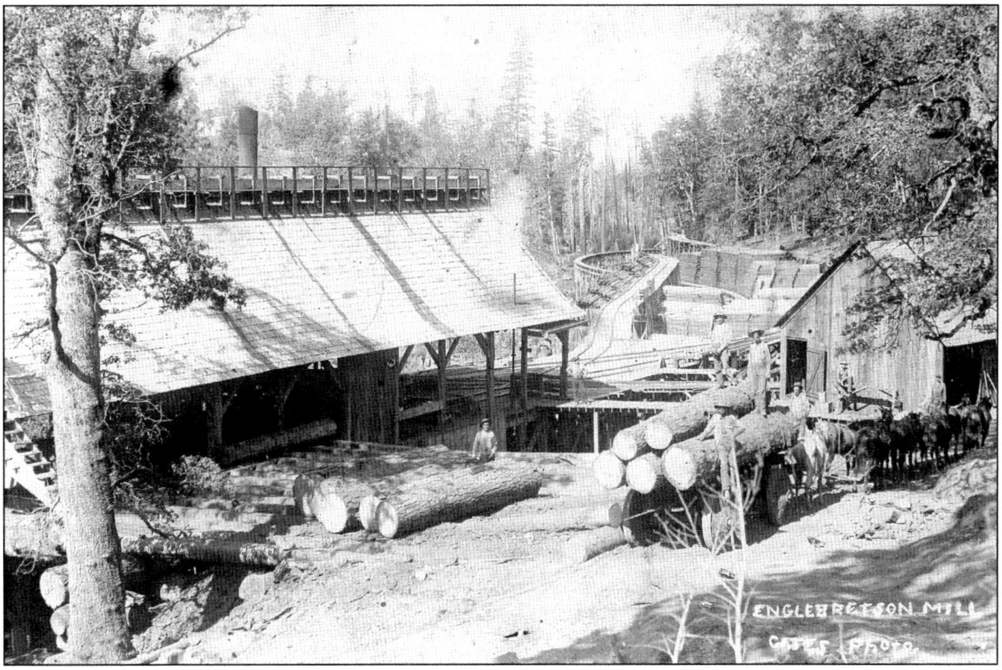

The Engebretsen Mill was at least one-third smaller than the new Champion Mill at Lyonsville but was said on several occasions to rival "the Champ" in board feet sawn during one day.

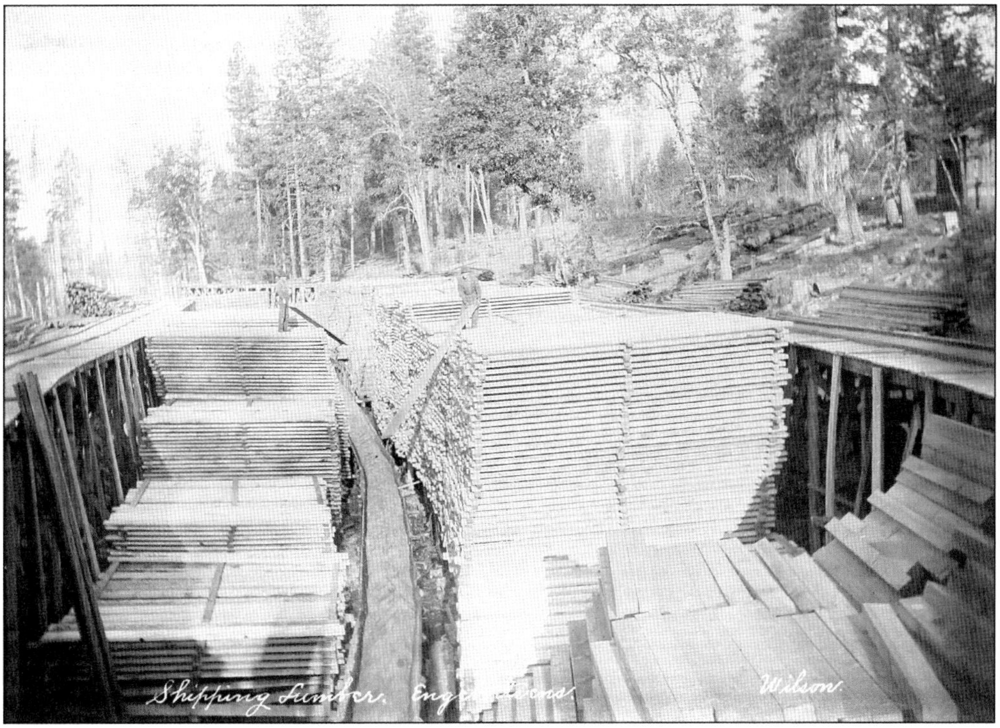

As fast as the "flume dogs" could send lumber down the flume, more was piled in great quantities by three, eight-hour shifts. Adolf had many private valley contracts that required an almost unquenchable supply of lumber. Among this clients were Huntington and Hopkins of Sacramento City.

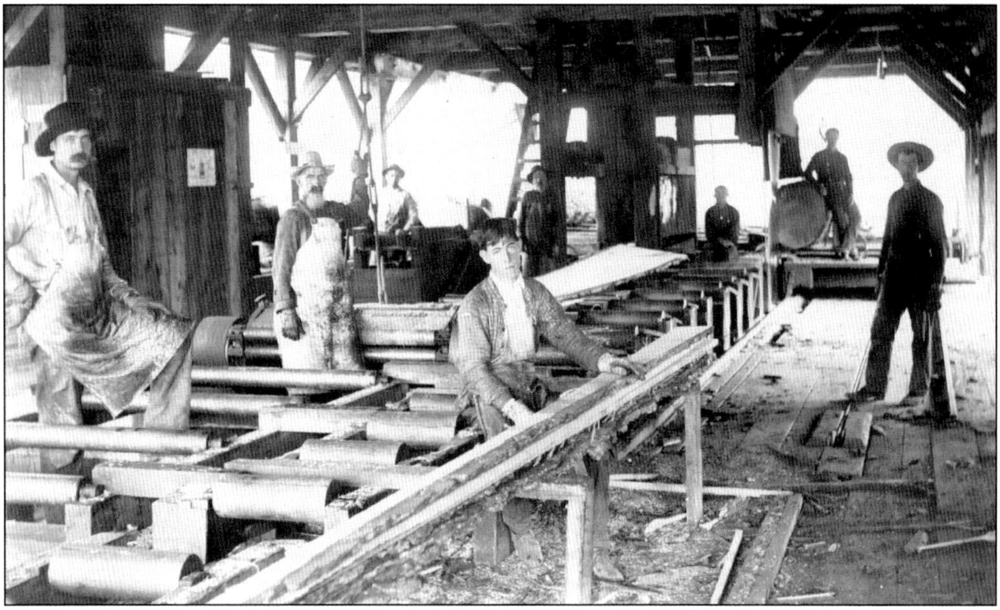

Shown just after it was completed is the upper deck of the Engebretsen Mill. The wooden short rollers had shafts of three-quarter-inch water pipe as axles. Shown is the planer, which is a Griswold and is being operated by James Gray (with beard). James's grandson Emory Shelton (foreground) is stacking shims that will be cut up to feed the steam-powered boilers. The tree men on the right, from left to right, are Tom, Jim, and John Shelton (in hat); to the left is Cletus Jensen.

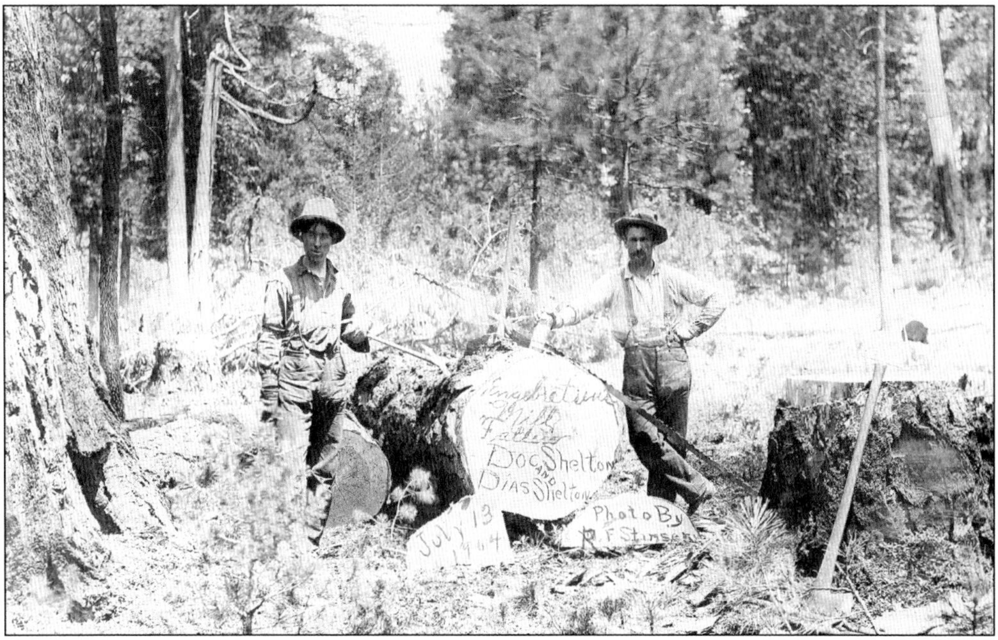

Early fallers were paid by the day for footage fallen and estimated scale. Trees were chalk marked with a signature butt cut to indicate who cut down the tree to ensure payment from the lumber mill. Here in this 1904 Stinson photograph, Doc Shelton (right) and son Dyas pause on a hot summer day at Shelton's Camp for this photograph. The bottle Doc is holding is not whiskey, but saw oil.

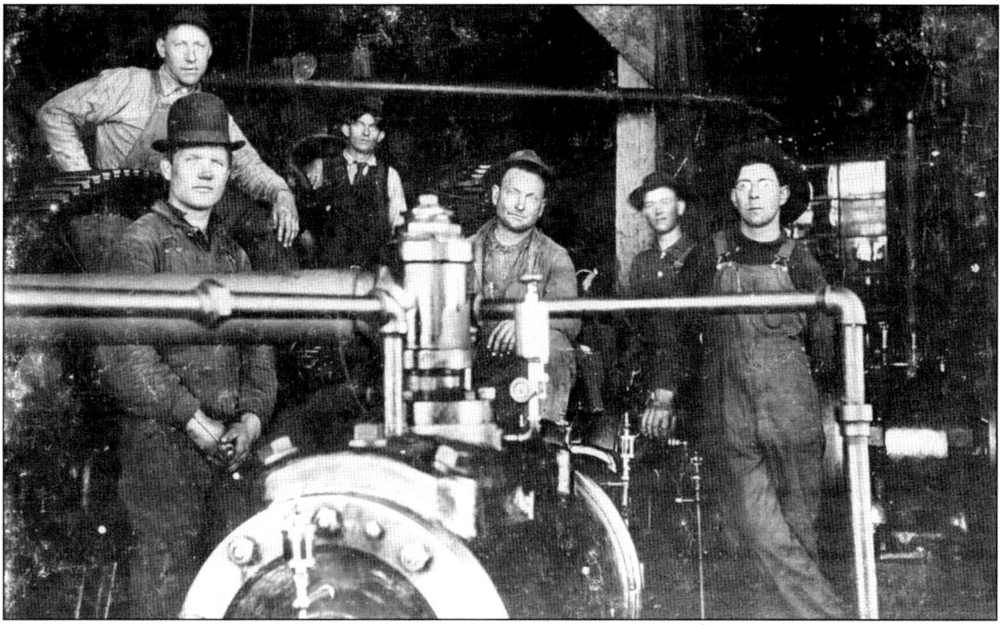

The steam crew worked on the lower level of the mill to feed sawdust as well as scrap to the boilers that powered the mill. The fires were kept going 24 hours a day. The chute above in this photograph was directly under the huge circular saw and conveyed sawdust to the lower level.

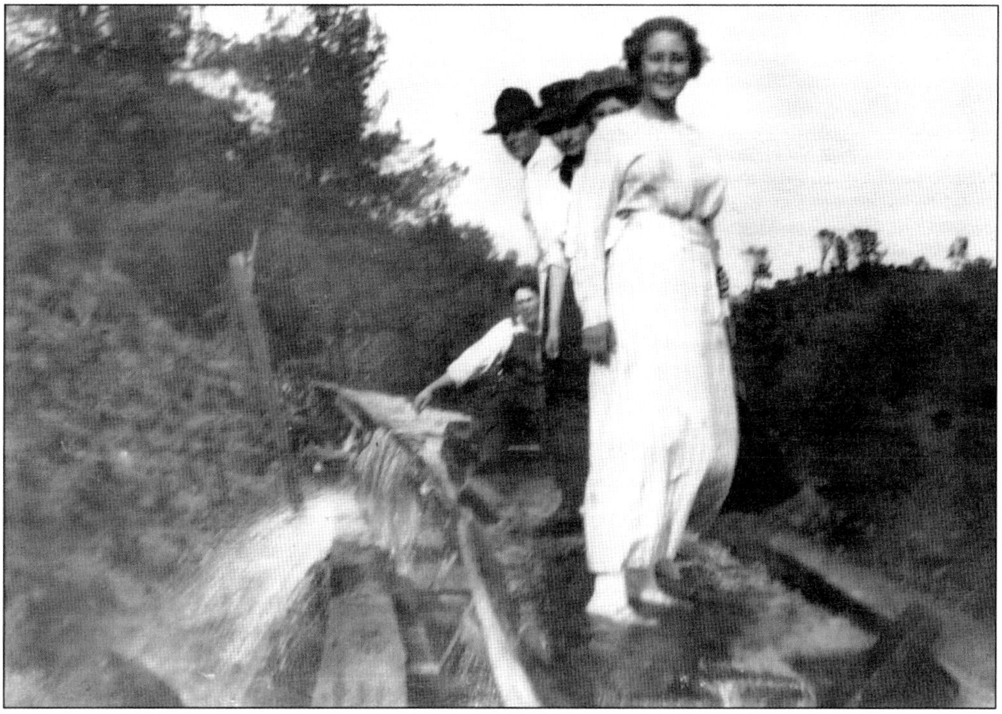

Riding wooden flume boats was a weekend pastime as well as a means of transportation and could easily move two people from place to place. These same flume boats were used in dry shutes and pulled by cables from attached rings. Two of these flume boats from the Diamond Maych Company have survived and are in the author's collection.

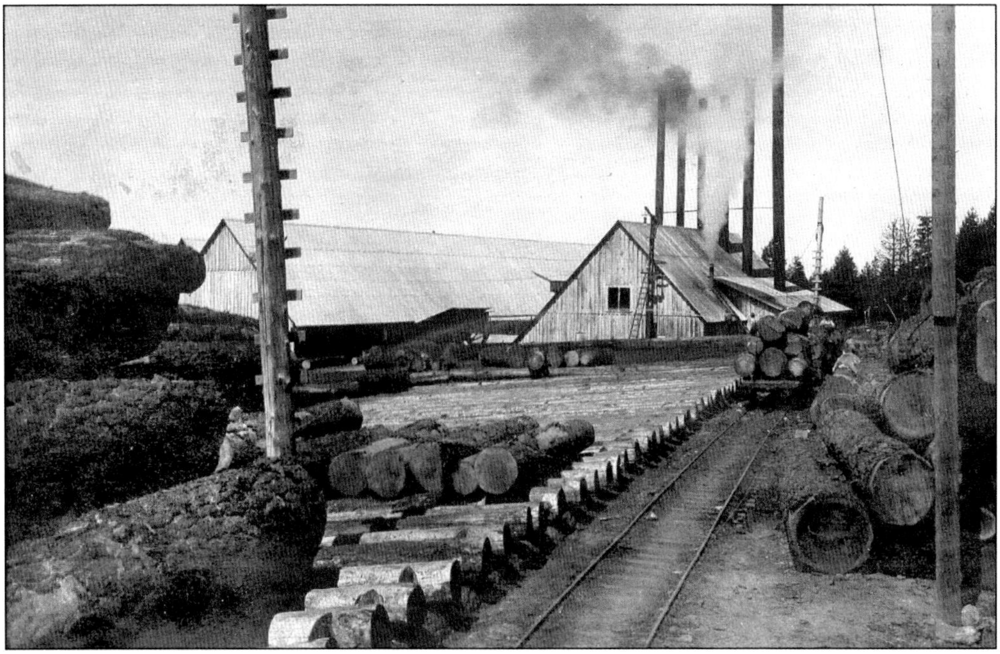

Built in 1864, the original Belle Mill was named for Belle Shelton, whose family lived nearby. The boards for many of the original Lyonsville were sawn here. It had four boiler stacks to begin with. The later Engebretsen Mill only had one stack.

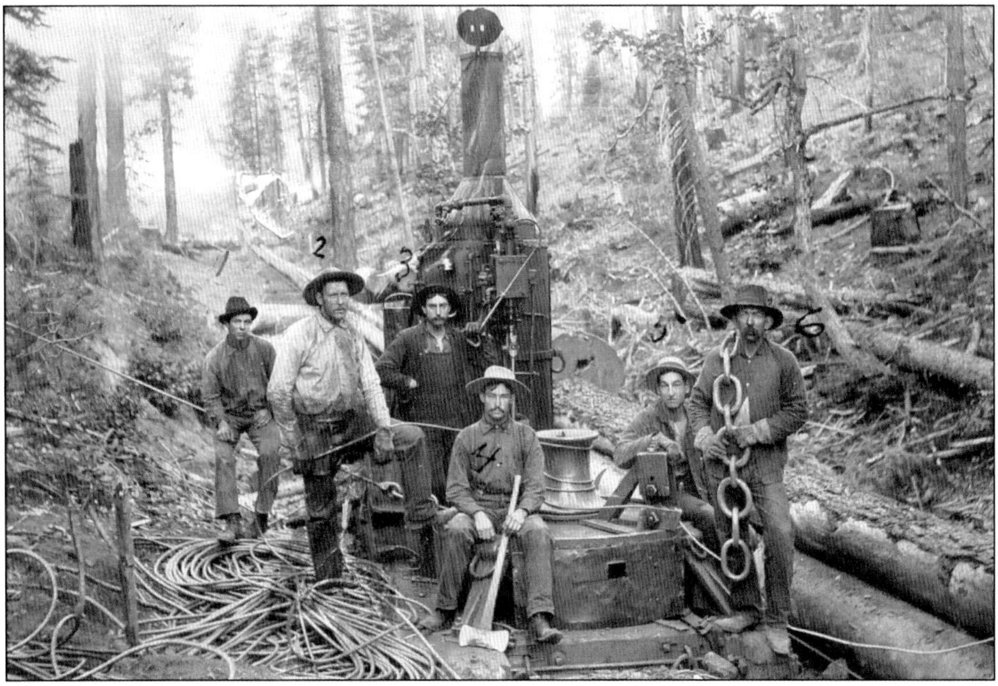

Here the bulltender crew from Engebretsens Mill poses as they prepare to go to work. A Dolbeer Donkey engine was always kept near the mill to help with large tasks. This engine and crew are shown on the hill just above where Engebretsen Town would be built. The crew are "straight lining" logs to the actual Mill site at Lymans.

Four

LYONSVILLE
SIERRA LUMBER COMPANY'S HUB OF COMMERCE

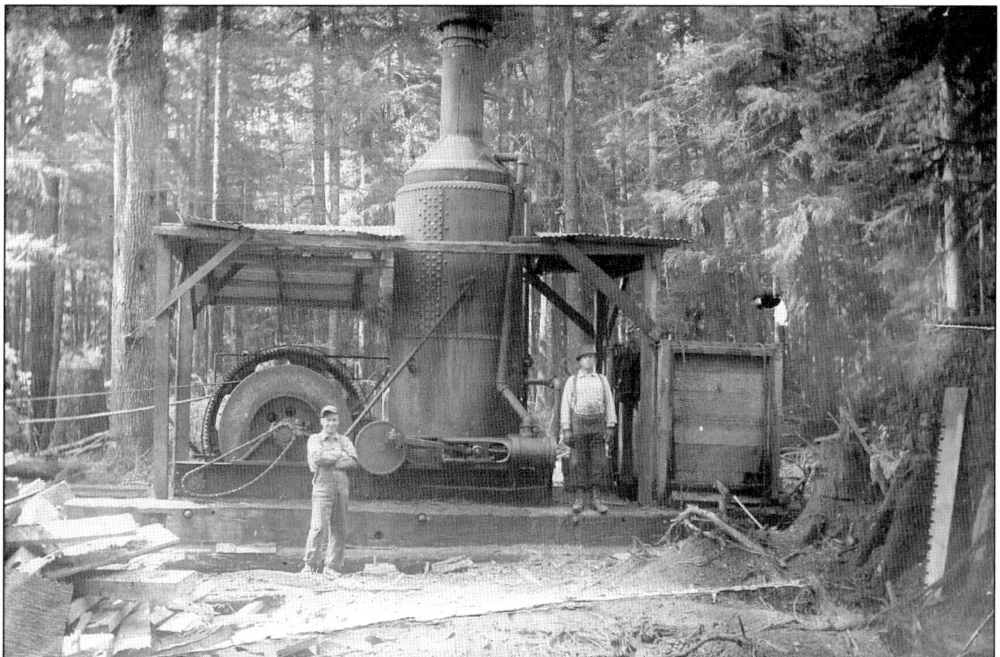

Arthur Molton (left) is standing in front of a Stirling donkey engine. Arthur's mother was Lizzie Turner, the sister of Jack and George Turner. George Turner was a lively figure around Lyonsville and the famous 101 (or Turner) Ranch, where the Belle Mill Cemetery is located, is named for him. The other man in the photograph is Walter Gosney. This was one of the first trials between Stirling steam and belt-driven donkey engines.

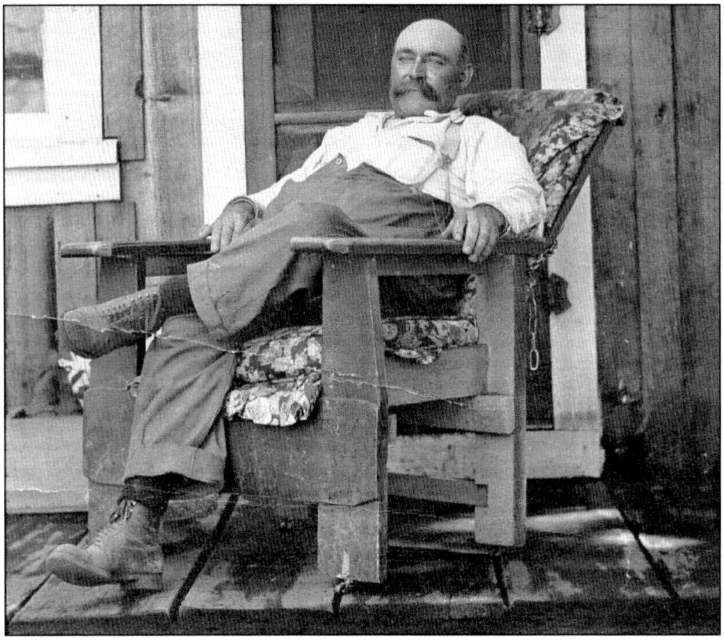

Jack Turner acquired a huge amount of property around Lyonsville. His famous 101 Ranch, named such because he painted the numbers on his barn roof, still stands today. Here he relaxes in his favorite chair that the crew at the Champion Mill made for him. Turner was a big whiskey boss and owned rights to the distillery at the Cliff House Saloon. Being a good boss, he was known to give most of his stock away.

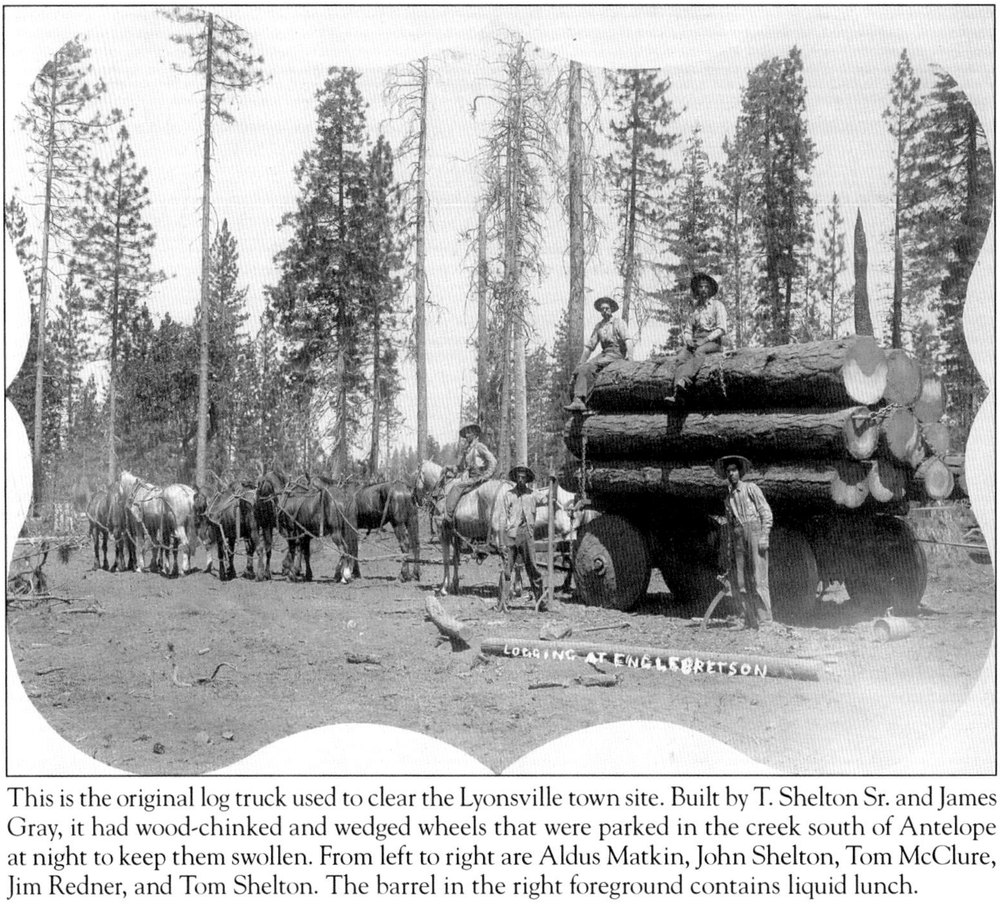

This is the original log truck used to clear the Lyonsville town site. Built by T. Shelton Sr. and James Gray, it had wood-chinked and wedged wheels that were parked in the creek south of Antelope at night to keep them swollen. From left to right are Aldus Matkin, John Shelton, Tom McClure, Jim Redner, and Tom Shelton. The barrel in the right foreground contains liquid lunch.

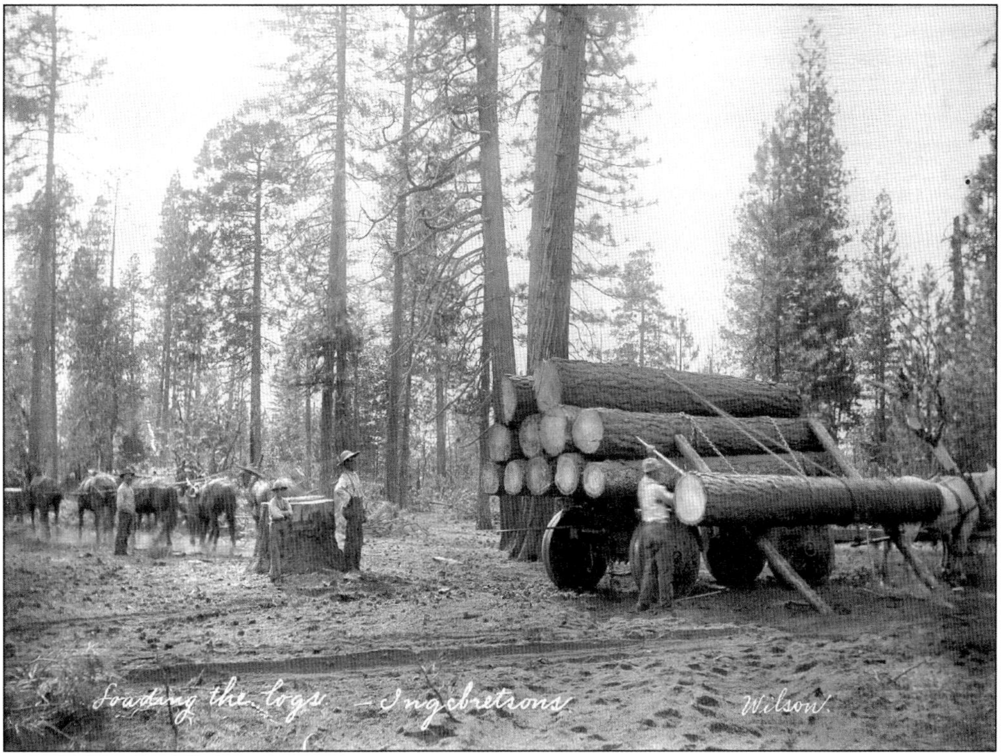

Logs were loaded in several ways in the woods. They were often "yarded," or "pulled" by cable, to the truck by horse or oxen and then rolled up ramps by chains and horses. Some were pulled up by Dolbeer Donkey engines. This was very dangerous, and several graves at the Belle Mill Cemetery are attributed to chains or logs breaking.

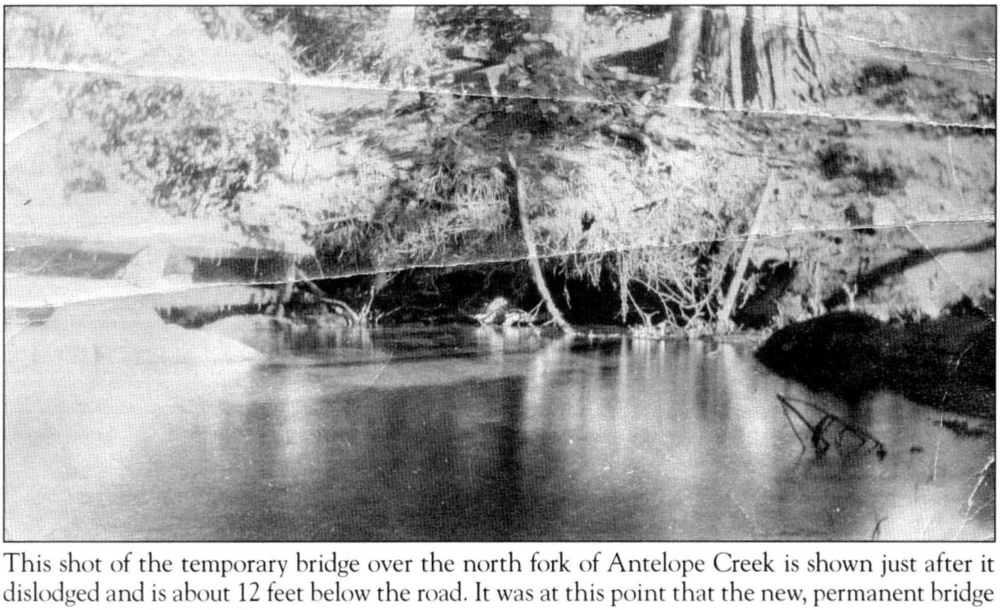

This shot of the temporary bridge over the north fork of Antelope Creek is shown just after it dislodged and is about 12 feet below the road. It was at this point that the new, permanent bridge at Boots' Bend was built.

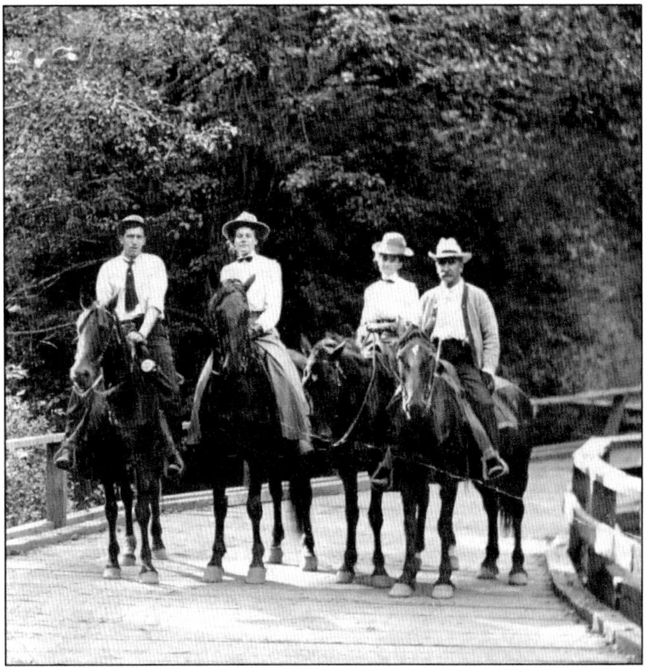

Boots' Bend was named for Thomas Boots, who first accompanied the Olson family to the spot on a fishing trip in the 1880s. A natural pocket sat near the creek and the old North Fork Bridge. This large flat afforded a perfect camping spot. Though the creek was small in size, it offered 10- to 12-inch trout from its pools. The bridge and approach to the town site of Lyonsville were built prior to the clearing of the land. The horseshoe-shaped bridge formed the approach to the steep grade to the town site a quarter-mile away. Pictured from left to right are Tom McClure, Nancy Westrope, Belle Moulton, and Jack McClure.

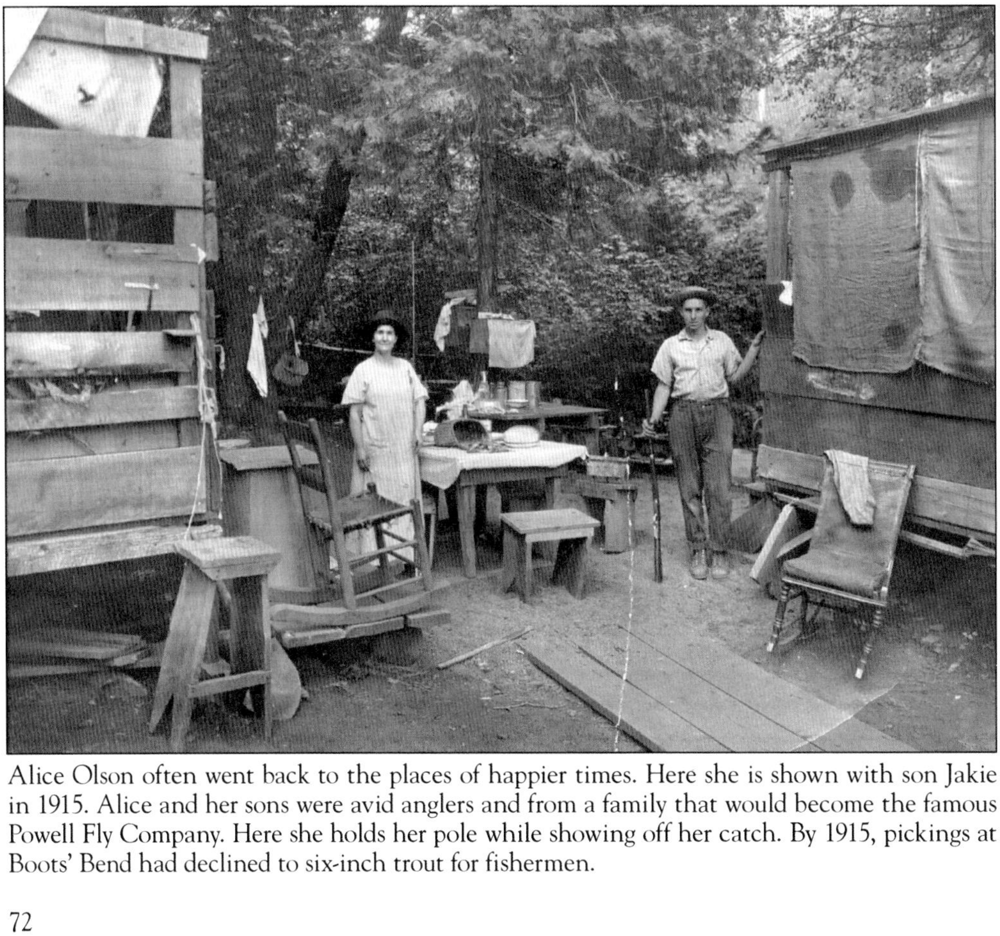

Alice Olson often went back to the places of happier times. Here she is shown with son Jakie in 1915. Alice and her sons were avid anglers and from a family that would become the famous Powell Fly Company. Here she holds her pole while showing off her catch. By 1915, pickings at Boots' Bend had declined to six-inch trout for fishermen.

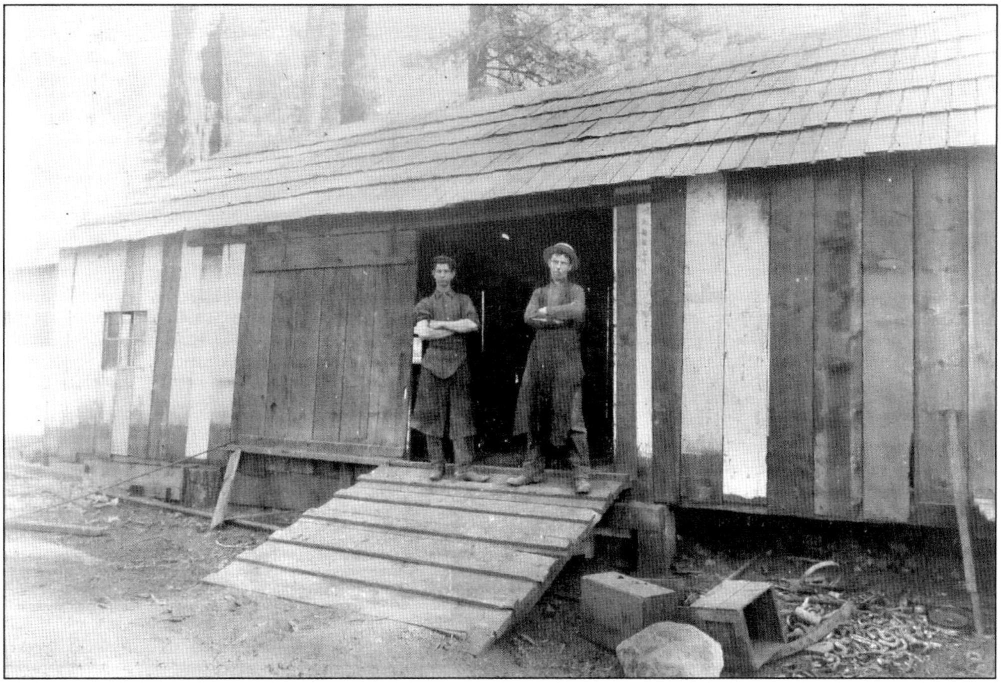

From Boots' Bend, the road climbed abruptly to 200 feet above the creek in a quarter-mile. From above the bridge to the town, a conglomeration of exposed pipes lay on the hillside. These carried water to Wells and Moores Blacksmith Shop, the Cliff House Saloon, and the White Angel Bordello. These were the first structures to be seen on the right-hand side (west) of the road in Lyonsville.

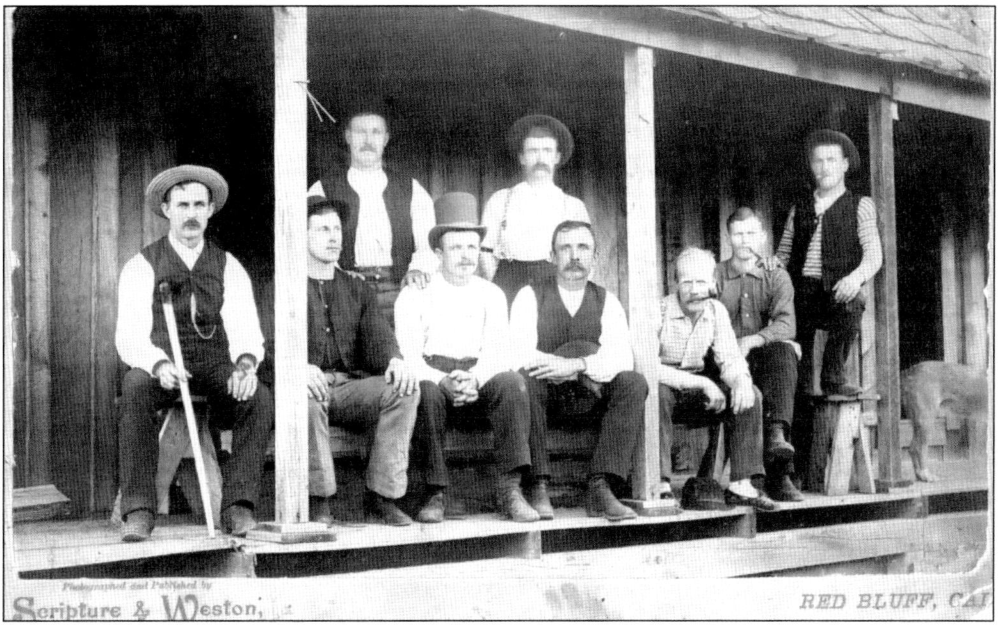

The Sierra Lumber Company store did a good service for townspeople, holding charges on groceries until payday. The post office, connected to the company store, was a magnet for the locals to congregate and socialize in Lyonsville.

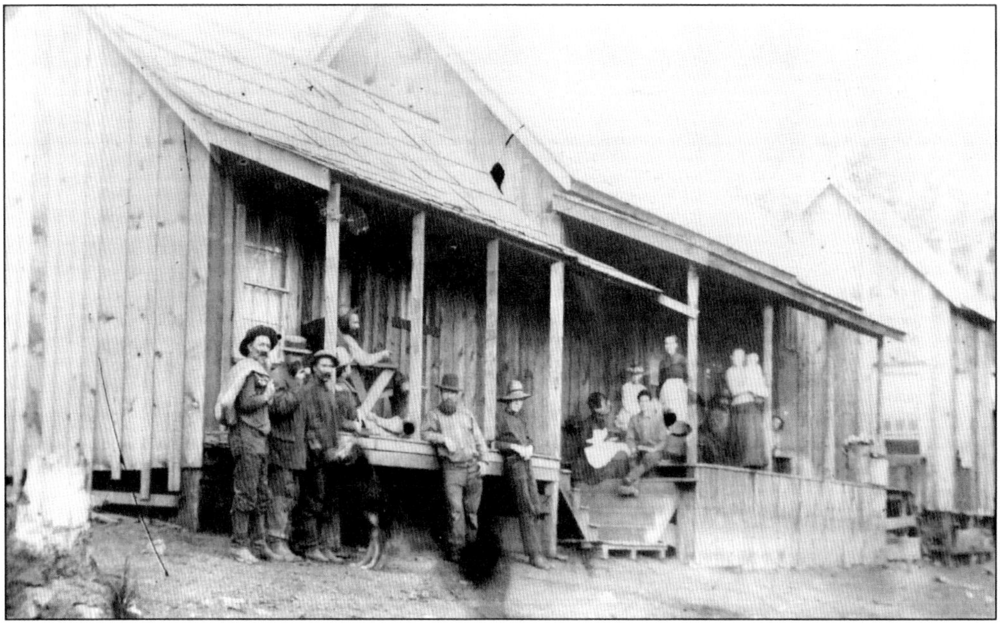

These row buildings, including the post office and adjacent company store, all backed up to a road that bordered the log yard for the Champion Mill and had large sliding doors for easy access by wagon or train.

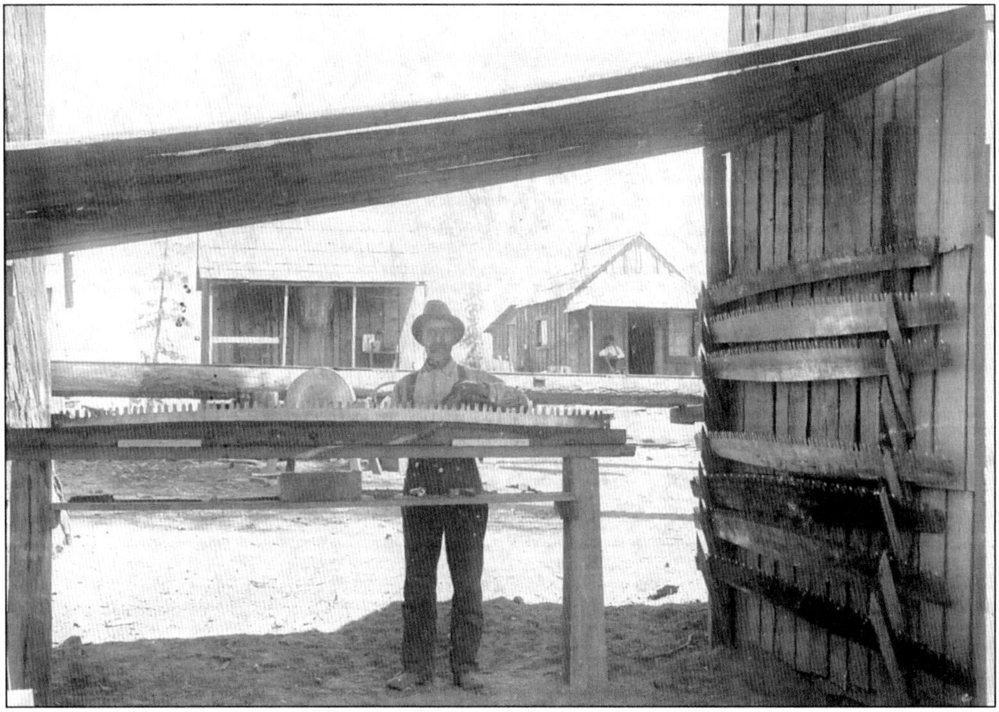

The saw filer for the Champion Mill was Eldus Johannsen from Sweden. His saw shop sat above the Champion Mill and below the elevated track on the switch siding. Note the train rails for meter-gauge mounted on the logs. Eldus's cabin is behind him amid other cabins for the men in the community.

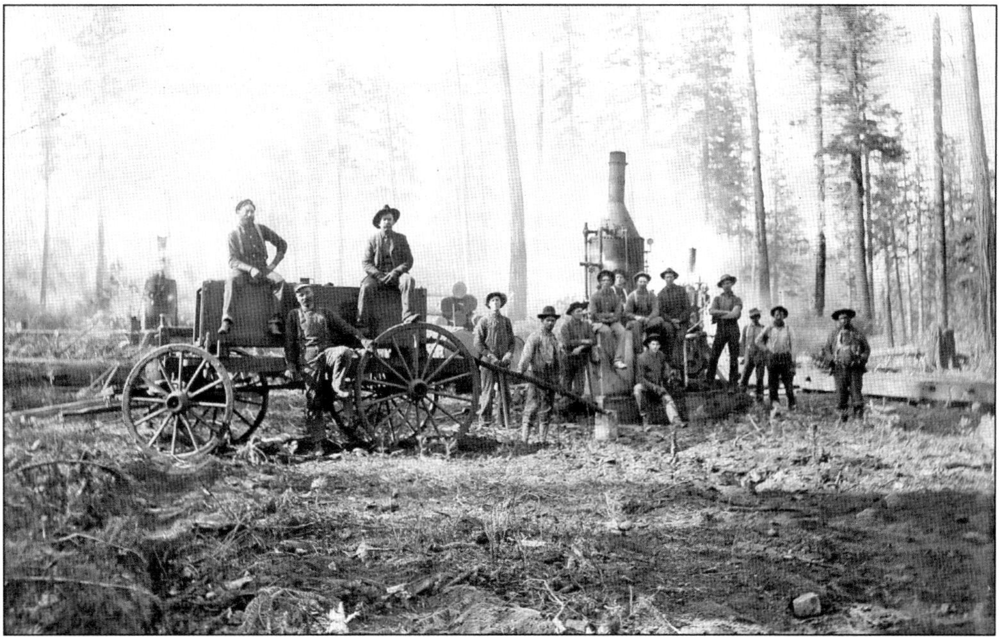

Men clear the town site of Lyonsville by Dolbeer Donkey engine. These "yarders" were used as a convenience, as previous work had been done by hand and oxen. Shown are crews from Engebretsen's mill. The very lumber from these trees was sold to Sierra Lumber Company and used to build the original Champion Mill. The original box flume in the right of photograph supplied earlier structures that made up the town.

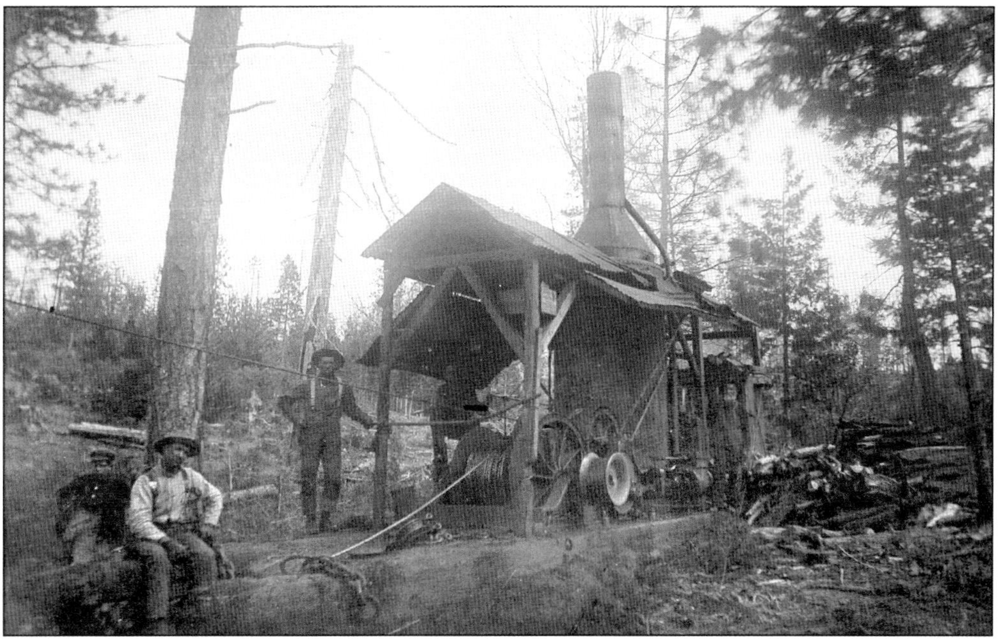

Just past where the Lyonsville Mill was to be built, the clearing of the roadbed was done by hoist logging. The slope on the left is where the land near the point fell off to the south fork of Antelope Creek and the postpile. The Dolbeer Donkey engine sits where the saw filers' cabin would be built.

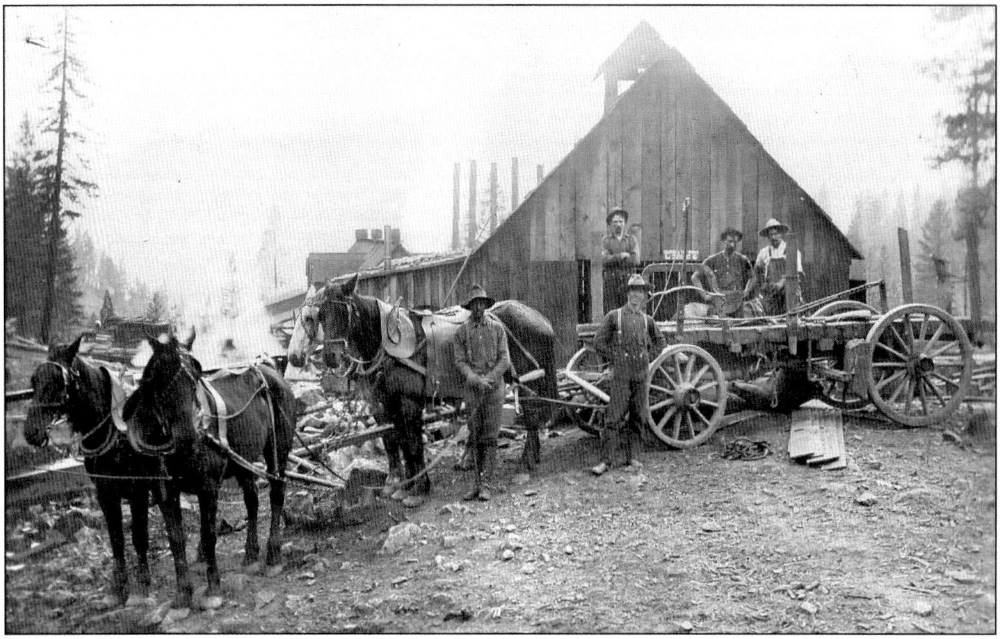

This is one of the most incredible Lyonsville views in this photograph from the James Gray Collection. Men are unloading sacks of grain, used for a still that supplied the Cliff House Saloon, in front of California Saw Works machine shed with the Champion Mill in the background. The large woodpiles pictured behind the horses' heads primarily supplied the boilers to the mill.

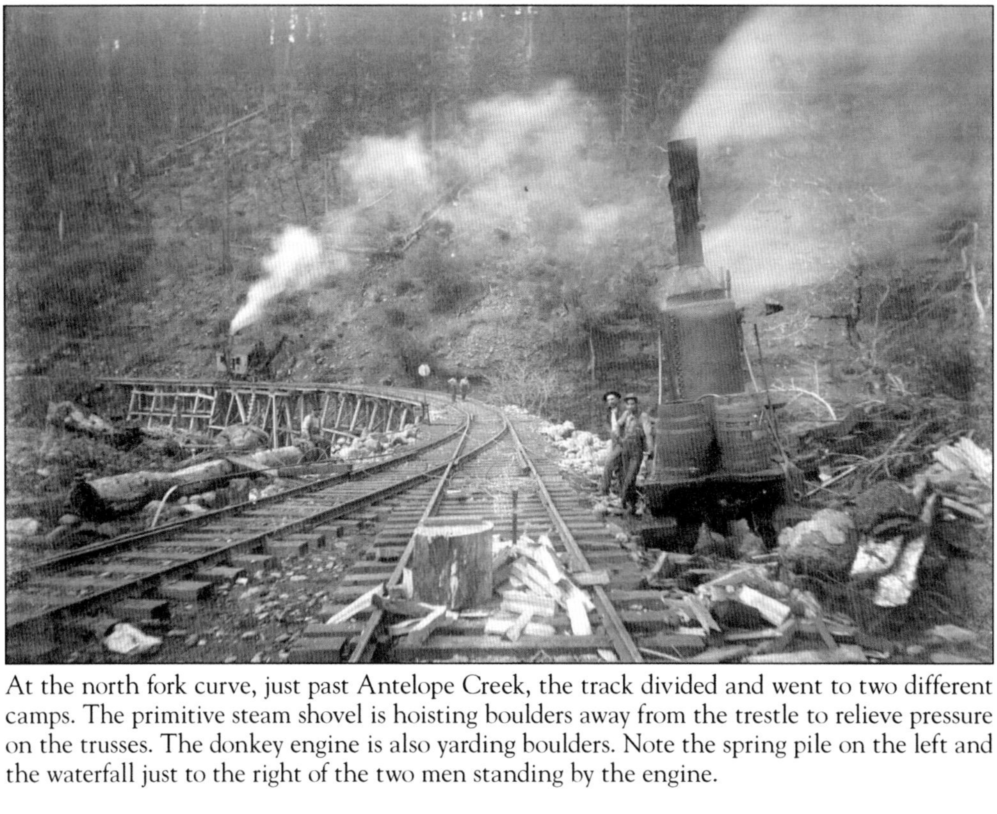

At the north fork curve, just past Antelope Creek, the track divided and went to two different camps. The primitive steam shovel is hoisting boulders away from the trestle to relieve pressure on the trusses. The donkey engine is also yarding boulders. Note the spring pile on the left and the waterfall just to the right of the two men standing by the engine.

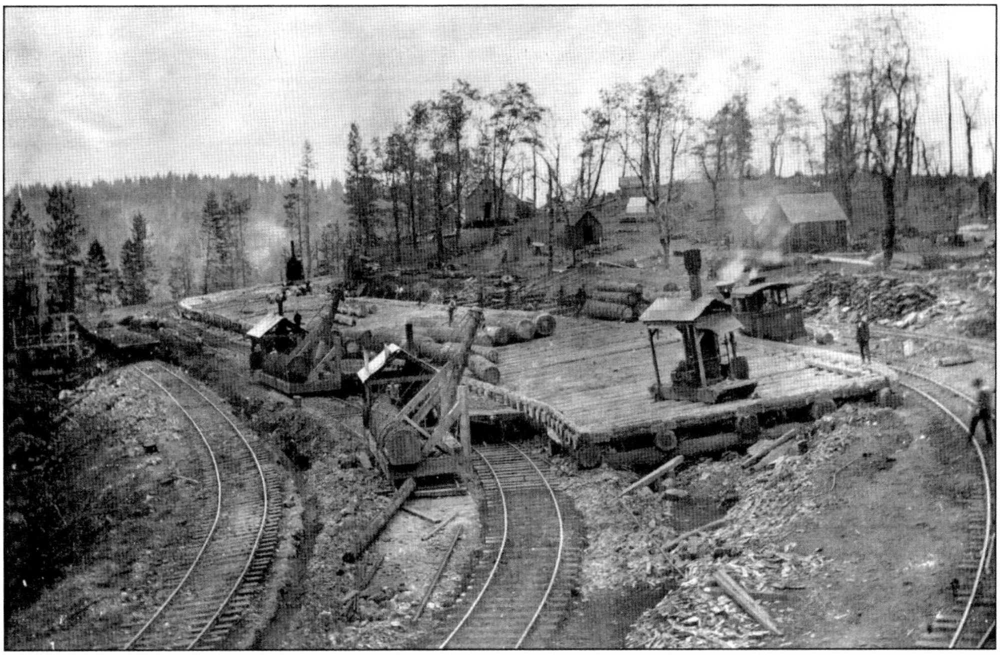

Here are three spur lines for the narrow gauge in Lyonsville. The right line was soon removed and later the other two tracks became the main road. The greaser's shingled shack sits in the center at the ridgeline, and the small building to the right of it is the dynamite shack. The No. 2 Shay engine, the first engine in Lyonsville, is preparing to back out after pushing a carload of logs into the landing.

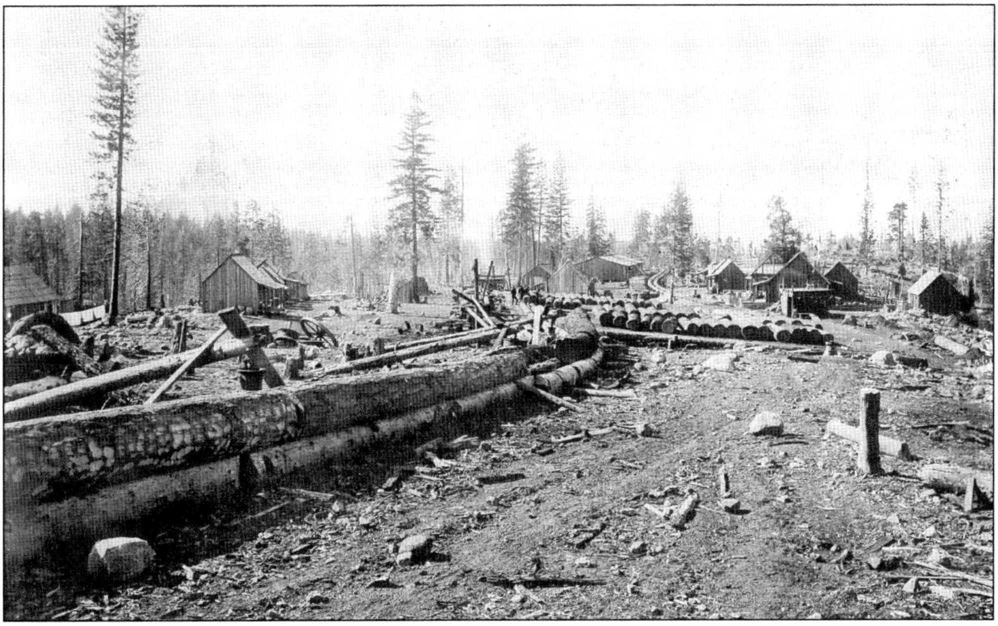

Gears, cogs, spools, and the No. 2 Shay engine (partially disassembled and hauled on a special wagon) were already snaking their way up the Hogsback. This was the final clearing of the town site, which extended all the way up to the steeps to Lyon Hill. The saw filer's wife has hung her white sheets out to dry, and on the far right are the stock pans of Adolf Olson.

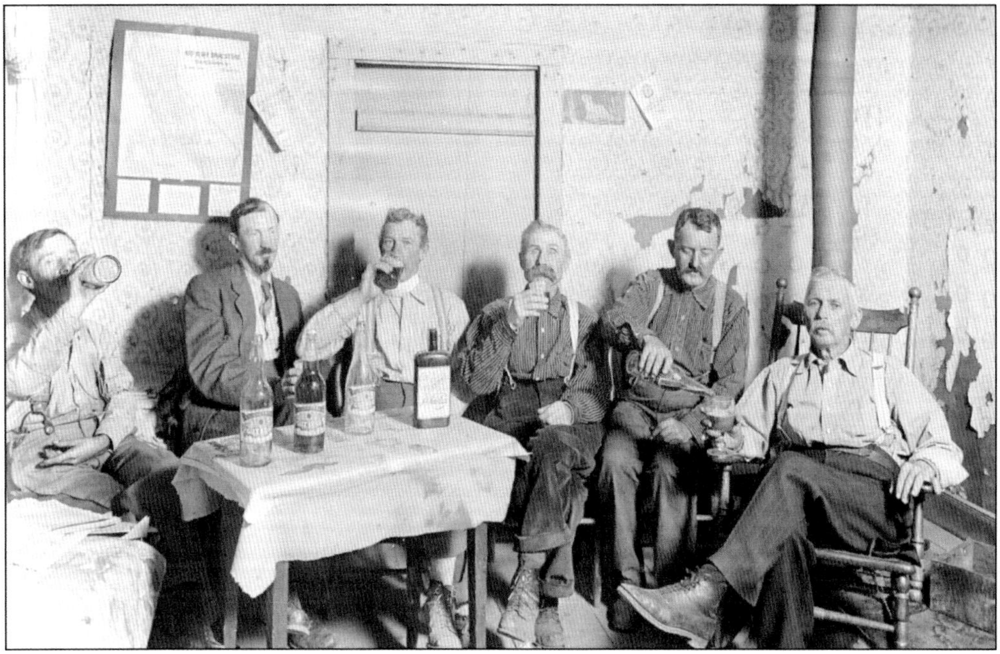

The office of Dr. Connell was located near the school and off Champion Street between some residential houses. Dr. Connell was the company doctor for the Sierra Lumber Company and was housed, equipped, and employed by mills in the area. Seated in this 1900 interior photograph from left to right are Bill Greer, Dr. Connell, Bob Greer, Adolph Olson, Abe Watson, and George Britt.

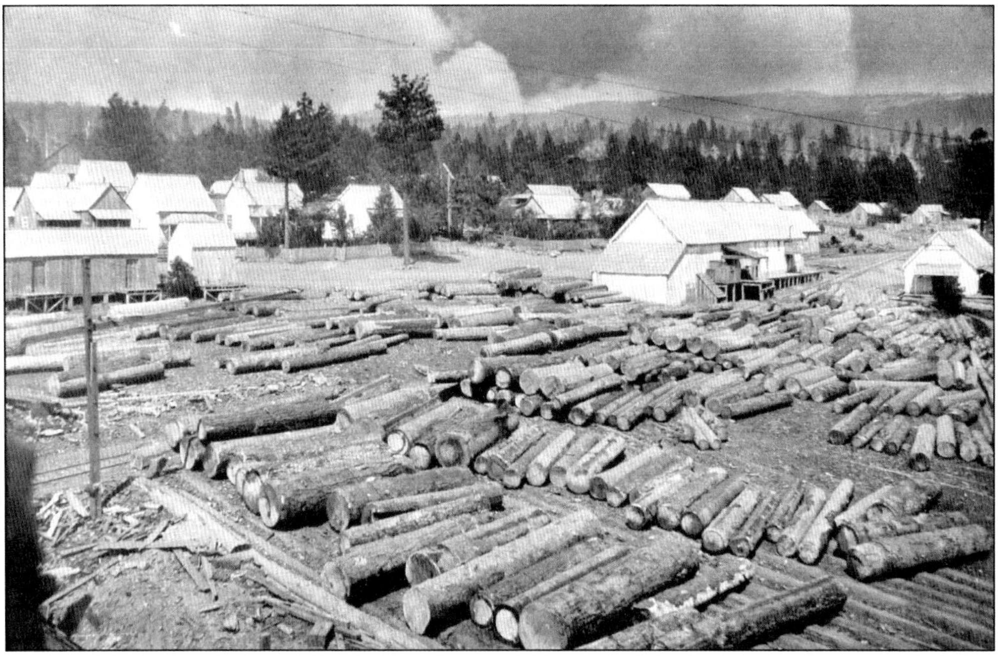

This photograph of Lyonsville was taken in 1892 from atop the whistle tower of the Champion Mill and looks up toward Lyon Hill. Beyond the rolling yard, where logs were rolled down platforms to the great saws, are the houses and cabins of the early town.

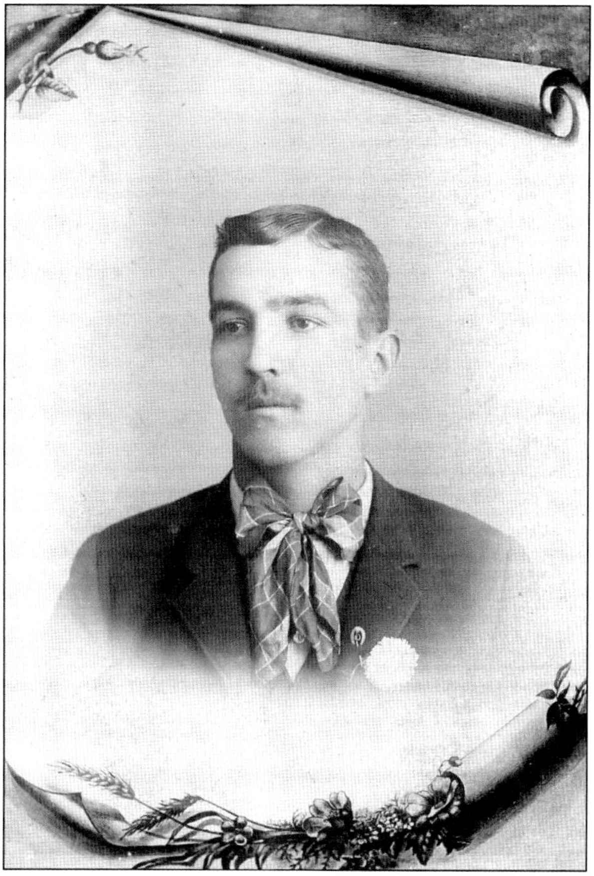

Jacob "Jake" Shelton was a coupler on the No. 6 line behind the No. 2. On September 9, 1898, a sudden jolt threw 25-year-old Jake beneath the trains wheels. His legs were severed, and he died within minutes. An elegy in the *Red Bluff Daily News* read, "There's sorrow in the household now / Grief fills each aching breast / A Darling son and brother dear / Has gone to his last rest." Jacob is buried in the Shelton plot at Belle Mill in Lyonsville.

This is one of the earliest photographs of the Champion Mill just after completion and at full production. "The Champ" also boasted a fire flume atop the mill. Notice the water running down the roof, but after two serious shingle fires on the roof, it was repaired with galvanized steel. As the caption states, "Capacity av. about 75,000 [board] ft. pr. day" was sawn on one 24-hour shift.

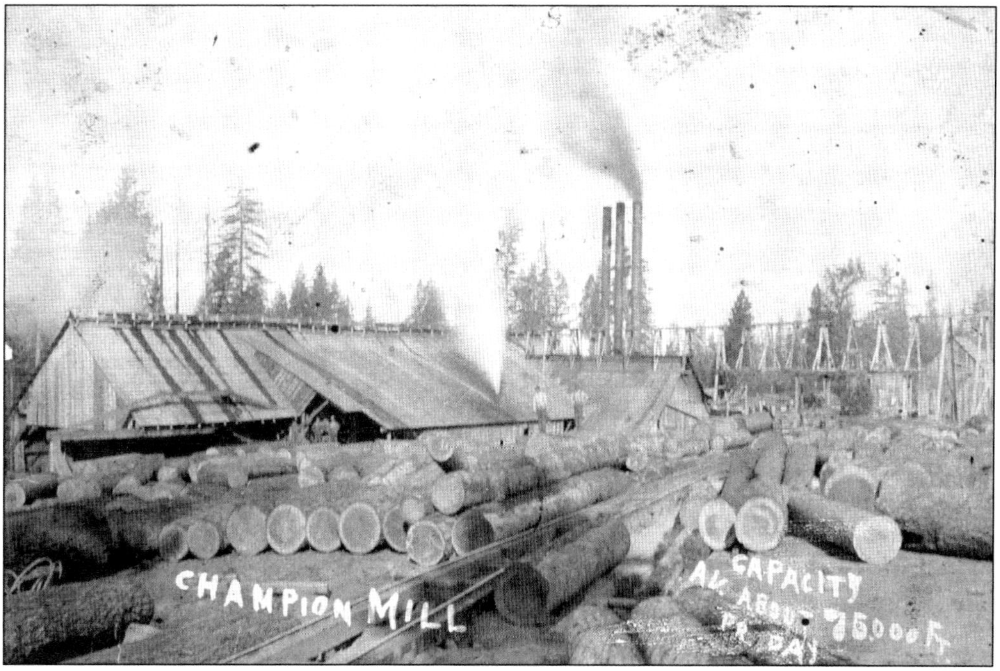

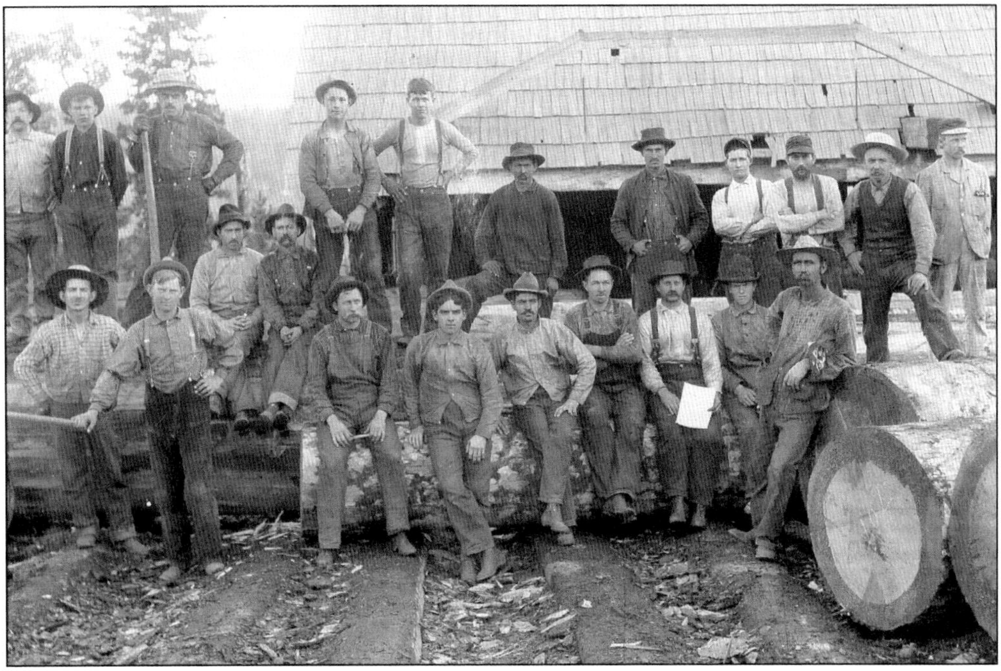

The crew at the Champion Mill poses in 1896, and foreman Herman Burr holds a certificate of appreciation from Sierra Lumber Company. A day earlier, the crew broke the record of 75,000 board feet with a whopping 92,000 board feet cut and stacked. For years, the certificate hung in Dr. Connell's office; he poses second from the far right in the hat. The imposing Tom Boots, with a cowboy hat, is below Dr. Connell.

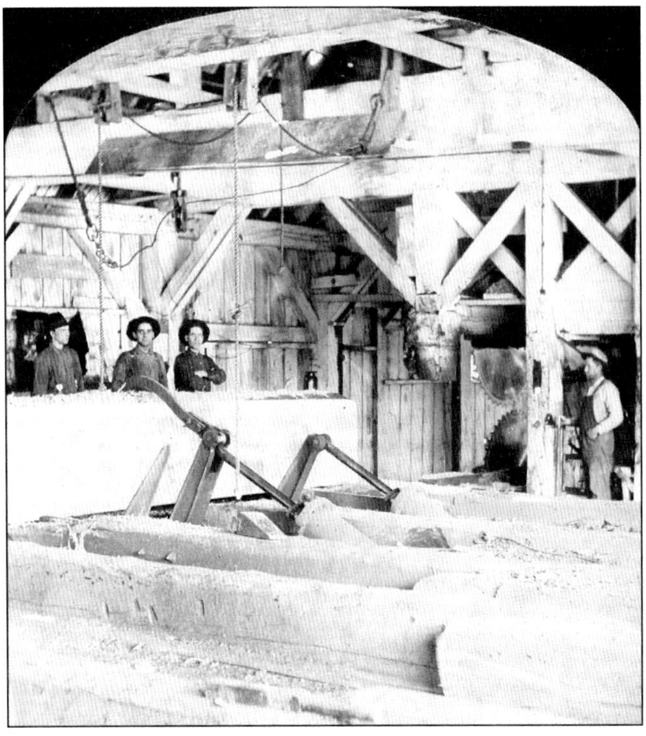

This stereoscope card of the saws at Champion Mill shows the production line and piston-driven hooks for holding and turning logs. Two slabs of 30-foot-wide lumber were saved by Adolf Olson from this log and are preserved to this day in the author's museum. Daguerreotypes, tintypes, and stereo cards were luxuries.

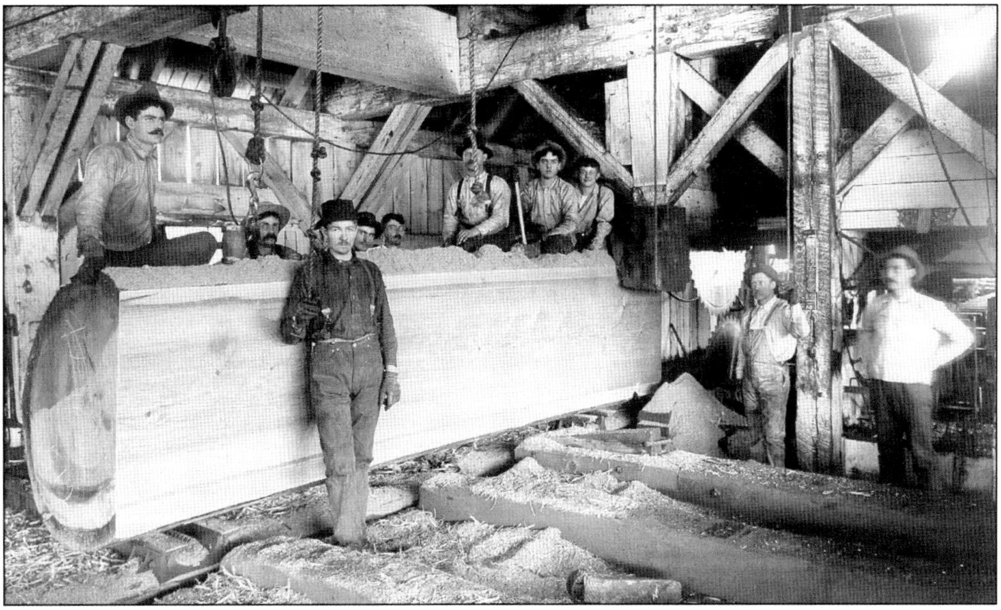

This photograph is from the collection of Hannah and James Gray. It shows the men of Champion Mill celebrating as they have just broken the daily production record for the mill by 17,000 board feet.

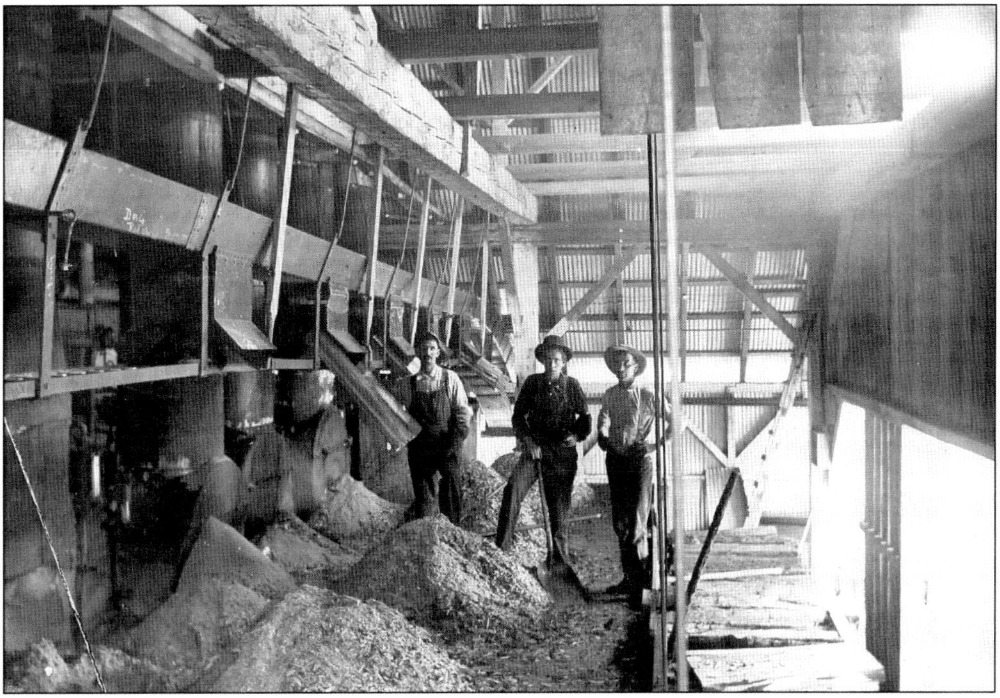

Contrary to what many people have thought, the Champion Mill and Lyonsville actually had electricity in a limited sense. The boilers were fed with sawdust and scrap sent down chutes from above. Excess sawdust was sent down a giant chute behind the mill to the giant sawdust pile that eventually ran a quarter-mile down the hill to the south fork of Antelope Creek and encased entire trees. The sawdust pile grew to 200 feet deep.

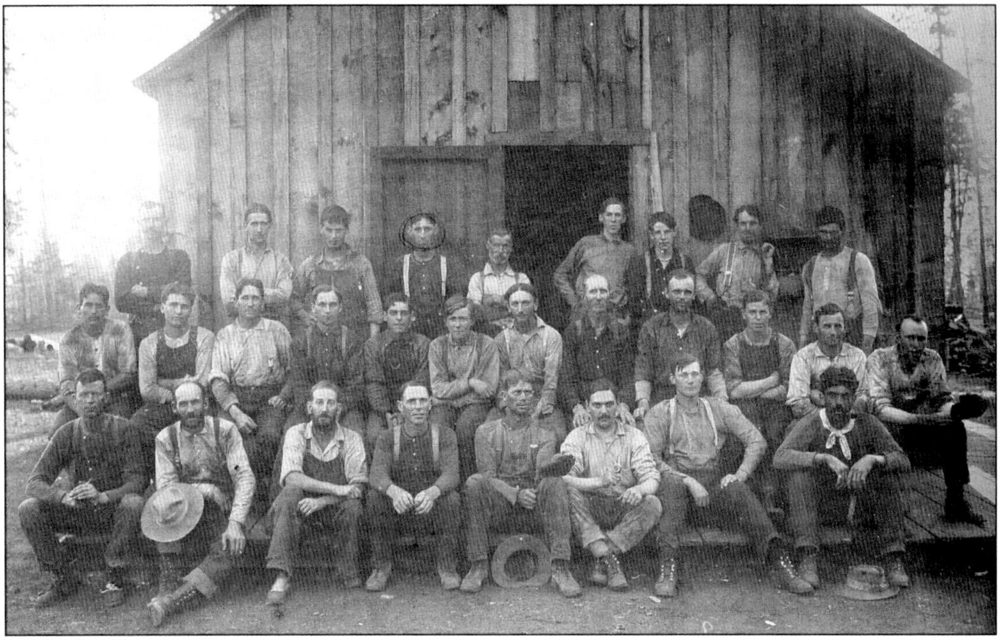

Here is a cookhouse at Shelton's Camp in 1899. Camps and outposts were more distant as time went on and near-lying timber was cut. This necessitated on-the-spot camps that could only be reached by train. Most company camps operated a cookhouse that offered a hot breakfast and dinner; lunches were portable and could be carried into the woods. Breakfast was at 5 a.m., and dinner was at 7 p.m., often serving up to 50 men.

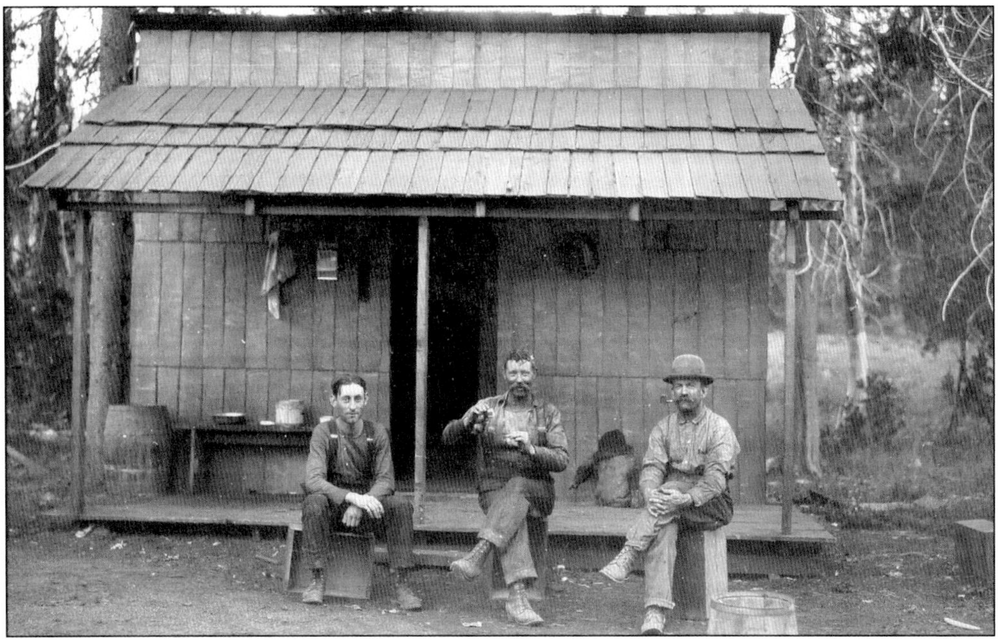

This is one of the single men's cabins at Shelton's Camp. Most single cabins were 9 by 12 feet and housed four men. This cabin is a frame cover with froe-cut, sugar pine thin shakes. Pictured from left to right are Dyas Shelton, Will Shumaker, and Ed Shelton, who was the woods boss for the aptly named Shelton's Camp.

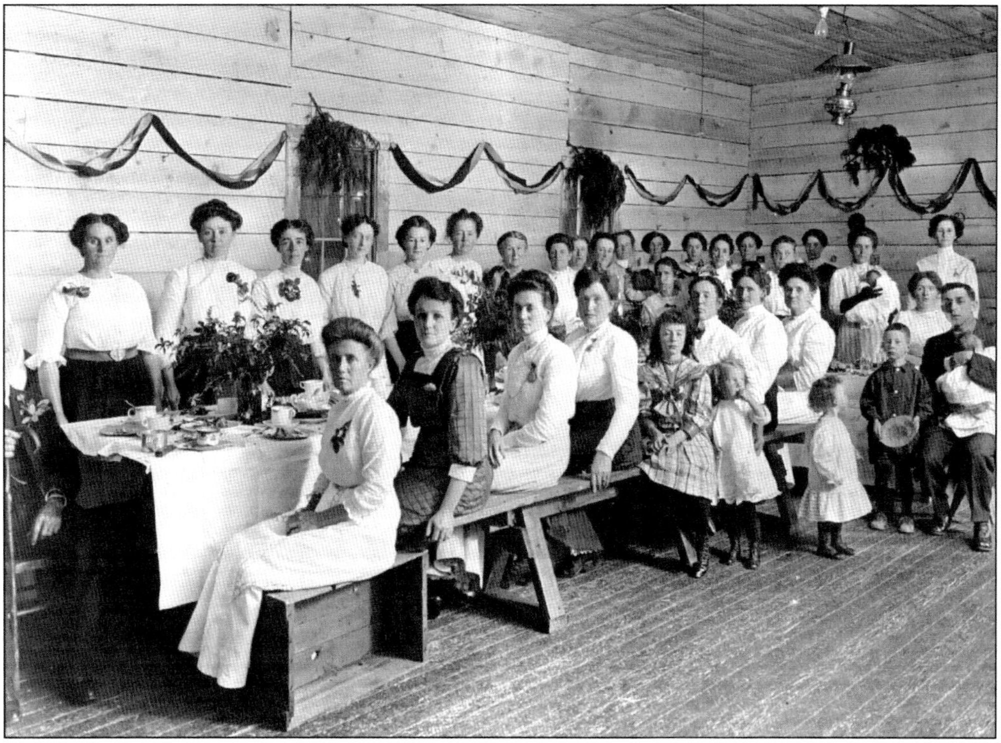

The Lyonsville Social Hall and community center was one of the largest buildings in town and had been thrown together as a barracks for crews clearing the town site to stay in. As with all lumber coming from Engebretsens, the planking for the walls was cut to eight-foot lengths for easy transport to town site. The ladies of the town have gathered in 1896 for Dr. Connell's birthday party.

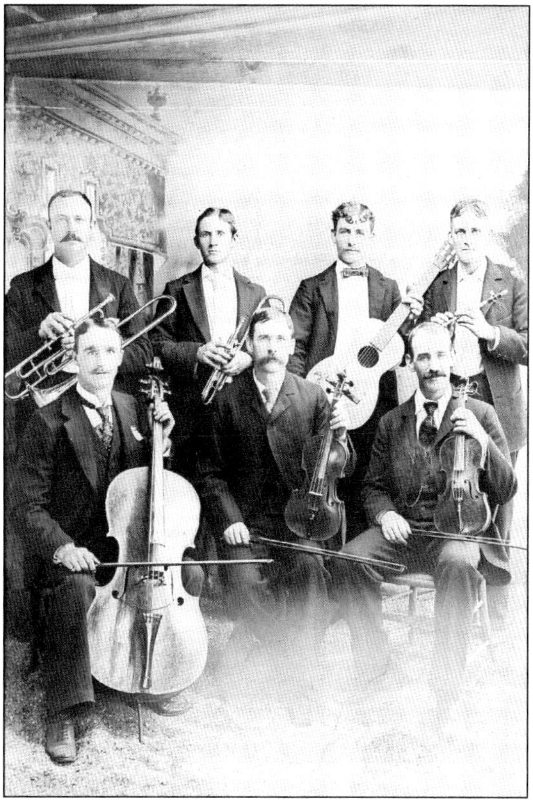

In 1885, a dance was hosted by the Lyonsville Hillbillies Orchestra at the community center. The orchestra members from left to right are (first row) Myrtle Knauss, George Turner, and Charles Shelton; (second row) Bill Cook, Albert Hughes, Lawrence Estes, and Harry Hughes. Though they were all cousins, only Charlie Shelton lived in Lyonsville at the time.

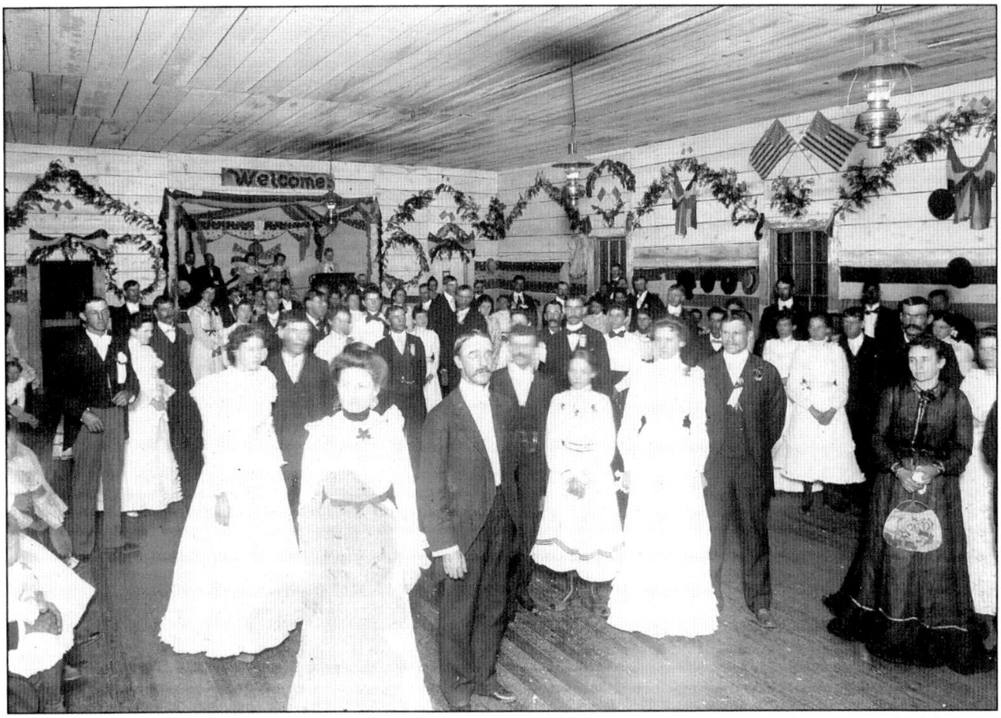

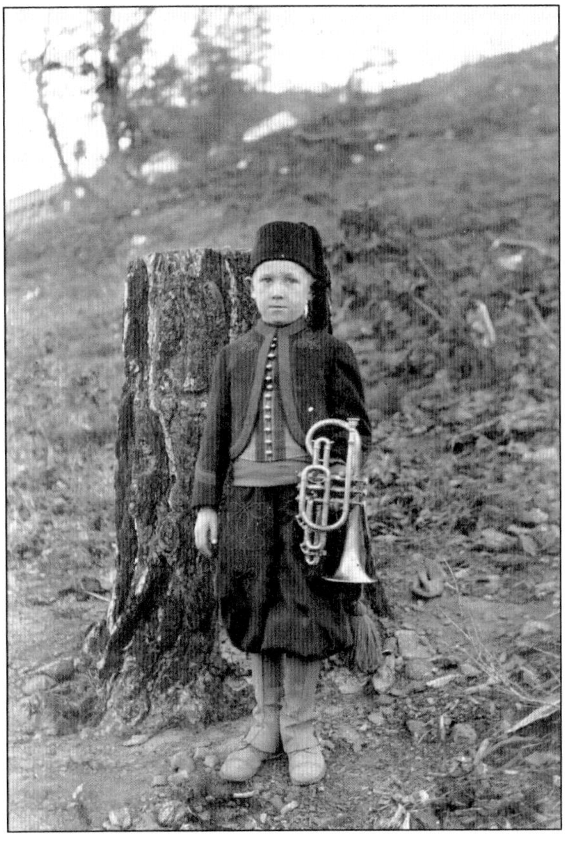

This July 4, 1893, dance was held at the Lyonsville Community Center. The orchestra is the Nanney Orchestra and is comprised of Lulu and Olive Nanney on violins, Abner Nanney Jr. and Charles Shelton on guitars, and Anne and Ida Nanney on the pump organ.

Danny Shelton, pictured at seven years old, was band mascot for the Lyonsville band as well as Mammoth Mine, which was partially owned by his parents, Charles and Eva Shelton. Danny had one sister, Doris, who married John Pangborn.

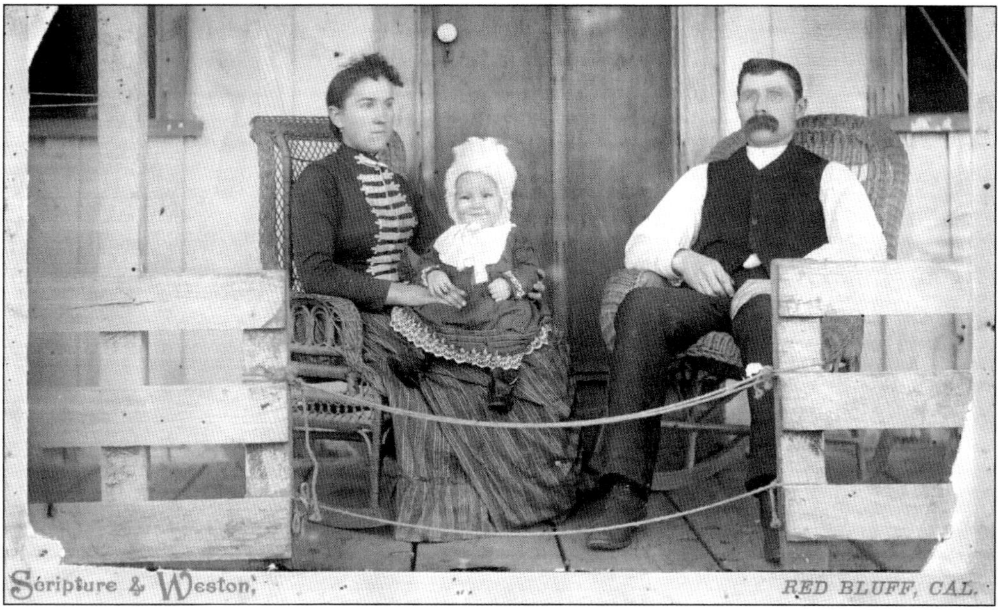

Adolf Olson and wife Alice Elizabeth pose on the front porch of their Lyonsville home in 1888 with the first of their three sons, Eddie, at 10 months of age. Adolf was the head sawyer at the Champion Mill for 34 years. The Olsons were a bit more affluent than some Lyonsville folks because of side businesses that they both had. Alice did washing and ironing, while Adolf home-brewed beer and raised sheep.

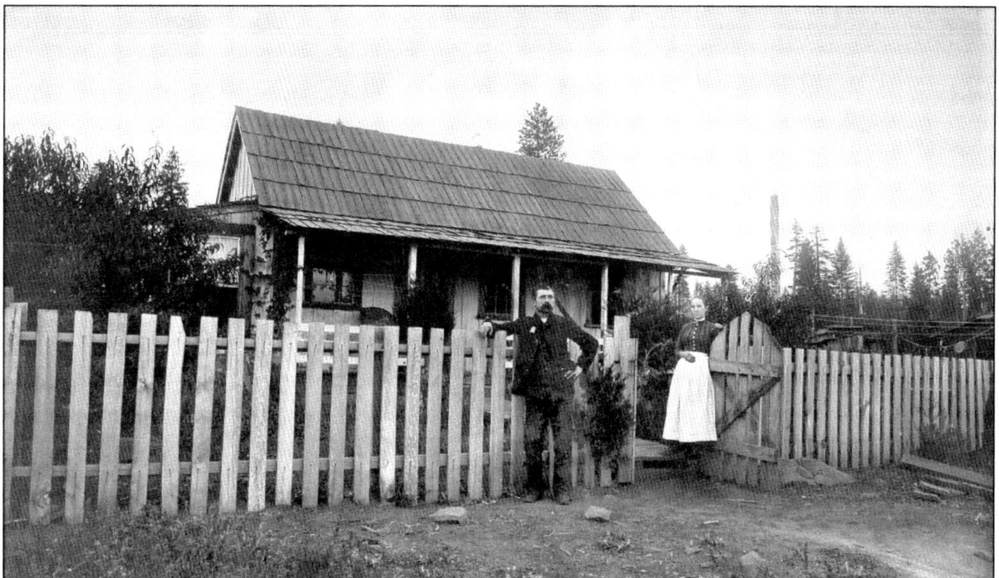

Another view of the Olson House shows native Cedar trees as well as hops and peaches planted by the Olsons. One amenity of the Olson home was the far left kitchen wing, which could be closed off from the rest of the house during hot summer days. Letha Jane Shelton's clothesline and wash shed can be seen on the right.

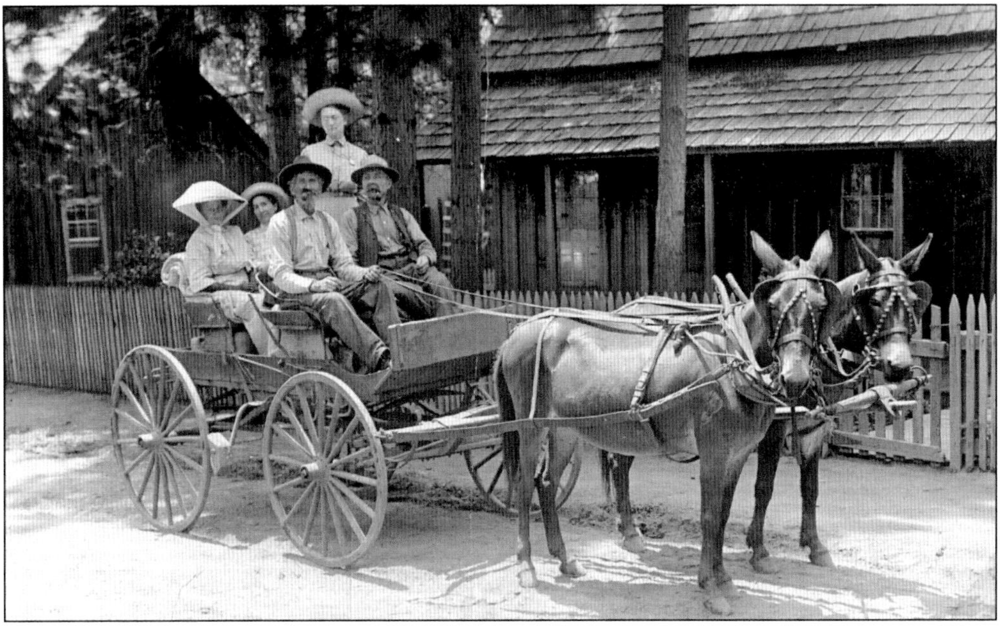

After many years of living in Lyonsville, the Olsons, shown in their wagon, are accompanied by their friends. Pictured from left to right are (first row) Jim Lucas and Adolf Olson; (second row) Pattie Lucas, Alice Olson, and Minnie Walker. The mules, Elmer (left) and Winnie (right), were companions of the Olsons for more than 30 years.

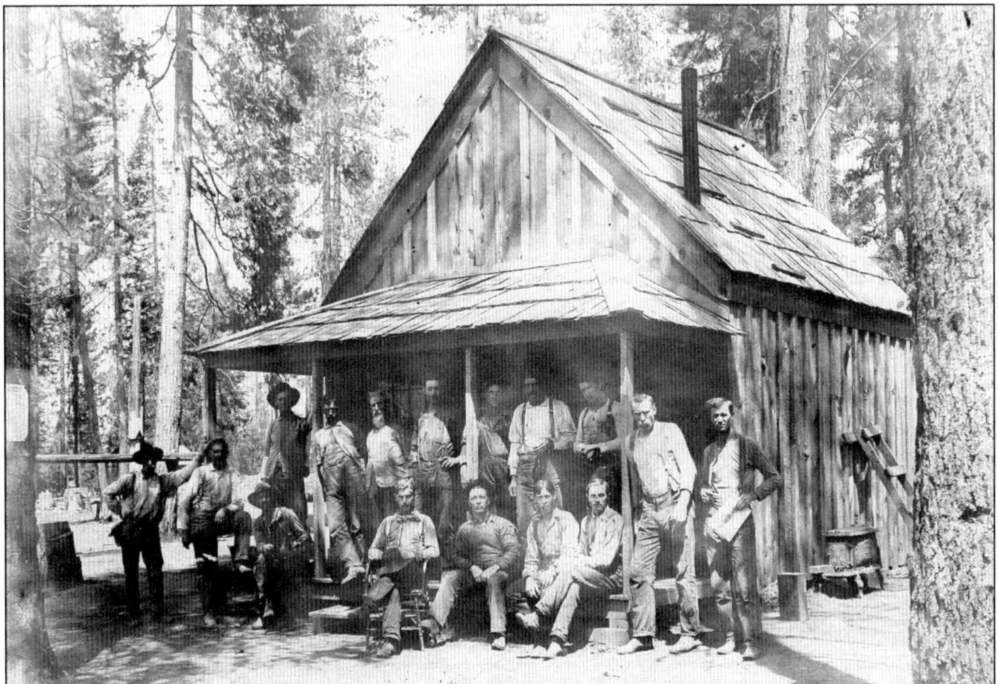

Next to the family homes were the single men's cabins. Most single cabins, Dolbeer Donkey engines, and large pieces of equipment were mounted on skids for easy moving and loading onto the flatcars for camp relocation.

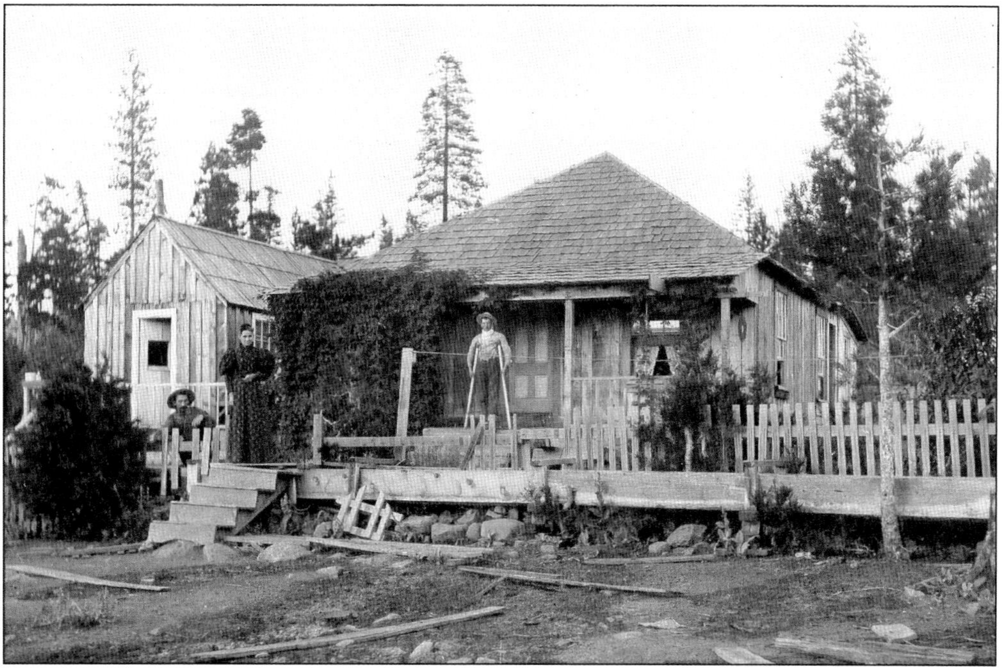

The Thomas Shelton home sat on Center Street, which was near the very center of town and was the first road built. The Shelton and Olson homes were the first structures to be built before the town of Lyonsville existed. Dr. Letha Jane's office is the building on the left. The saw blade on the porch is the dinner bell. The flume supplied water to the house. Thomas Jr. is on crutches.

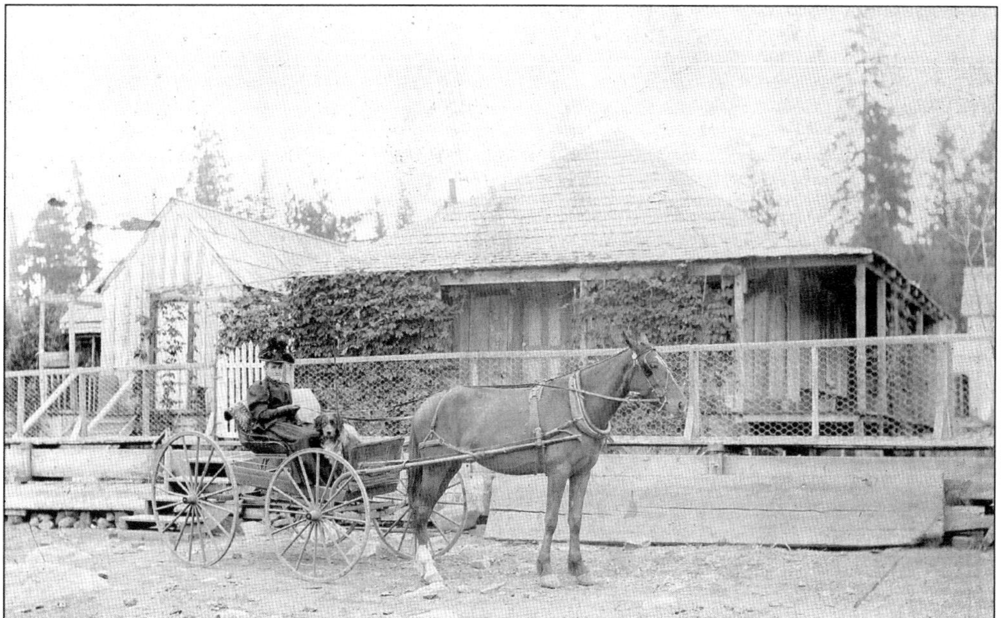

"Weep not for Mother. We all have the same ordeal to pass," read the words from the epitaph of Dr. Letha Shelton printed in the *Red Bluff News* and pasted on the reverse of this photograph. Dr. Shelton died at her Lyonsville home on March 17, 1900. She is pictured with her dog and horse in 1898.

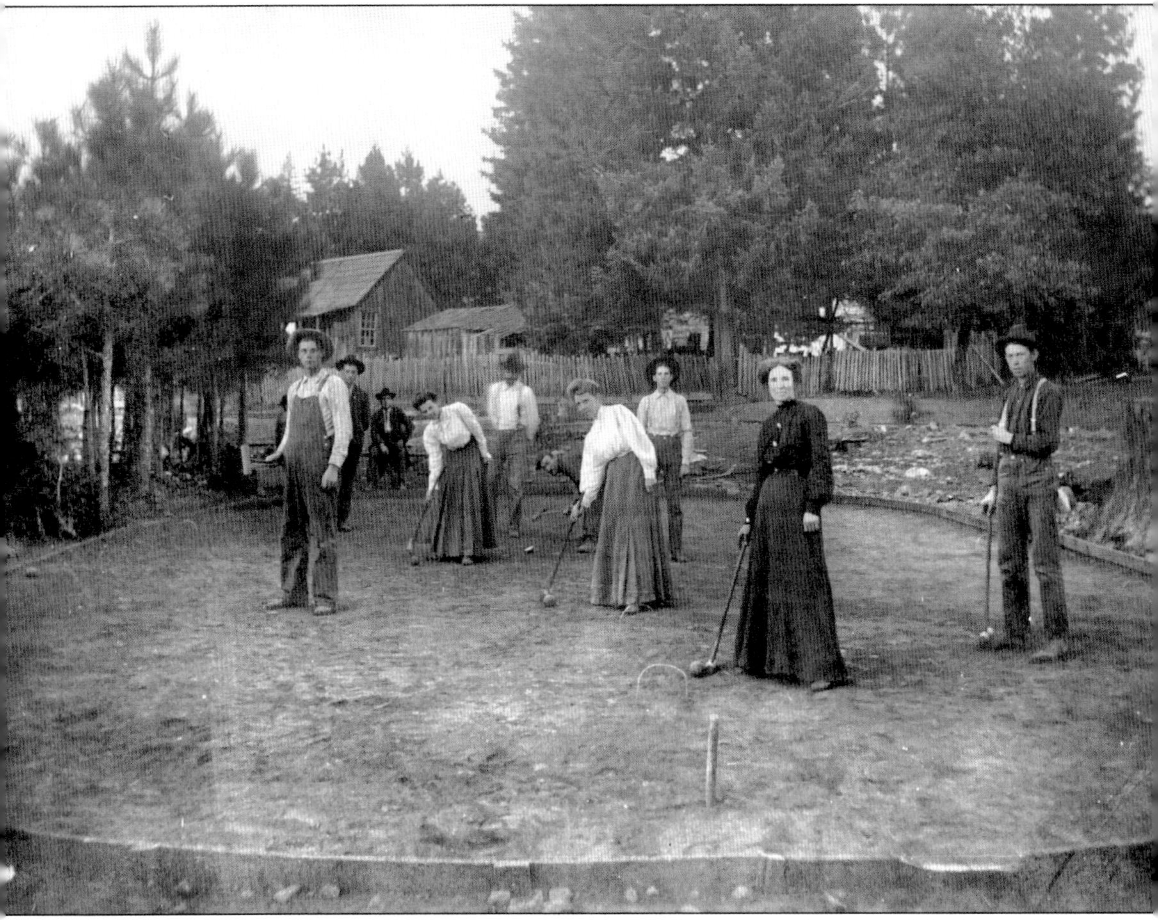

Annie and Nancy Westrope were from a pioneer family that came to Lassen and the Mineral area, finally settling near Lyonsville. Shown here playing croquet are the two Westrope girls in white blouses just before they married the two Shelton brothers; Thomas is seated, and John is to his left, both with a hat on. Croquet tournaments were big in Lyonsville on Sunday afternoons.

High Point, as it was called before Lyonsville was built, was first settled by Thomas J. and Letha Shelton. Shown in their wedding photograph, the Sheltons were married June 2, 1854. By the time Letha and Thomas arrived in California, Thomas's brother, James, was a wealthy landowner in Newville near Orland, California. He promoted river commerce and Thoroughbred racehorses and had a racetrack on his extensive ranch.

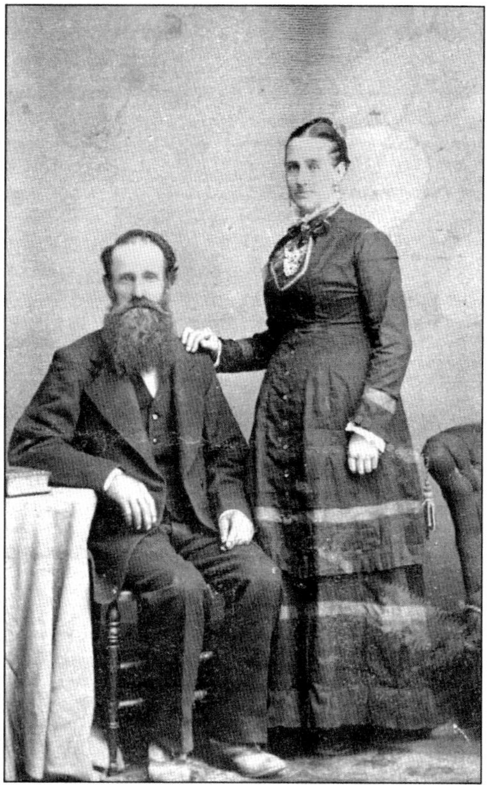

Later in the day, the croquet players arrived at the Thomas Shelton Sr. house for dinner on September 18, 1898. Trout as well as meats were kept fresh in a cool rain barrel that a trickle of water ran through. Shown from left to right in Letha Jane Shelton's lush garden are Tom Shelton, Annie Westrope, John Shelton, and Nancy Westrope.

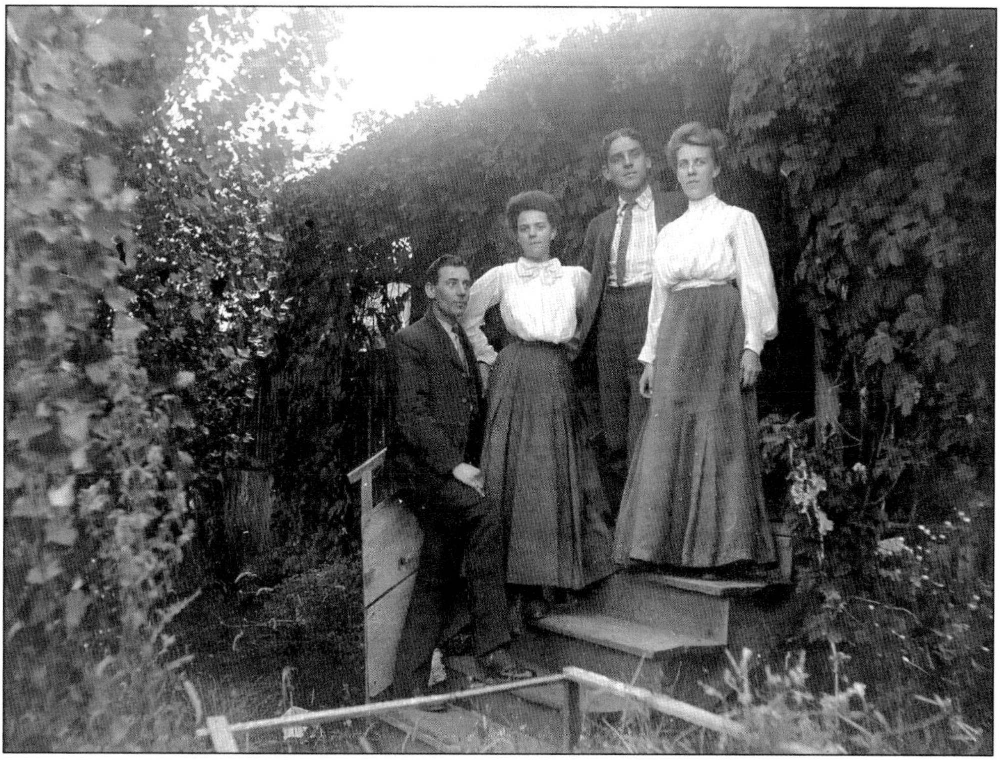

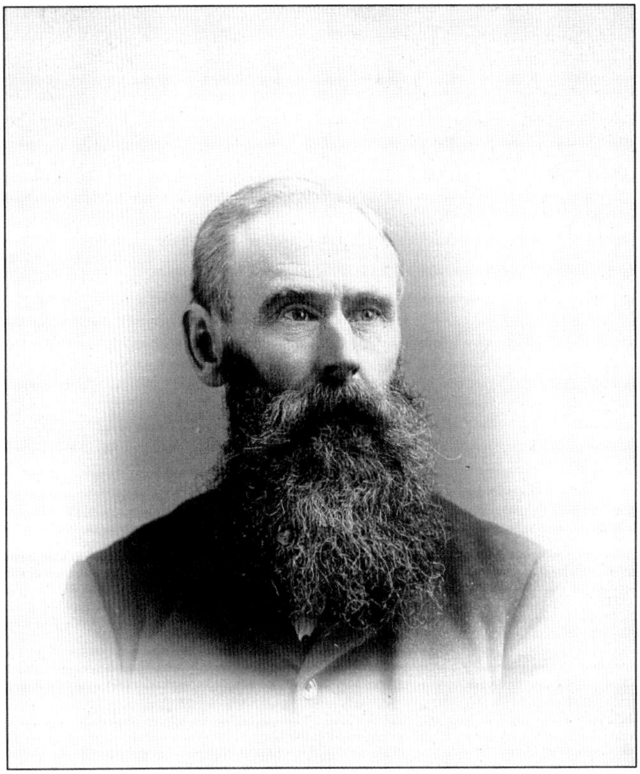

Born in Gladbrook, Iowa, on November 25, 1831, Thomas Jefferson Shelton came to California in 1849. Thomas died at his Lyonsville home of heart failure on March 25, 1891. In December 1886, his children all pitched in money when the photographer was in town and had these photographs taken as a Christmas present. Thomas was a shake splitter most of his life in Lyonsville and split the shakes for the Champion Mill.

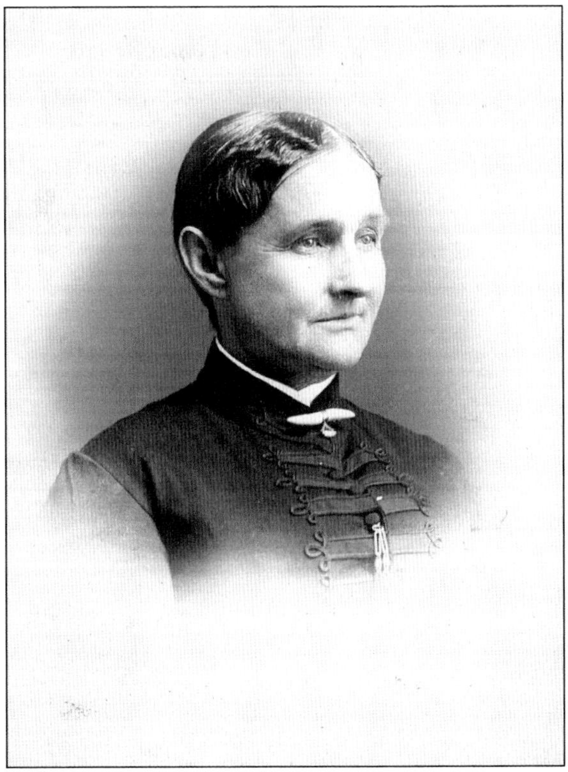

Letha Jane Shelton, born October 4, 1836, studied medicine in Iowa before becoming a midwife and moving to California. Letha was the mother of 13 children. Her youngest child, Jacob "Jake" Shelton, a train coupler, was killed in a train accident, and she was 35 miles away. Her family attempted to console her, saying that she could have done nothing to save Jake's life, yet she mourned for two years until her death on March 17, 1900.

Adolf and Alice Olson proudly pose here on their wedding day before Mr. J. D. Gaines's camera. Adolf Olson achieved the highest office in the Lodge Club and was a member for over 40 years.

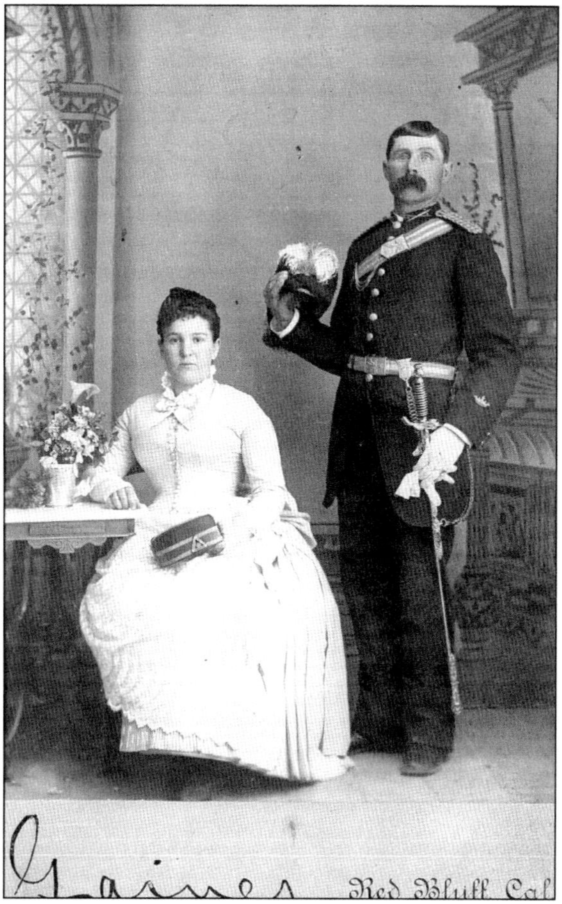

The greatest court trial in Tehama County history to this point was over whether Thomas J. Shelton Sr., who was accused of "stealing and carrying away" 12,600 pine shingles from J. R. Markley, was guilty. He was consequently found not guilty for lack of evidence. This was mainly because the shingles in question had disappeared, having been flumed down to the Sacramento River the previous night. R. A. Martin (a distant relative) was the presiding judge. On the day of the court trial, photographs were taken as many people from Lyonsville were witnesses for both sides and put on their best for court, which was held in the community hall. Here Ed Shelton (leaning on a bench), a witness for the defense (as well as Thomas's son), deliberates with other members of the community. Over half of the people in the photograph are related.

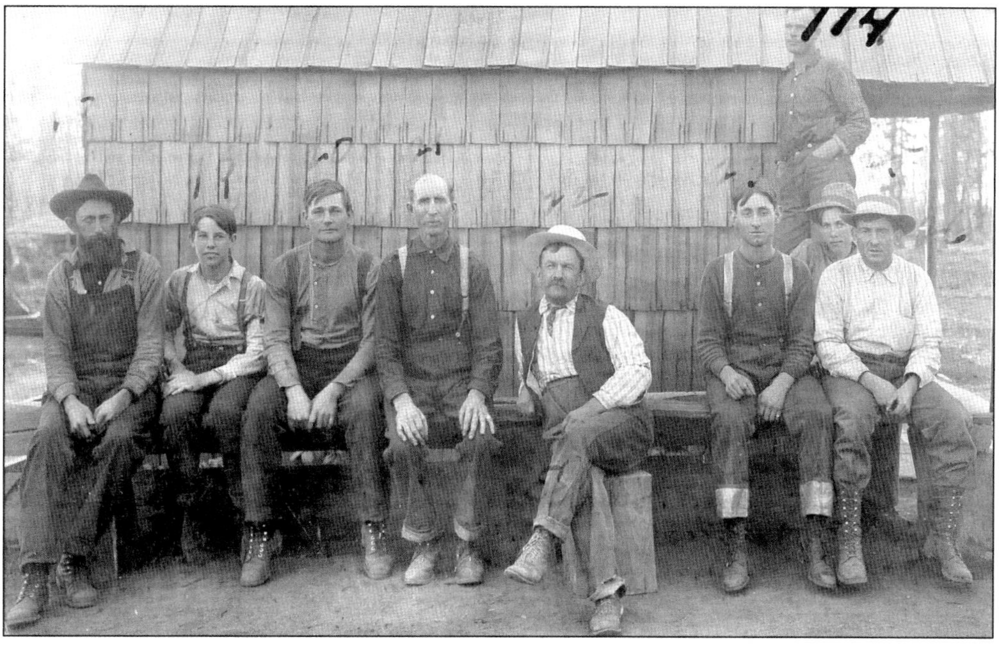

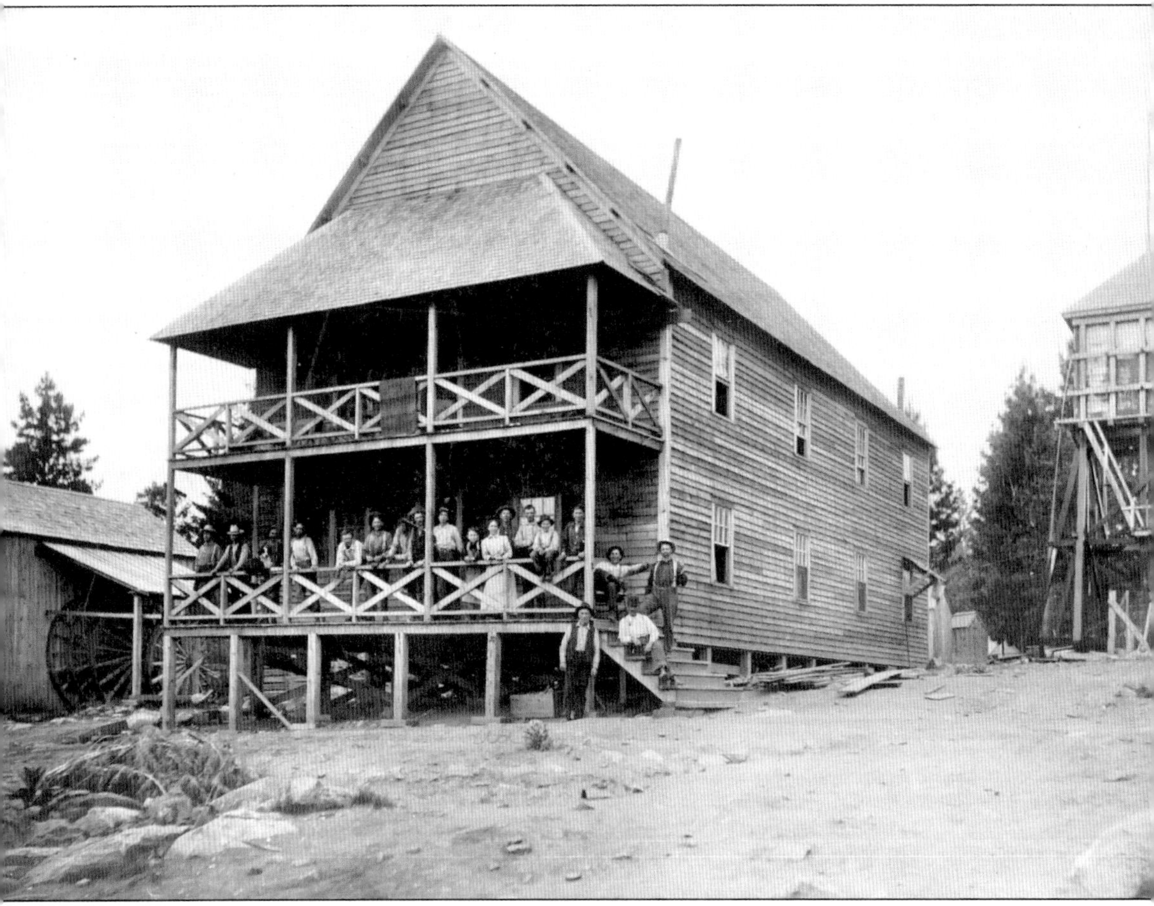

Alice Olson's Boarding House was the largest building in Lyonsville with two carriage barns and its own pressure-fed water towers, but the layout was ill-suited for community events. Pictured in this 1910 photograph are, from left to right, Tom Donnelly, John Boots, Tom Jensen, Dyas Shelton, Jim Sills, Tom Markley, Bert Hughes, Ed Boots, Mike Fatch, Jakie Olson, Alice Olson, Tom Boots, Jim Greer, Alva Olson, Frank Thorp, Dr. Connell, Eddie Olson, Ed Shelton, and Ned Williams.

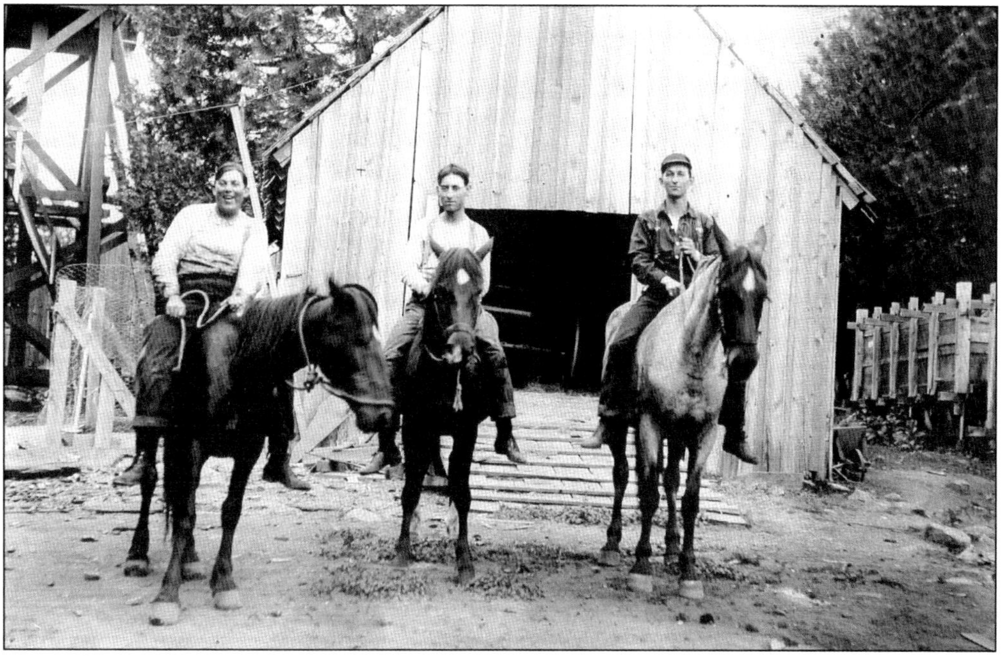

Taken the same day of the previous photograph, Eddie Olson, Dyas Shelton, and Lloyd Shelton pose from left to right in front of a carriage barn for an unknown photographer who used Alice Olson's camera.

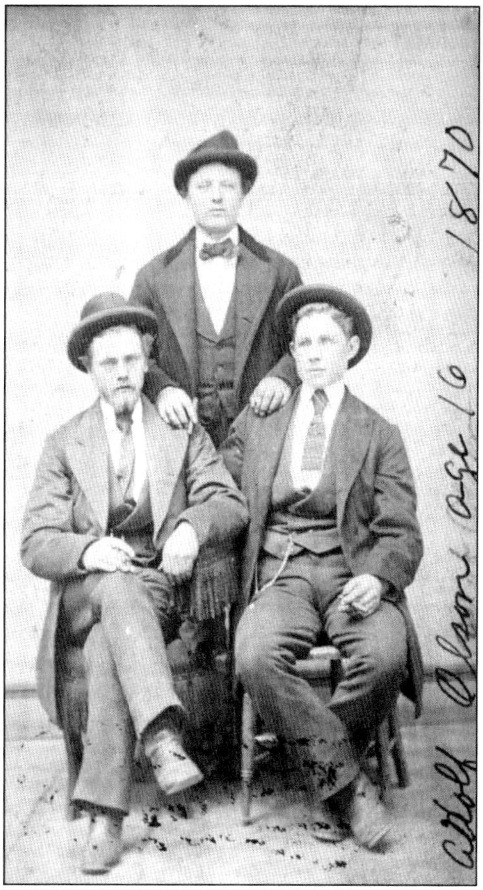

Adolf Olson, seated at right with cousins Lars, left, and Hans Hansen, was just 16 years old when this photograph was taken in 1870 after the three immigrated to this country with their other cousin, Jonas Jensen. This photograph was taken in San Francisco shortly before the group departed for Red Bluff. Adolf had been a mill worker in Sweden.

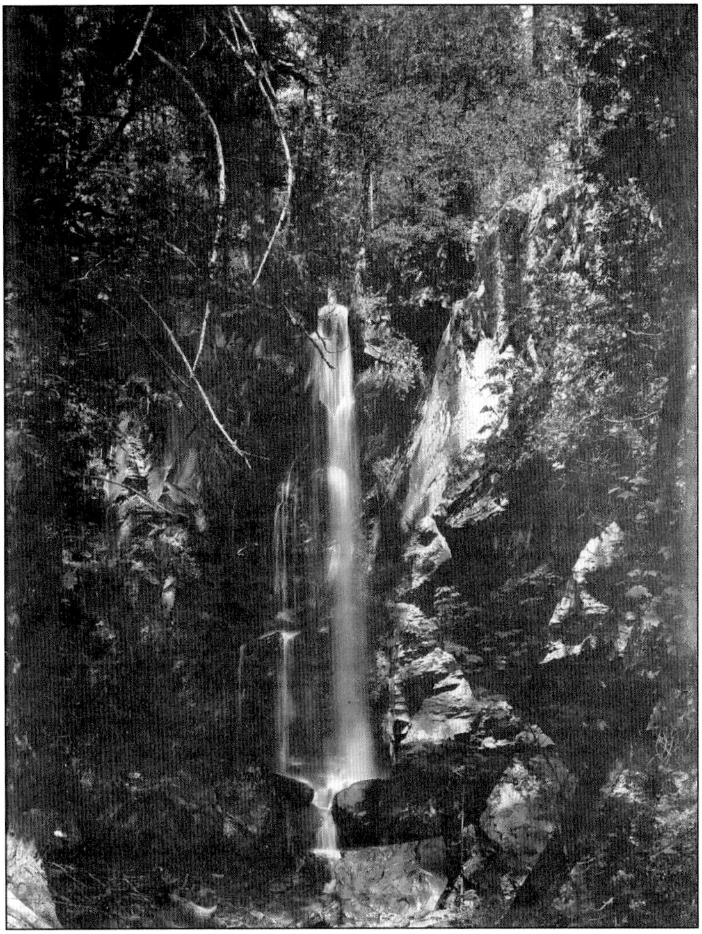

The 1884 image at left was taken by the Sierra Lumber Company as a promotional calendar photograph to show people out of the area the leisurely benefits the mountains had to offer. The following year, the lower photograph was used as a promotion during a slack time to try to lure people to Lyonsville to fill job positions. Most of the people in the lower photograph were business people, including Alice Olson (seated on the far left) and Dr. Letha Shelton (in the black dress). Just below the falls was a natural bowl. This bowl was extended by youths and built up with rocks to provide depth for those jumping from ledges on the falls. Any evidence of this has long washed away.

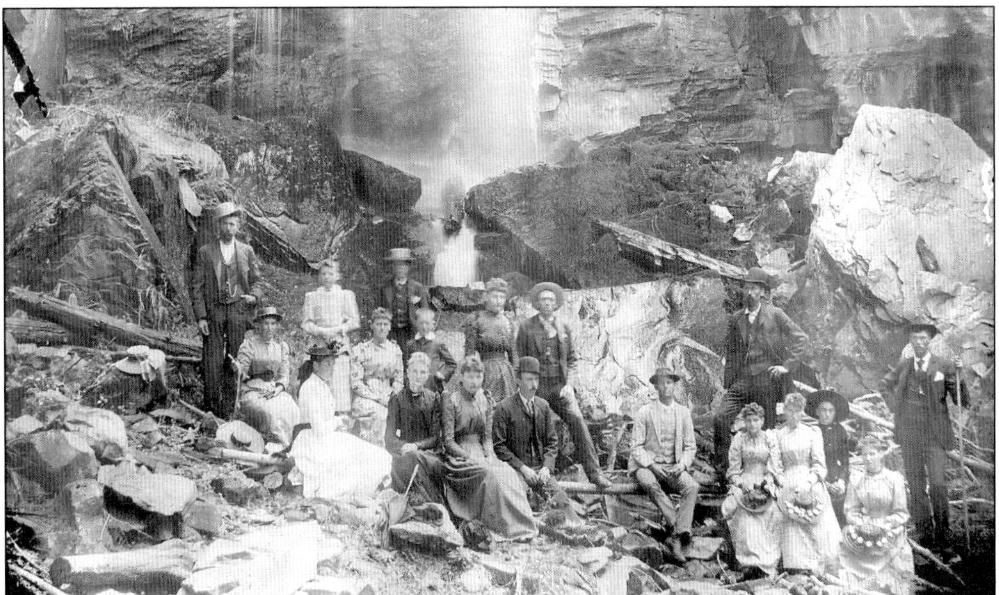

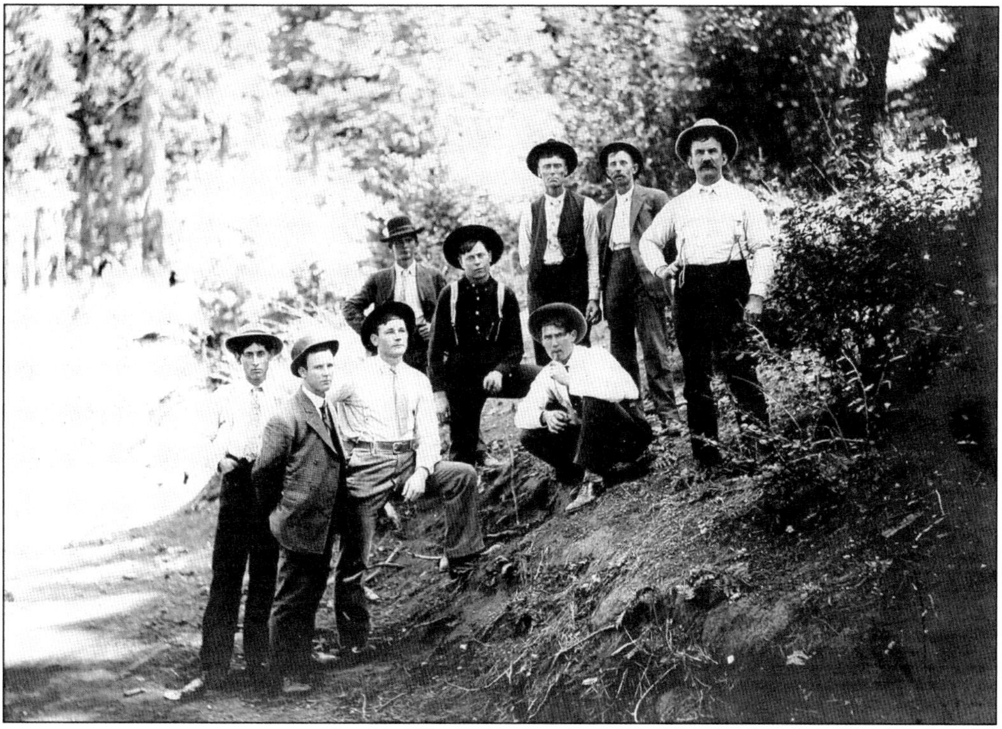

Other activities that were enjoyed on Sunday afternoons by the single men were walks in the woods. Here Ed Shelton and the crew of Shelton's Camp take a walk on the logging road. Sundays were a time to put on one's best clothes before the start of a long, hard work week. Sunday services were presided over by the Reverend J. J. Greer, who was the reverend at Lyonsville for many years.

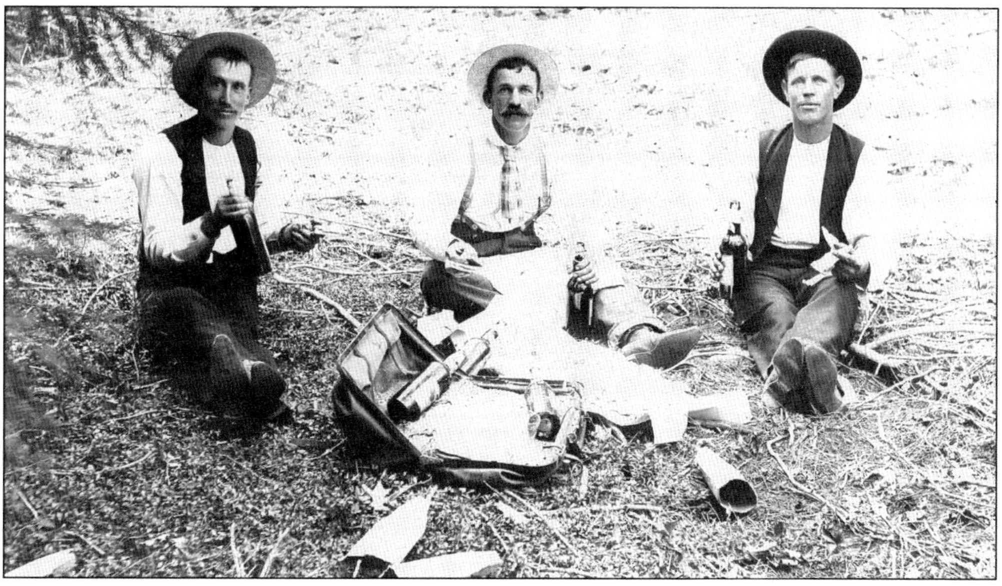

Throughout his life, Ed Shelton always had a weak spot for alcohol, which accelerated after the train accident and the death of his brother Jacob. Ed Shelton never married and lived most of his life in Lyonsville and his later years in Red Bluff. Ed Shelton, at 23 years, is pictured with his friends Jim Boots (left) and Jonas Jensen (right).

MALLOY'S CAMP

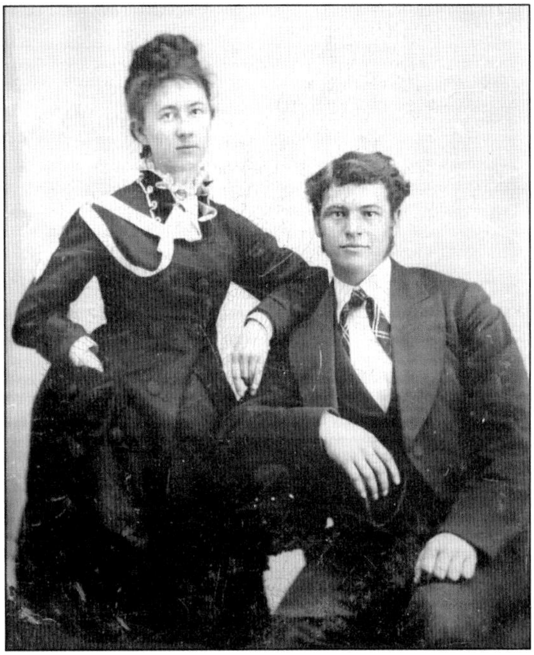

This tintype of E. S. Malloy was taken in New York before he and his wife, Phoebe, came to the West in 1860. As the story goes, Malloy had worked in the lumber industry in New York and was fascinated when landing in Sacramento City with boats followed by large spill booms, or rope lassos, that circled large groups of floating logs being moved from the Sierras. Malloy tracked the source to Tehama County and stayed.

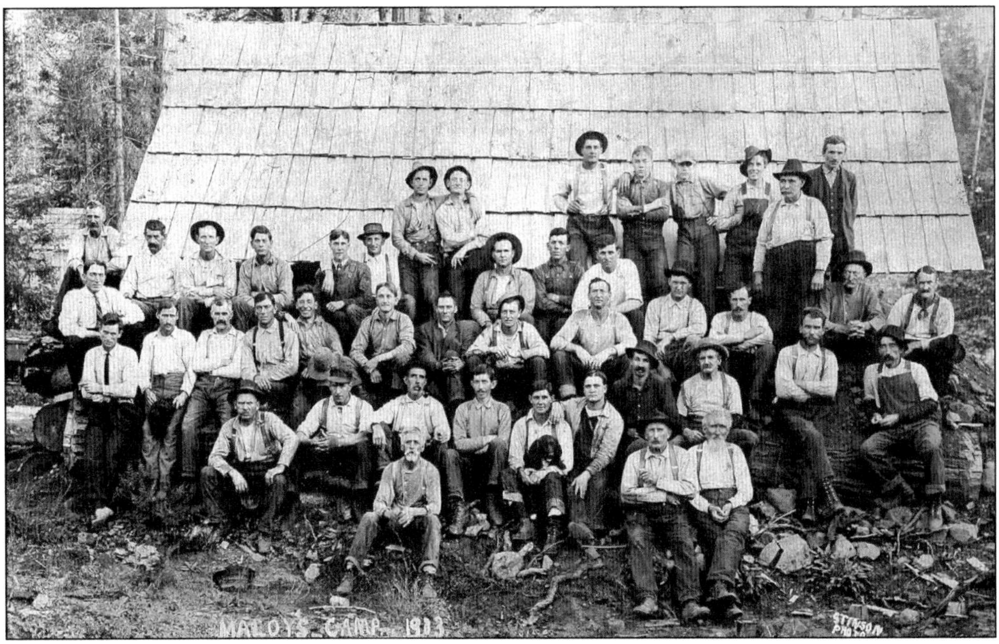

The post office and cookhouse were central to a camp. Here Malloy's crew relaxes while R. F. Stinson captures them on film in 1913. These were the final days of big timber before the decline of logging in the area. Tom Malloy, who is E. S. Malloy's son, smiles from the middle row (fifth from left) while Madison "Doc" Shelton relaxes (far right).

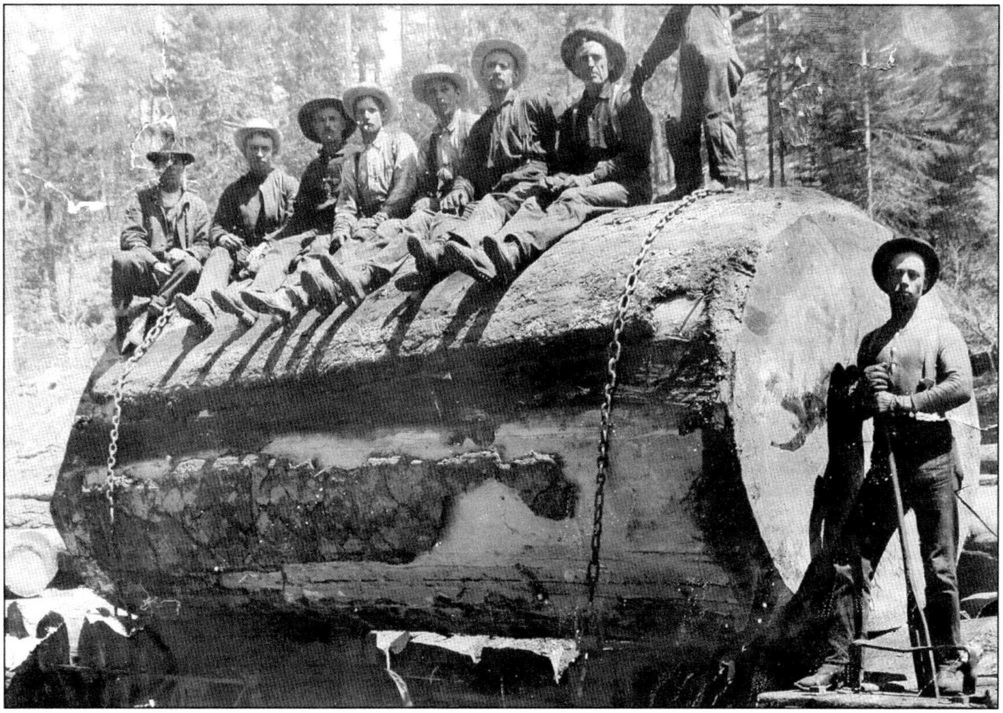

A spur of the narrow-gauge railroad swung out into the forests and reached Malloy's Camp. Serviced by the 101 and 103 engines, crews harvested the huge trees, often taking only the bottom, or premium cuts, of the trees and leaving the rest to rot in the woods. Most cuts of large trees were chopped into 16-foot sections for practical transport. This pine log is destined for the saws of the Champion Mill.

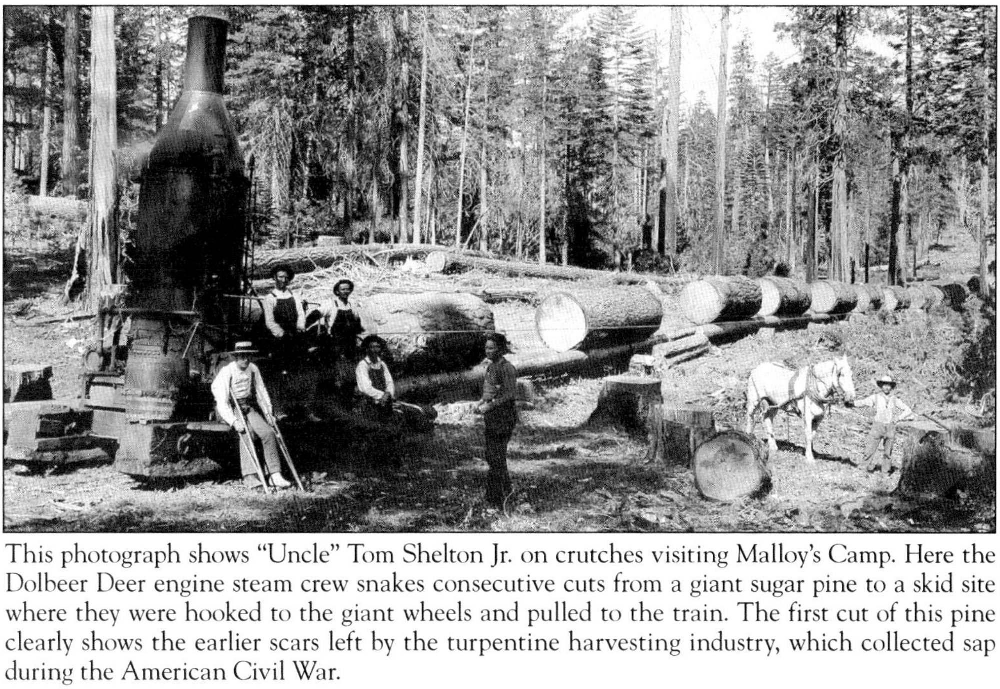

This photograph shows "Uncle" Tom Shelton Jr. on crutches visiting Malloy's Camp. Here the Dolbeer Deer engine steam crew snakes consecutive cuts from a giant sugar pine to a skid site where they were hooked to the giant wheels and pulled to the train. The first cut of this pine clearly shows the earlier scars left by the turpentine harvesting industry, which collected sap during the American Civil War.

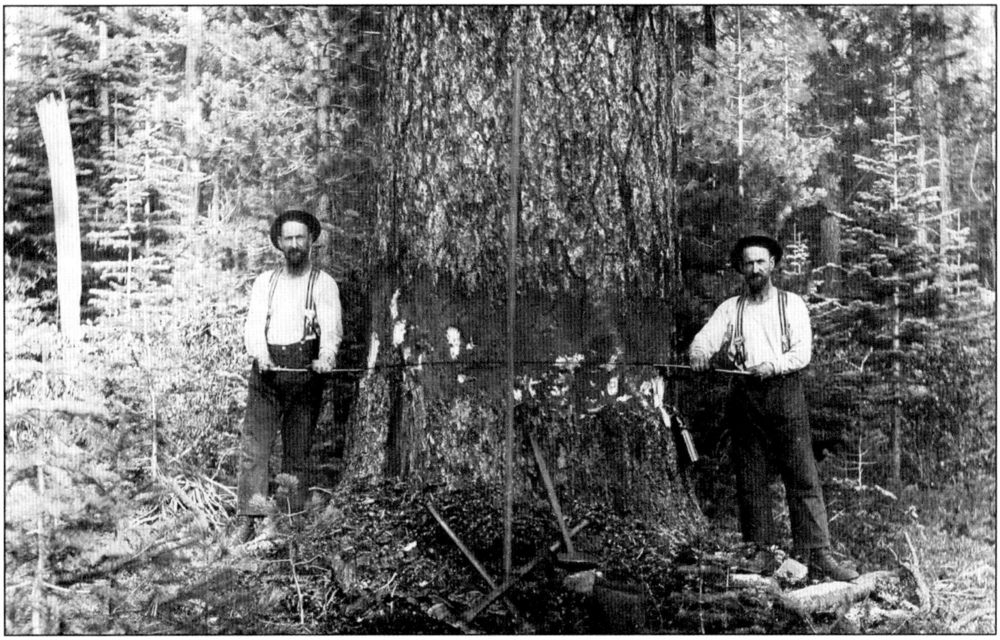

When R. F. Stinson did this split-and-spliced photograph of "Doc" M. V. Shelton felling a tree near Lyonsville, this saw cut was still in the safety zone with the undercut on the rear side with the lean of the tree. A good lumberjack could look up a tree and instantly know the "pitch and camber" (leaning) of the tree as well as the direction it would fall. The split photograph was spliced at the scale stick.

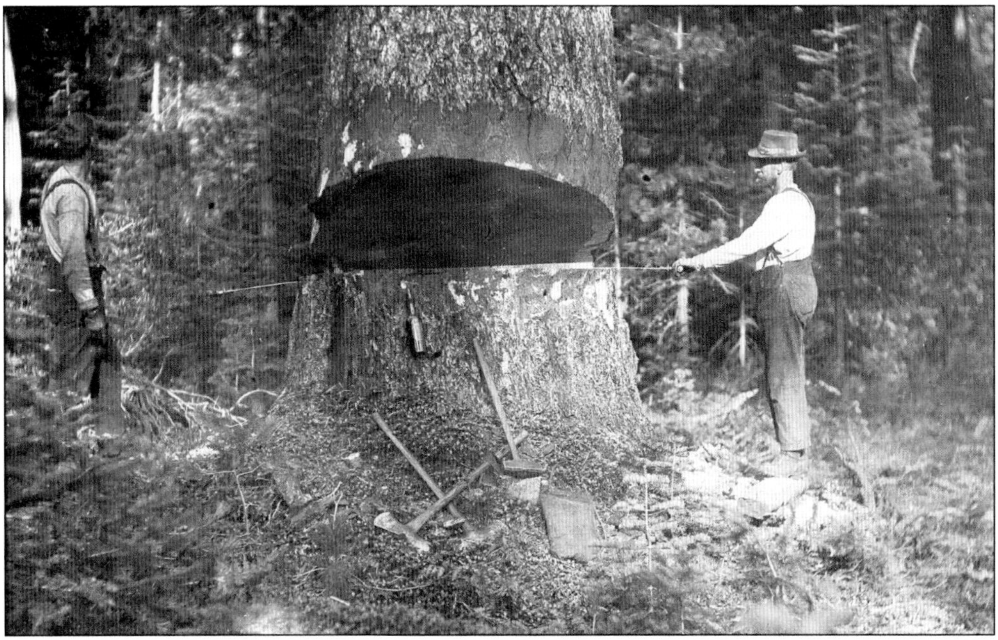

Since it took two men to put a tree of this size down with a double buck crosscut saw, Stinson captured this image a short time later. Frank Emerson, Doc's cousin, steps in to help Doc fell the tree. Trees were first ringed with an ax to remove bark and any embedded rocks that could potentially dull the saw blade.

"Shooting the Shutes" (or chutes) was accomplished by wooden flume boats, which were nothing more than half of an eight-foot log hollowed out with an adz, or hodadz. The boats were removed and put into the V flumes for water transportation, which was made especially easy by the buoyant and well-greased wood that repelled water.

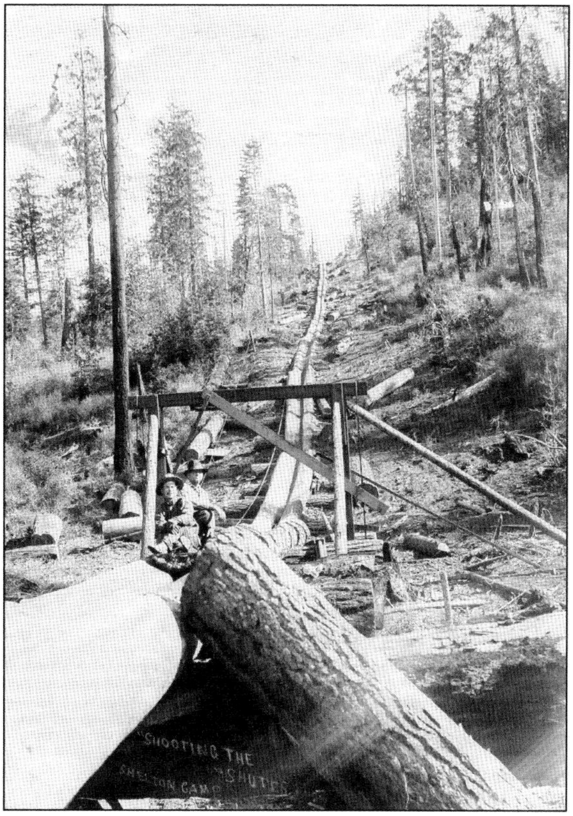

By the time the photographs on this page and the following pages were taken, Malloy's Camp had merged to become part of Shelton's Camp. The landing shown was more permanent than most, having two haul-back donkey engines and an elevated, mini–V flume that poured water into the spring box for camp use, both for steam donkey and men's personal needs. Ed Shelton (far right) is repairing a haul-back gear.

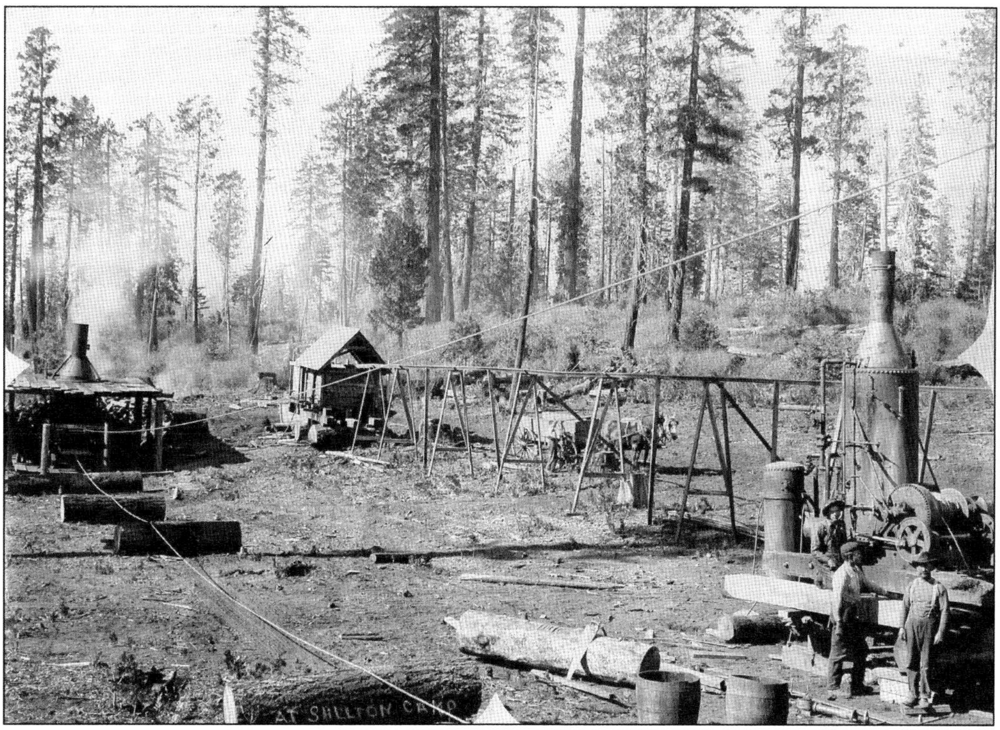

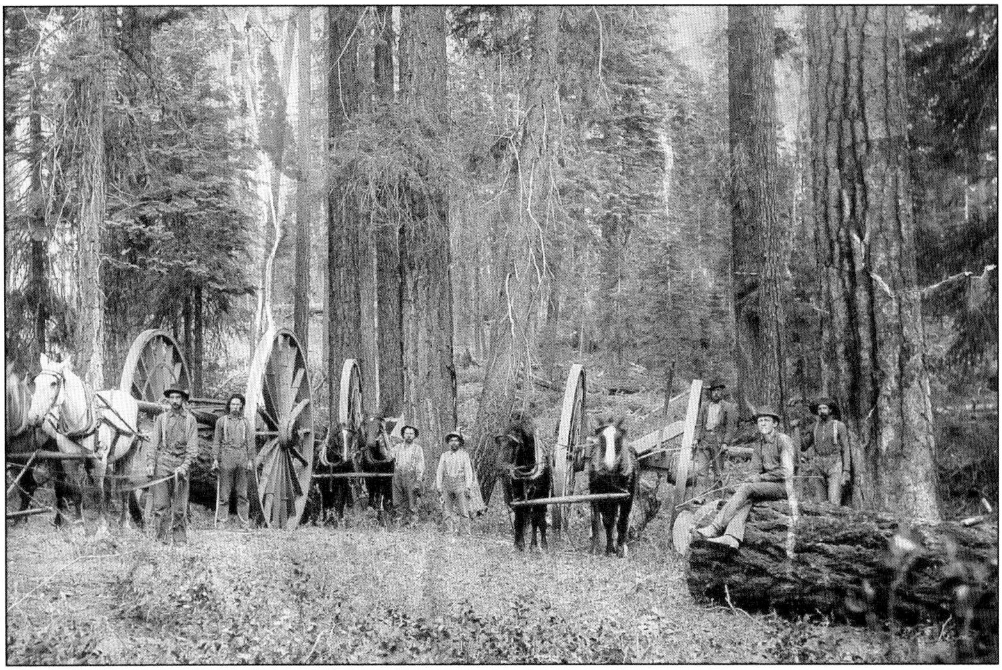

"Big Wheels" were employed to farm the woods and pull logs to the narrow-gauge tracks. Malloy's (Shelton's new) Camp was given the use of most sets of these wheels because most experienced men were dispatched to this camp that had the most timber groves with large trees to boost woods production. An interesting note here is that the fourth man from the right is James Rupert, a well-known Native American in the area. In this undated photograph, the harness tender sits on the log in the foreground with his hook to aid and prevent harness and chains from entangling horses and men. It was said that the harness tender had the most important job in the woods.

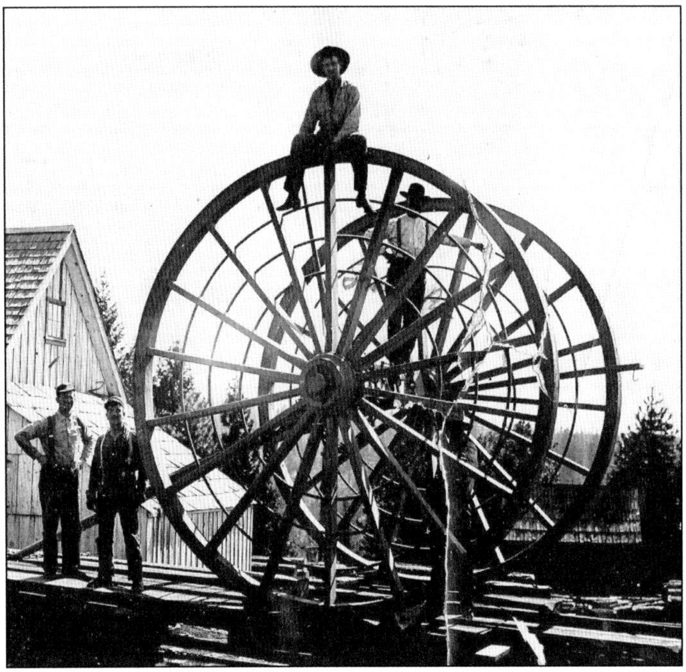

Big wheels were serviced at the machine shop at the Champion Mill. Though there were some wheels made of steel or iron, the wheels above have wooden spokes with wooden axles. This set of wheels is on its way back to Malloy's Camp aboard a flat car. The men pictured from left to right are Frank Thorp, Jonas Jensen, T. J. Shelton Jr., and the fourth man is labeled "Grampa" on the photograph. Standing inside the set of wheels is Lloyd Shelton.

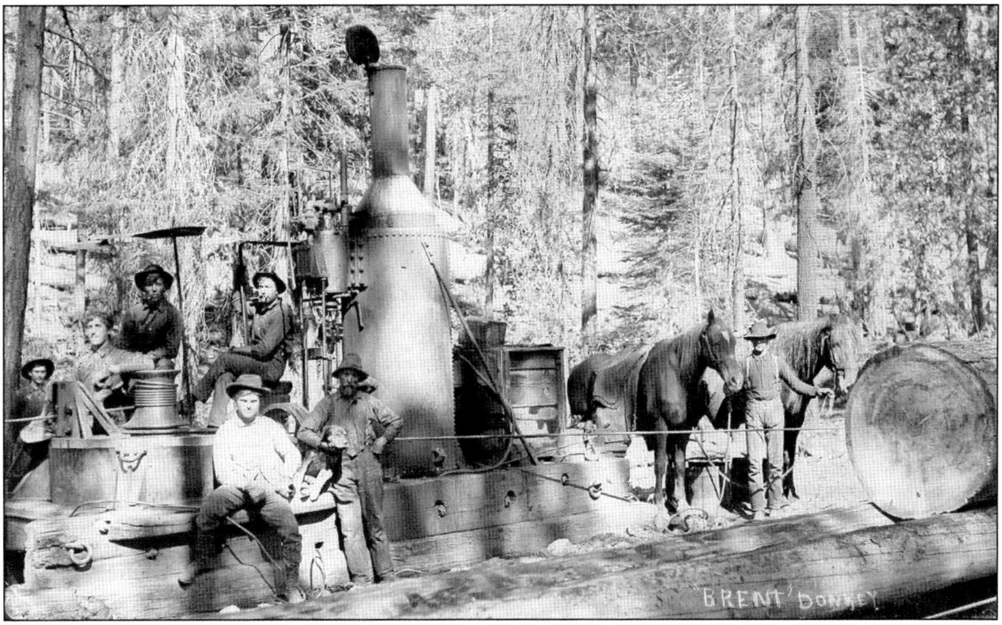

The Brent Donkey engine varied a little from the Dolbeer in innovation. It had a better system of gauges to regulate steam pressure and fewer men were scalded and burned. Though illegible and faded, the boiler has lettering of some of the men's initials. The Brent also had a water box mounted on the deck of the tender. The identities of these men at Malloy's Camp have been sadly lost to time.

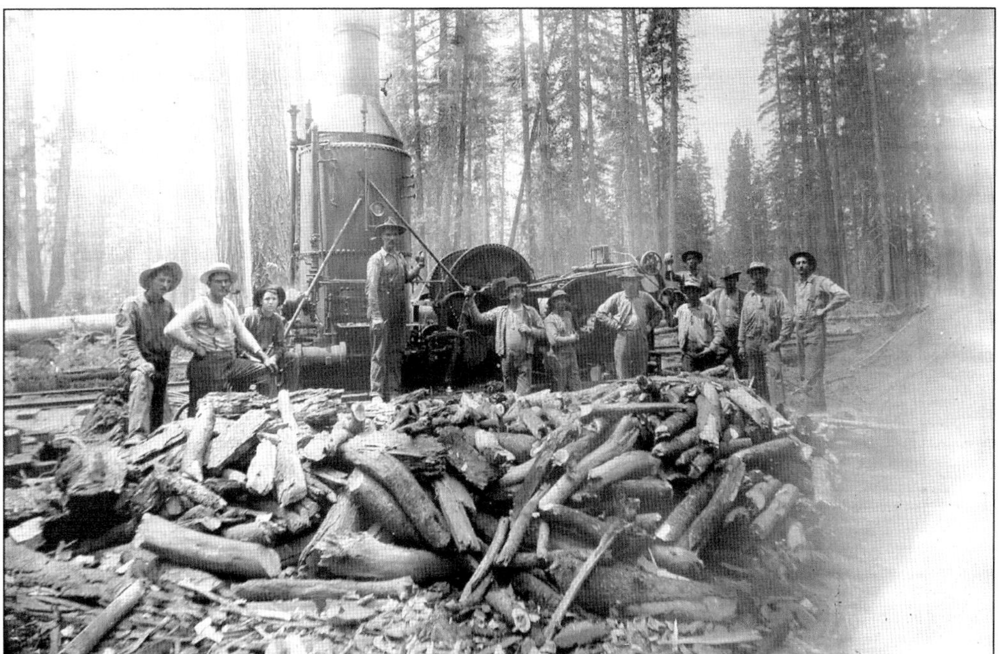

This double haul-back Dolbeer Donkey engine was photographed by Gates Photography Studio July 13, 1898, the same date as the top image. No one marked who these men were, but the number 40 is Gates's file number.

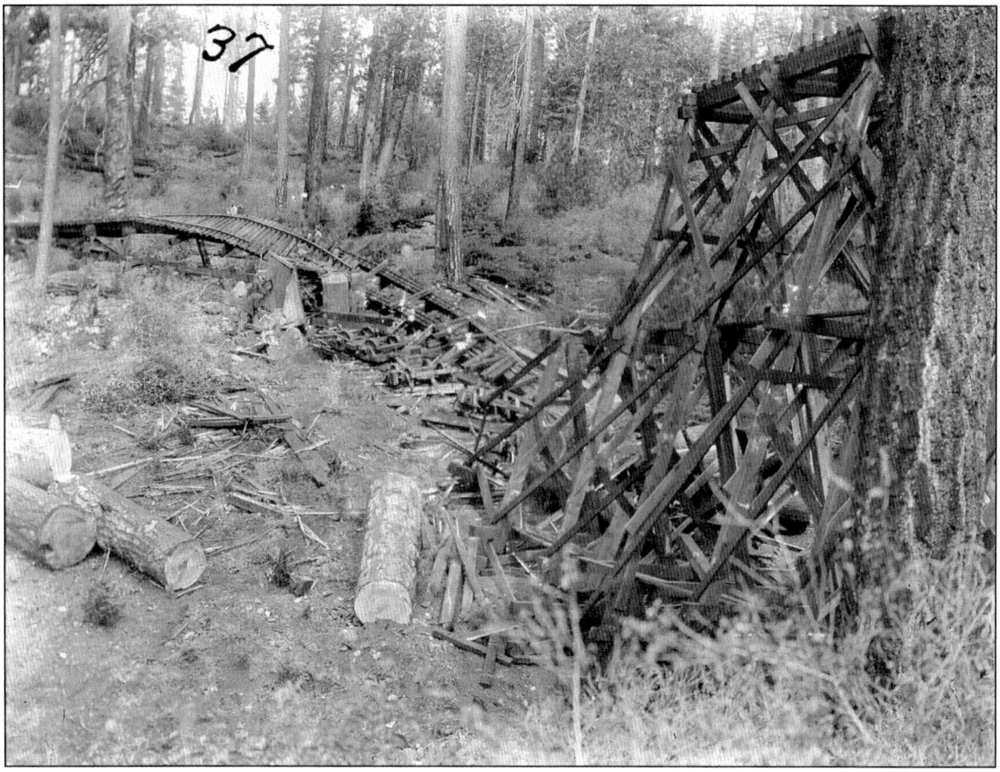

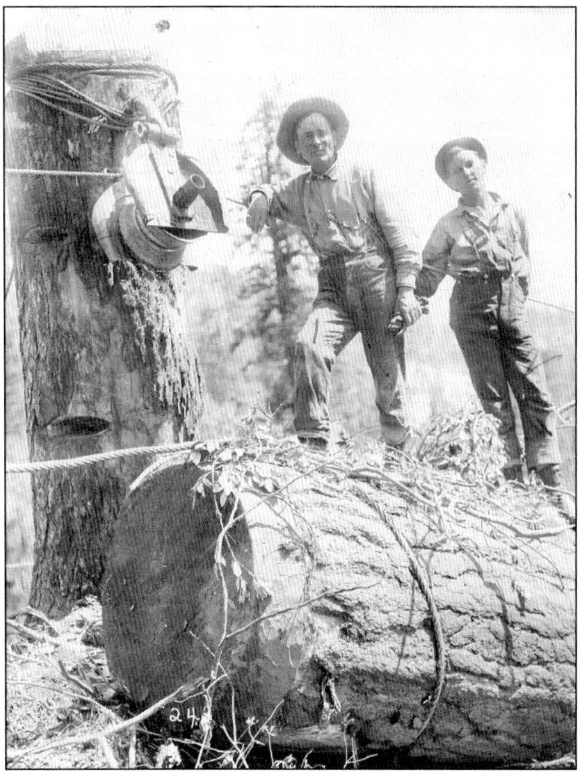

Trestle collapses were not a common occurrence but at times could not be avoided. Sometimes weight and speed were factors, and sometimes a single piece of lumber with the grain installed wrong would splinter, causing a massive collapse. Here the No. 2 lies where it fell in its last hour of service. It was not salvageable except for parts.

"Spar" (to hold cables) trees were cut high on the stump with the aid of springboards, which were three-foot-long boards with an iron catch that fit into the stump slots, as shown in this photograph. Perched upon this board required great balance. In this Gates photograph, a straw line runs through a haul-back pulley while "Shorty" Malloy and "Red" Sills stand atop a log that is choked for haul back. These precarious cables often snapped.

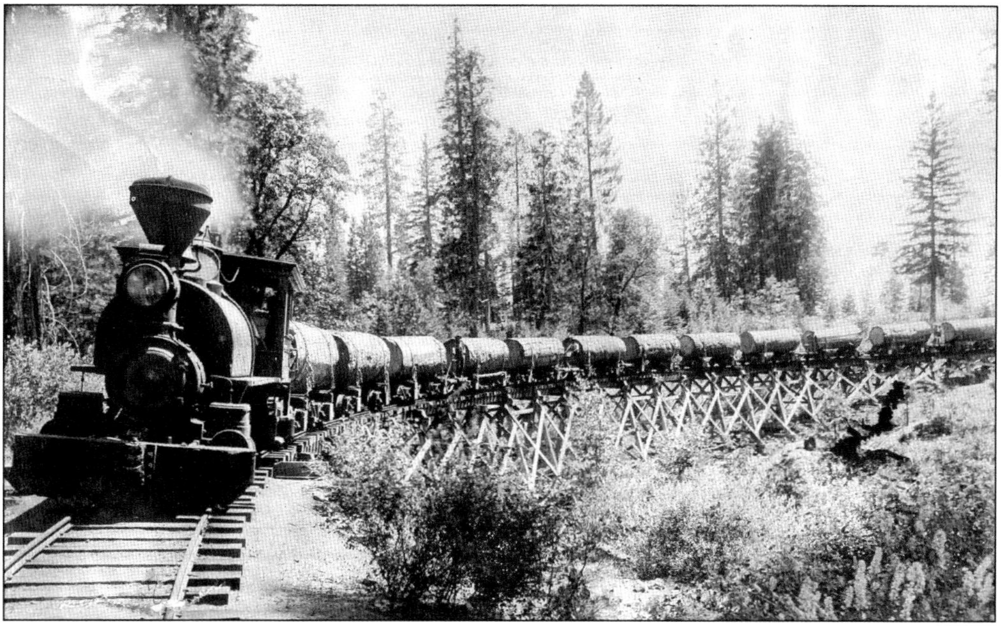

The small Shay engines were very powerful on a level track. This special train leaves Malloy across Yellowjacket Trestle July 3, 1896, for Lyonsville Siding as a centerpiece for the Fourth of July celebration that was held next to the croquet court.

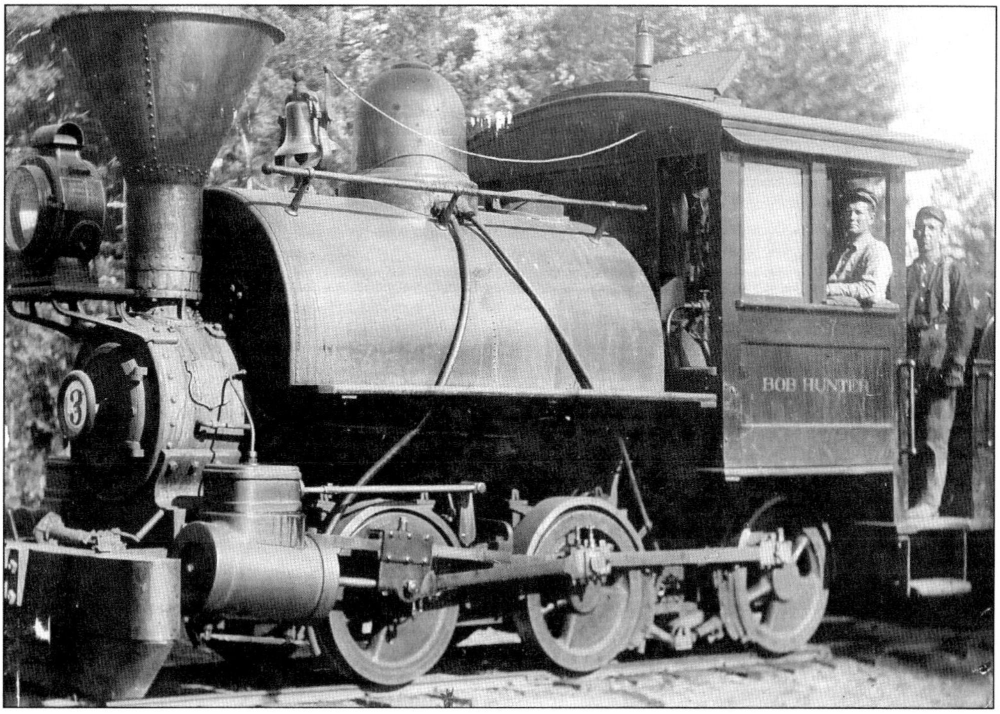

The "Bob Hunter" No. 3-669 was different from previous locomotives that had primitive wooden engine parts, like the coupler bumper. The No. 3 had all steel or iron parts and workings. This is the "Bob Hunter" on its first run at Lyonsville. Shortly before, the Sierra Lumber Company painted their name on the side of all their locomotives boilers.

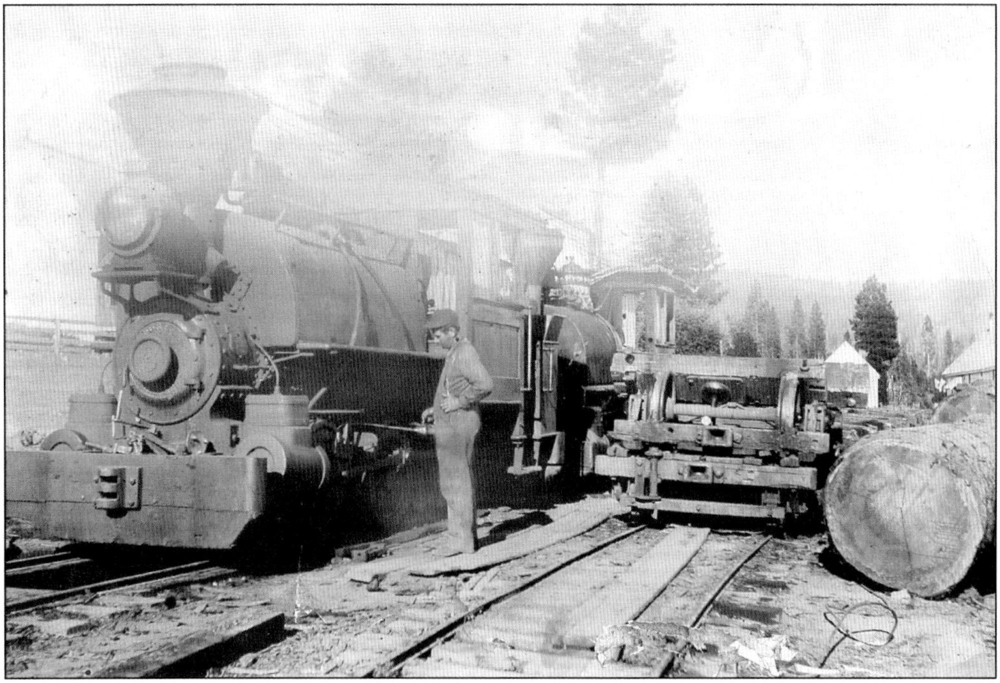

Sierra Lumber Company's No. 3 is pictured on July 4, 1896, as it was about to be decorated for the celebration. The No. 2, just behind, has already been festooned. The brakeman is oiling the parts with a pressure oiler.

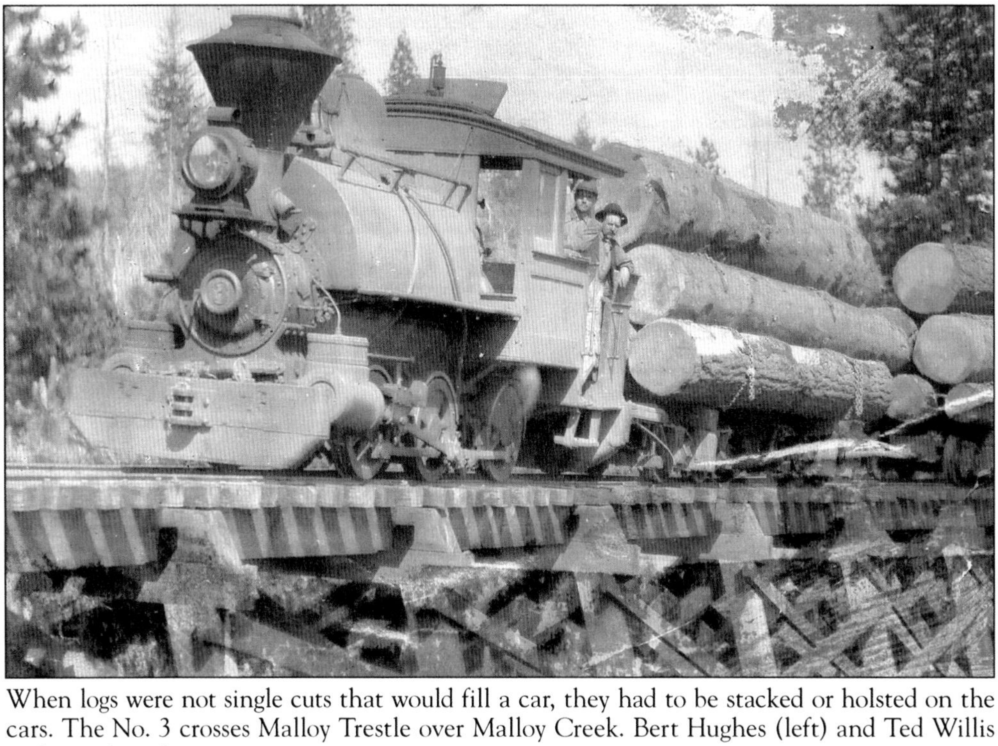

When logs were not single cuts that would fill a car, they had to be stacked or holsted on the cars. The No. 3 crosses Malloy Trestle over Malloy Creek. Bert Hughes (left) and Ted Willis make up the cab crew.

Beal's Camp

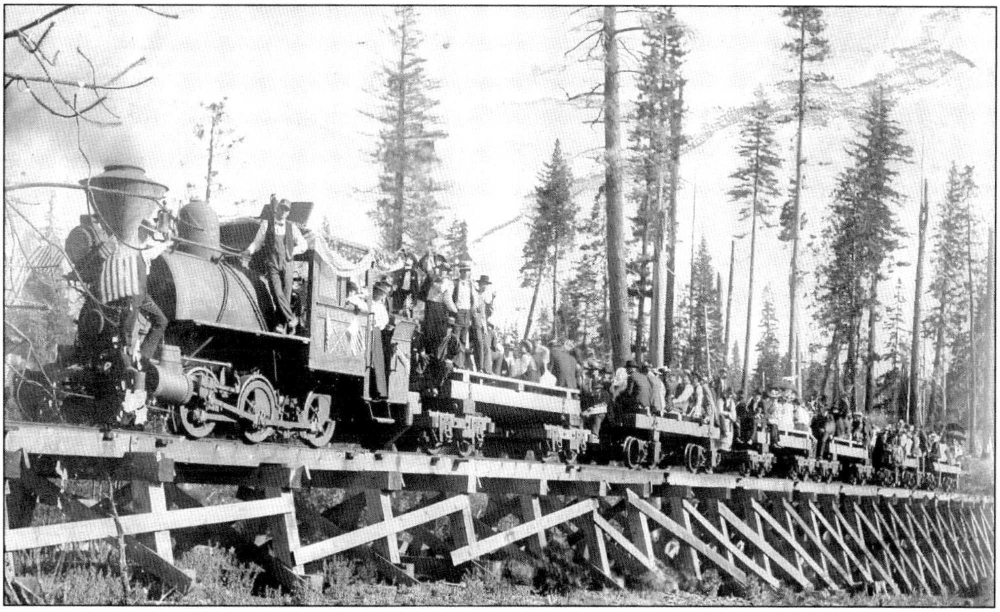

The No. 3 is pictured on July 4, 1898, after it was transferred to Beal's Siding. Shown on one of the many trestles is the excursion train full of picnickers. The trestle was built after the 1893 fire, and many snags, dead trees, and burned wood are evidence of the fire.

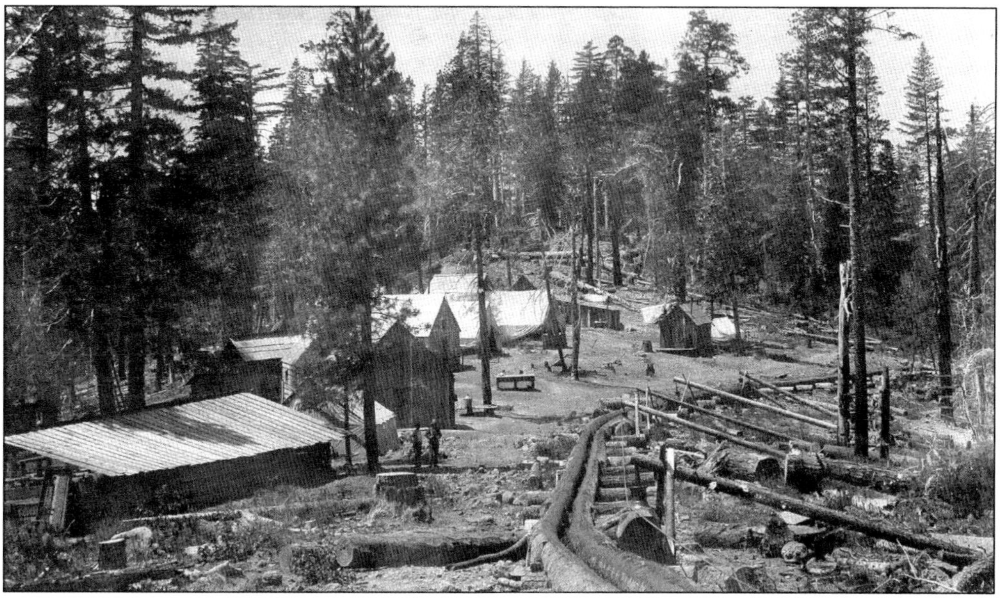

Just after Beal's Camp had been established, more men were needed, and a tent community, which would last three years, sprang up. A lean-to barn, on the left, and stock pens for horses and a few permanent structures are shown. Beal's Camp was more like a town a year later when approximately 80 people lived there.

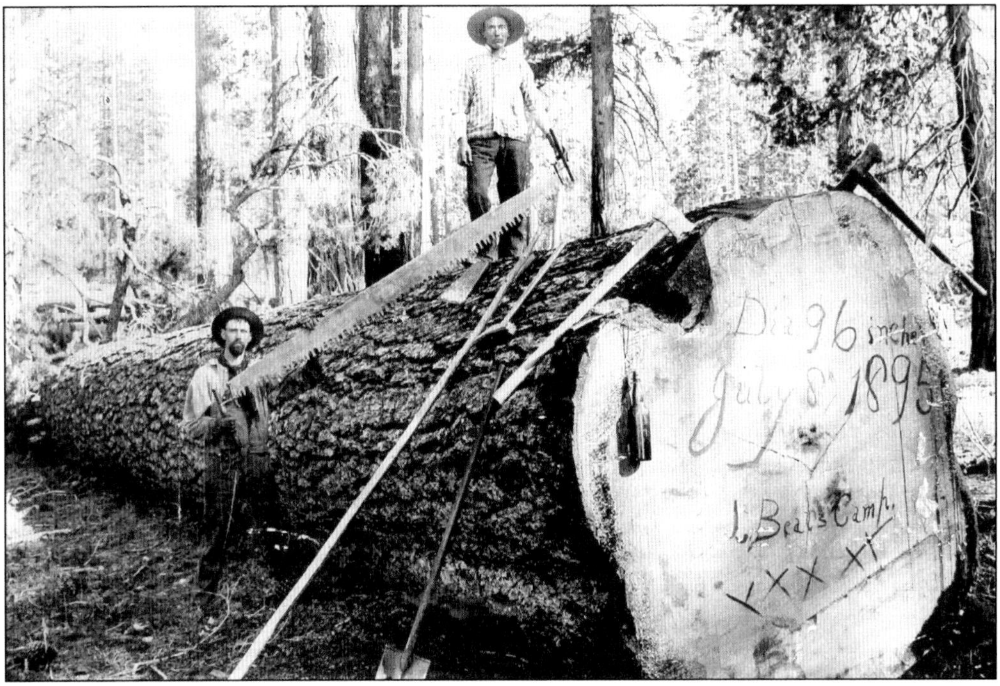

The second Beal's Camp existed high up in the mountains, moving cabins and men farther and farther out to timber. Only the most select trees were cut. This log measured 96 inches at the butt cut. The Y-shaped cracks in the middle of the tree were from "windshake." Often on premium trees like this sugar pine giant, only the bottom 40 feet were taken because of the immense work of climbing and bucking the tree.

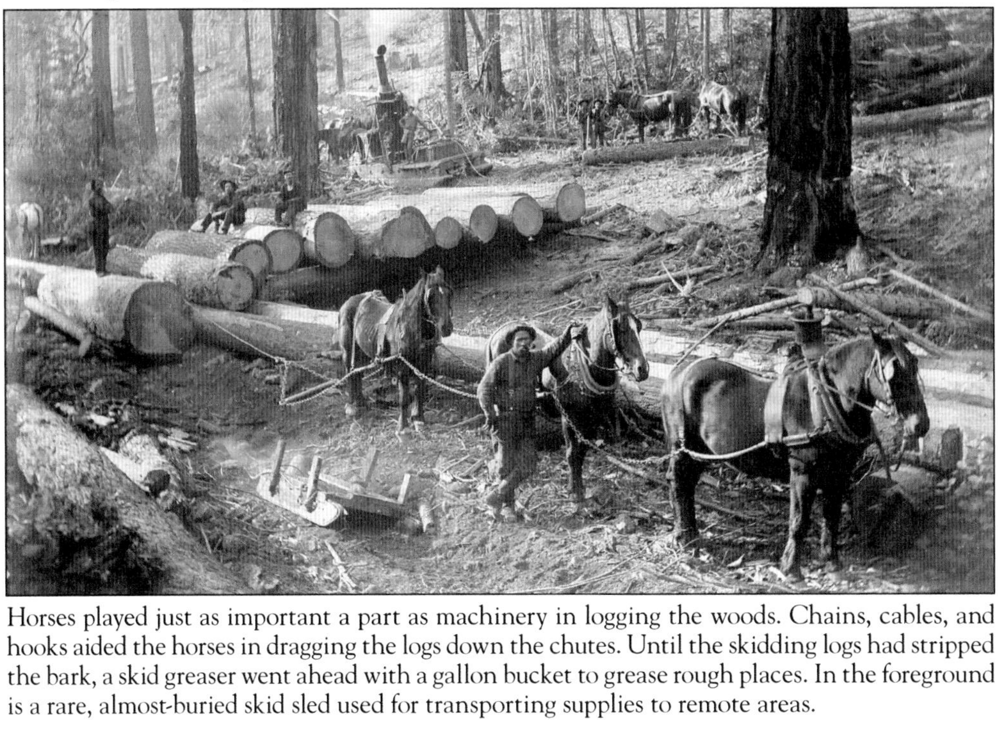

Horses played just as important a part as machinery in logging the woods. Chains, cables, and hooks aided the horses in dragging the logs down the chutes. Until the skidding logs had stripped the bark, a skid greaser went ahead with a gallon bucket to grease rough places. In the foreground is a rare, almost-buried skid sled used for transporting supplies to remote areas.

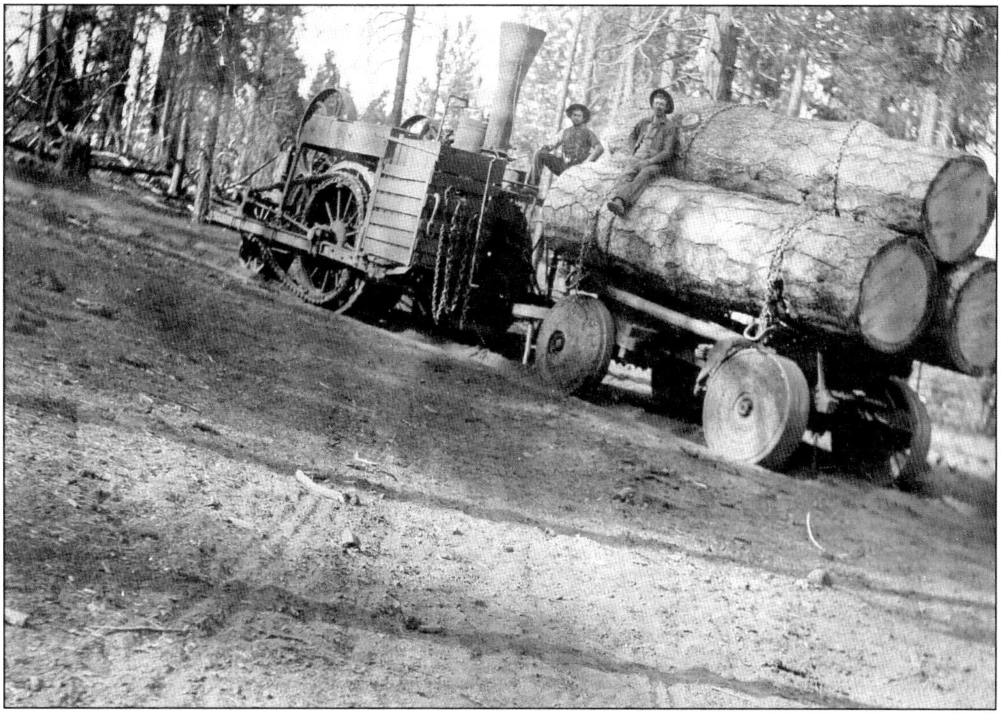

With the power of steam and the Dolbeer Donkey engine, it was found that with a little ingenuity the same engine power could be harnessed to skid logs another way. Shown here, and first used at Beal's Camp as a trial machine, a horse-drawn truck has been modified to be pulled by a crawler made by the Lima Locomotive Company. With all its cogs, pulleys, and belts, it was a wonder in its day with a 200-foot turning radius.

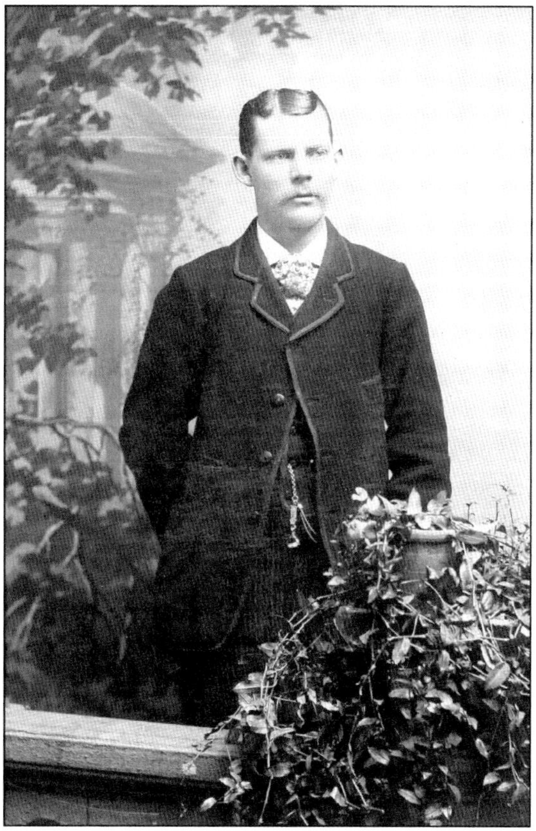

John Peligreen was Beal's Camp's woods boss for many years, setting records for production but always pushing the men. Peligreen angered Sierra Lumber Company officials on at least two occasions—the two disastrous trestle collapses shown on the following pages. These images show No. 3 being resurrected in pieces only to die a final death after overshooting the end of the track at Beal.

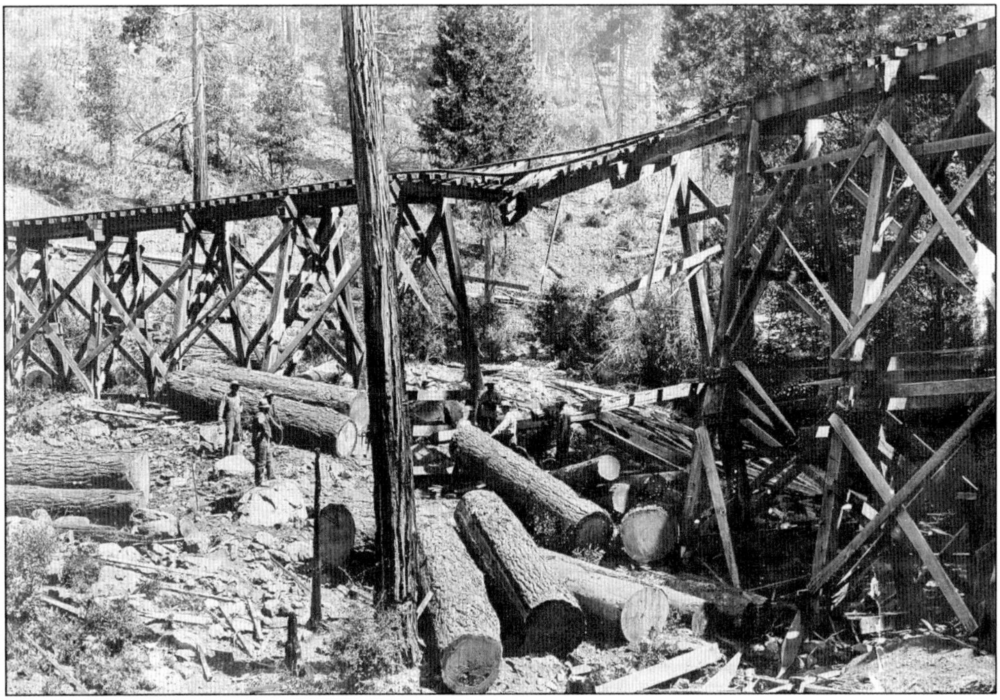

It was miraculous that engine No. 3 and most of its cars made it safely across the trestle at Jack Ass Gap. After a beam splintered, two sets of crawler wheels and two loads of logs were thrown 25 feet into the gap. Building outpost trestles was a huge feat. This trestle was five miles from the mill.

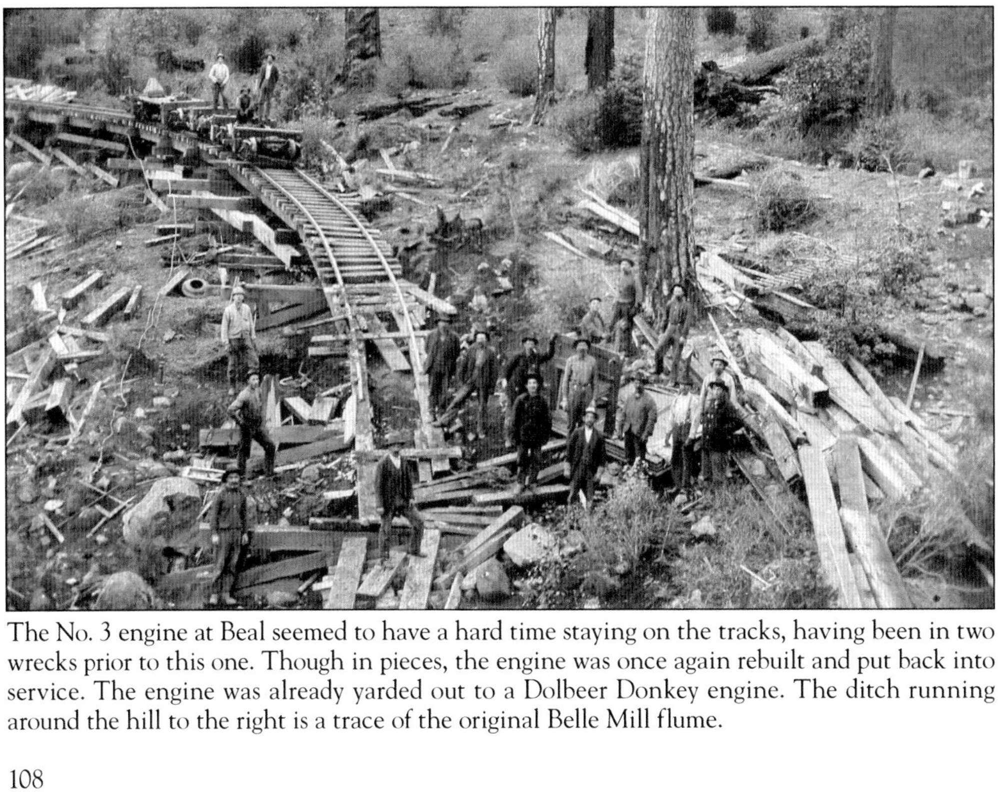

The No. 3 engine at Beal seemed to have a hard time staying on the tracks, having been in two wrecks prior to this one. Though in pieces, the engine was once again rebuilt and put back into service. The engine was already yarded out to a Dolbeer Donkey engine. The ditch running around the hill to the right is a trace of the original Belle Mill flume.

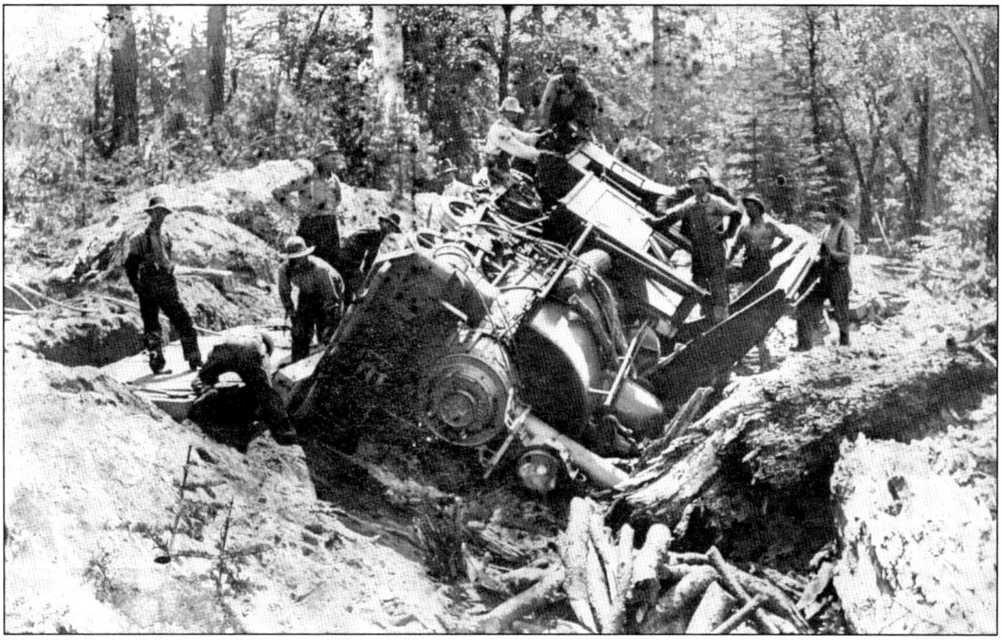

Lines, ties, and a large timber called a "chink block" are put in place here after the No. 3 came barreling down the track past the men and the landing where they waited with a siding full of loaded cars. The train overturned quite a distance past the end of the track. All that is known about this wreck is that it was blamed on a faulty gauge.

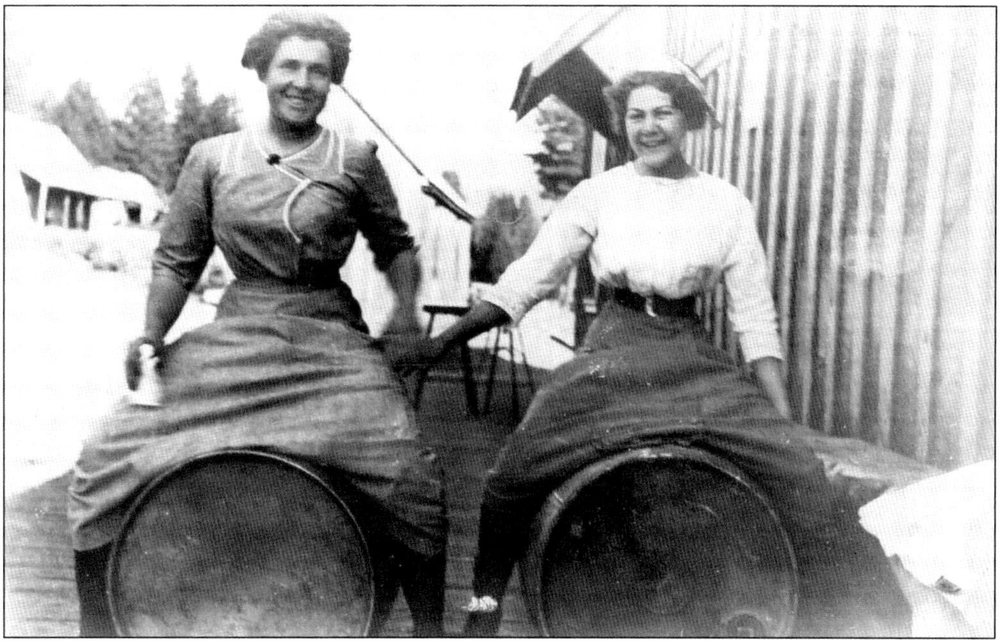

Maud Hoke, right, who later married Lloyd Shelton, poses with her friend Mary Hillhouse on the deck of the building that bordered the track where supplies were unloaded. By this time, Beal's was a well established camp.

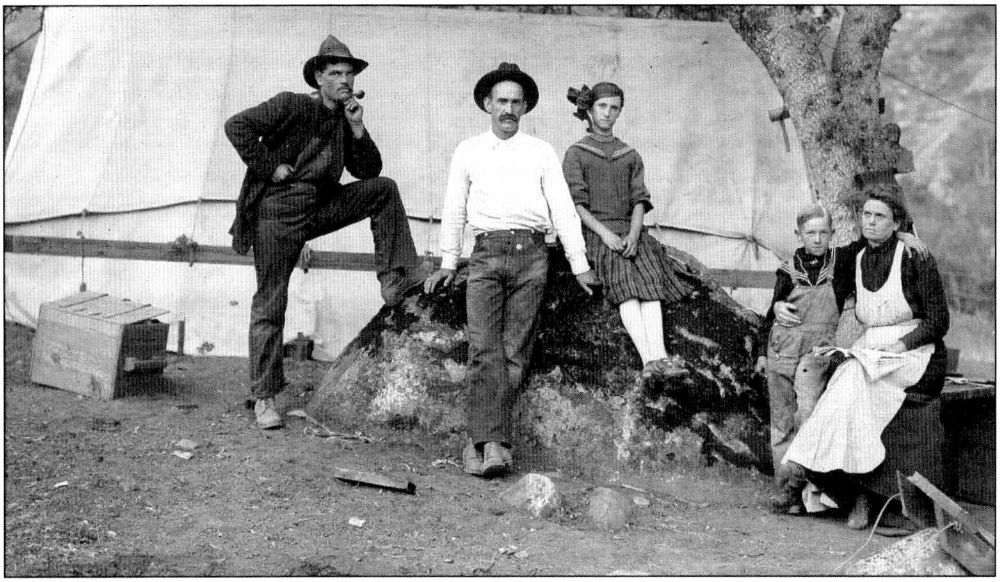

This photograph of Joe Martin, Charles Shelton, Charles's wife Eva, daughter Doris, and son Danny was taken at their camp near Beal. Charlie worked as a coupler on the train, like his brother Jake had when he was killed. The Shelton's enjoy a leisurely day off work. Like most families, they had a small transport sled, which can be seen in the right foreground.

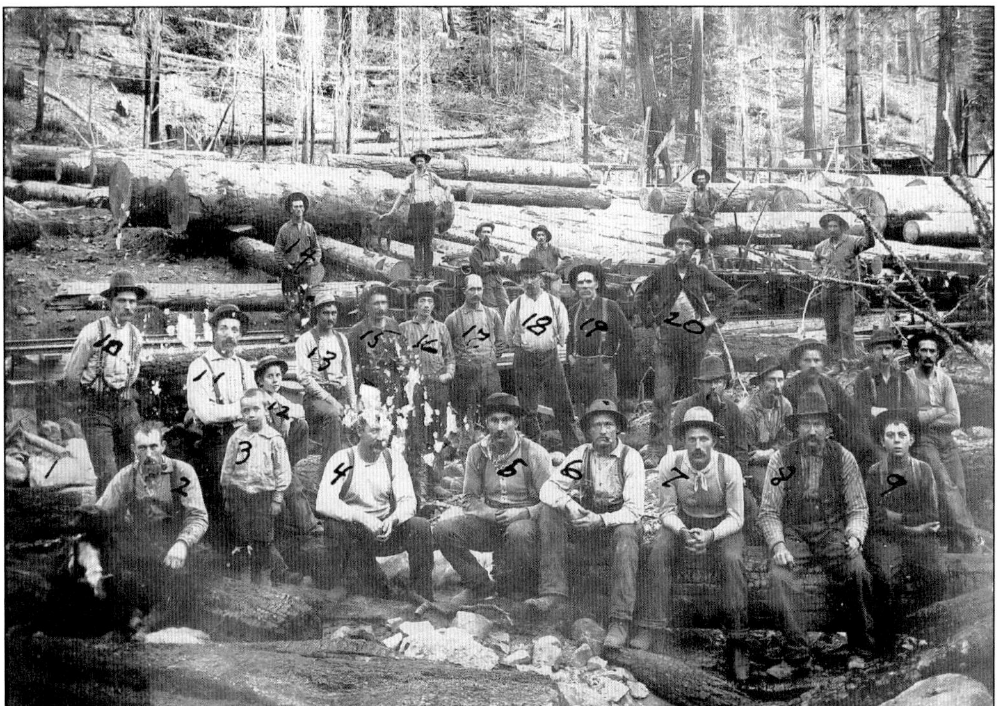

This photograph of the final days of Beal's Camp was ordered by Dr. Connell and taken by the Gaines Photograph Studio. A fire that summer had threatened the camp, and charred logs and trees surround the loggers. Most of the names have been lost, but known are Charlie Shelton (no. 2) and son Danny (no. 3).

SHELTON'S CAMP

Edward Shelton was born on December 10, 1866, and was the 7th of 11 children in his family to survive. Shown here in 1880 at Red Bluff, he had already started a career working for his grandfather, J. E. Gray, handling lumber for a flume from Rabbit Creek to the Gray House.

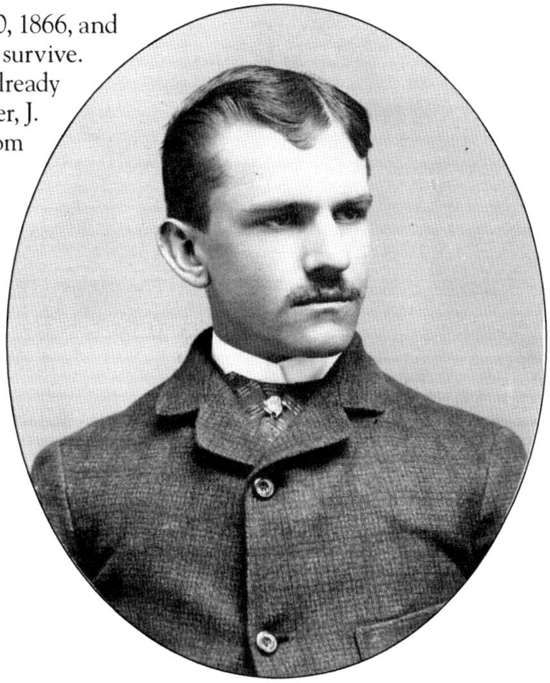

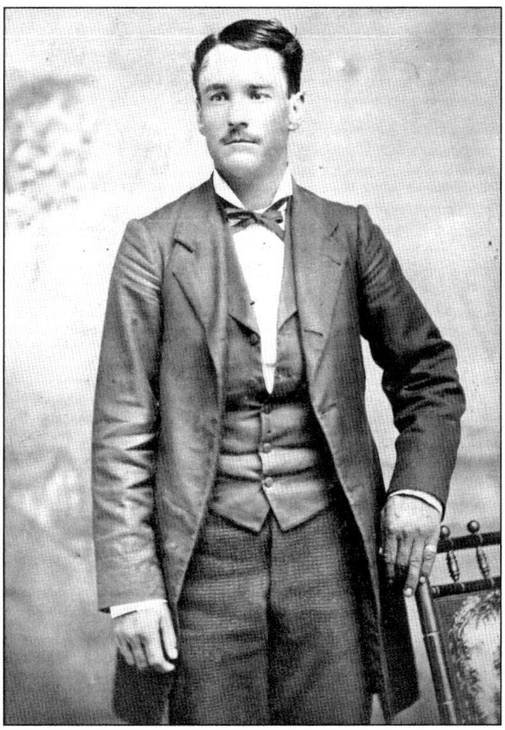

Shown here eight years later in 1888 at age 22, Ed already showed signs of hard work in his worn hands. Ed was well known in the saloons of Red Bluff and Lyonsville, but it was in 1898, after the death of his beloved brother Jake in a train accident, that Ed at 32 began to drink heavily.

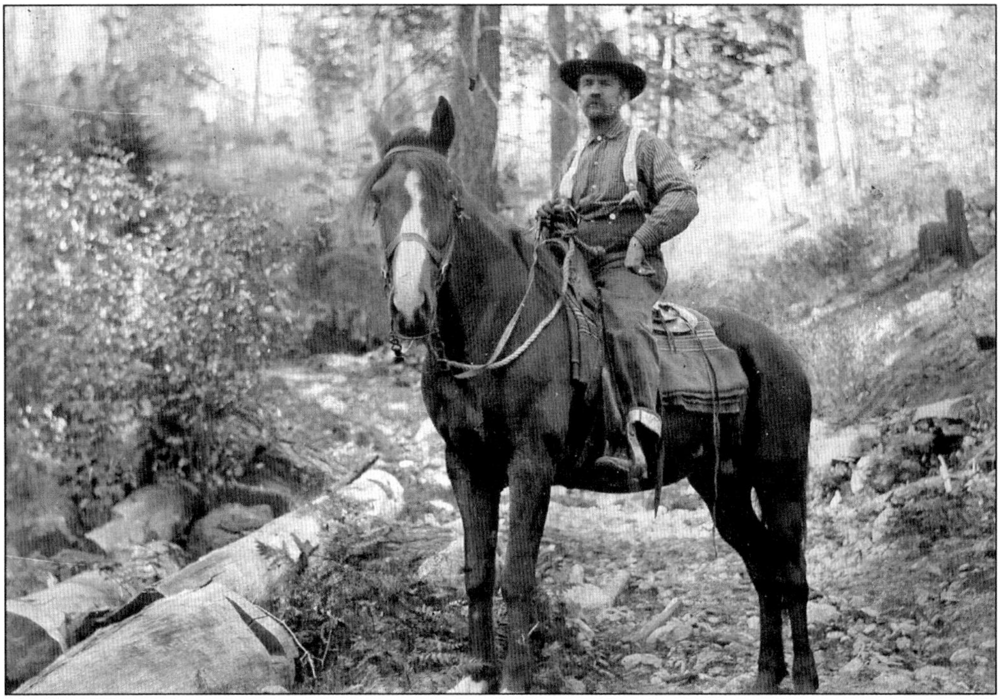

Shown at age 38, Ed Shelton was a seasoned woods boss in 1904 when this photograph was taken at Shelton's Camp. The years took their toll on loggers. Life was hard, and conditions were primitive. Shown here on his horse on Dry Gulch at Malloy's Camp, Ed poses by the remnants of Malloy's original cabin years after the camp closed, and people went their separate ways.

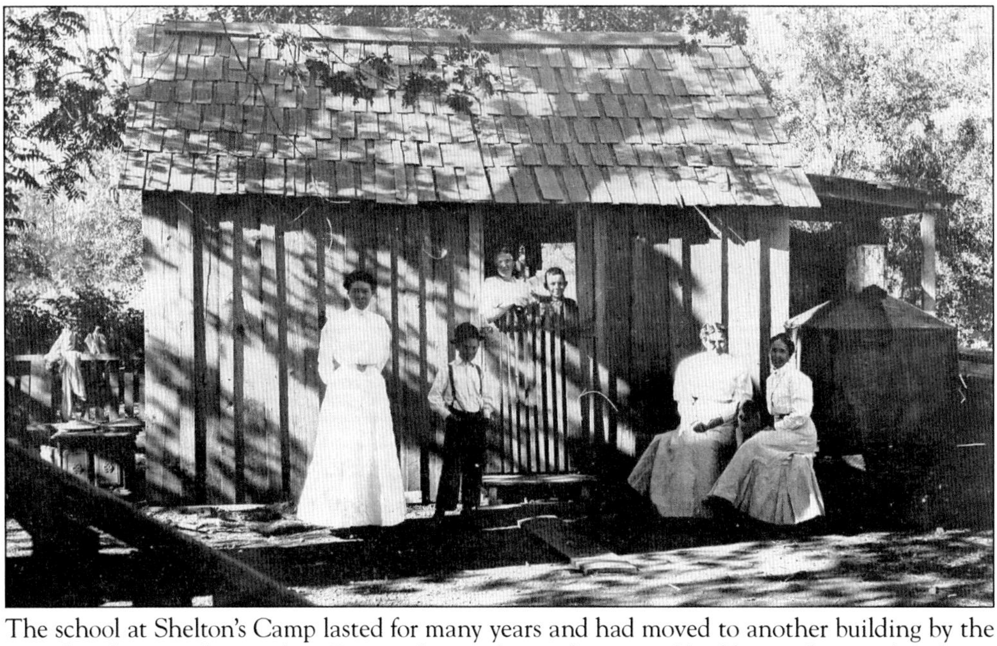

The school at Shelton's Camp lasted for many years and had moved to another building by the time this photograph was taken. Past teachers gather at the original building with several students, from left to right, including Mae Lucas, Mary Mae Bloxham, Jennie Frye, and Alice Olson. Except for Mae Lucas, all were sisters.

The canning kitchen at Shelton's Camp is shown with George and Annie McGowan, baby Josie, and their friends, George and Jennie Hartland. All camps canned foods for the winter. A variety of venison, beef, pork, wild berry jams, and jellies were preserved. The boiler hanging on the far right post is for submersing jars in boiling water to seal them. Notice the soapbox full of jars under the porch.

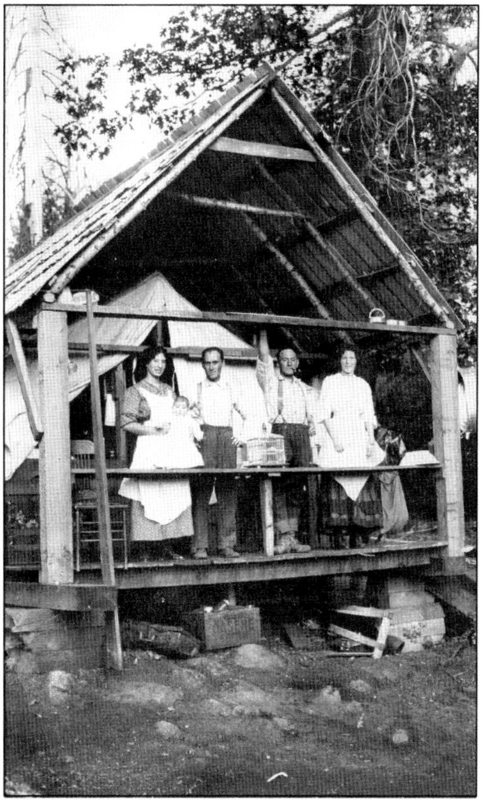

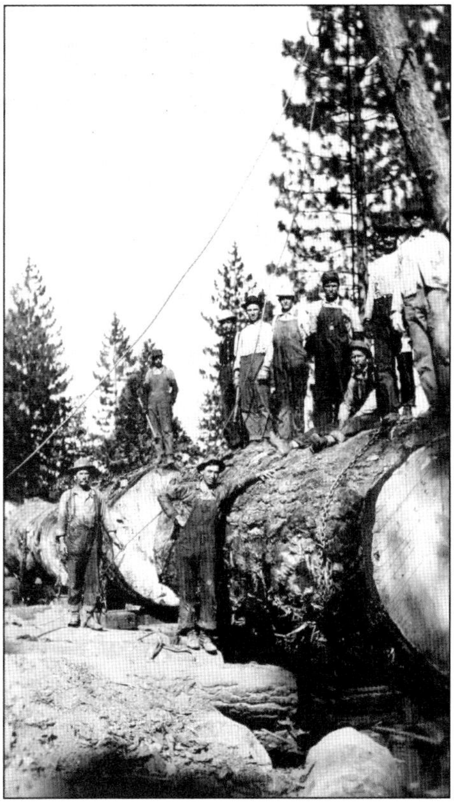

The largest tree ever to come out of Shelton's Camp was a red fir giant measuring eight feet at the base. Shown here loading 16-foot logs onto flatcars by means of block and tackle is crew No. 2. The final tally after the entire tree was limbed was 15 logs at 16 feet long, making the tree a whopping 240 feet tall after trim (cutting unusable base and top).

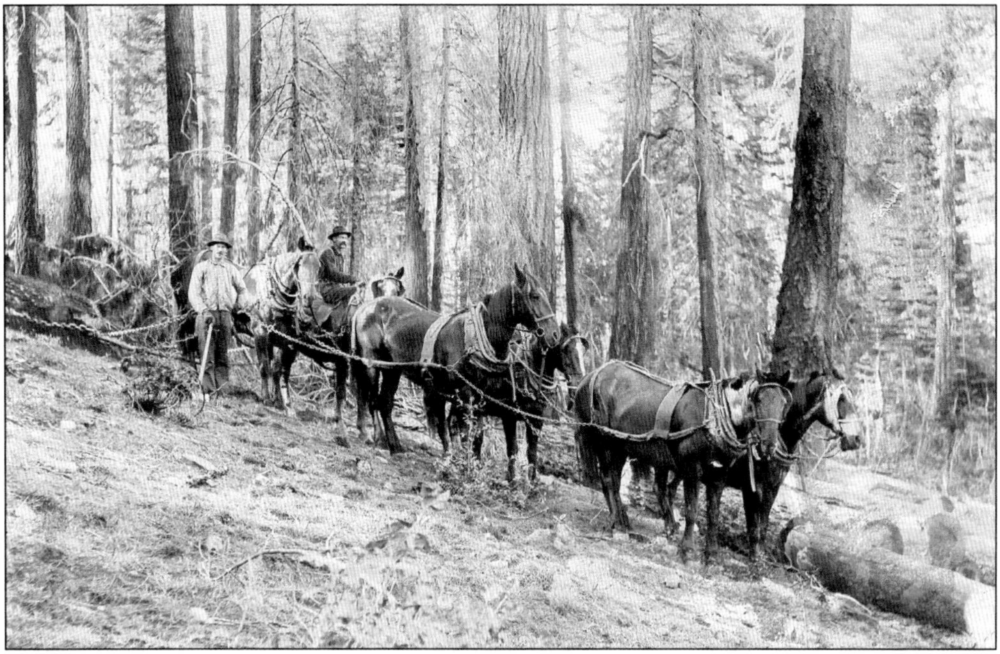

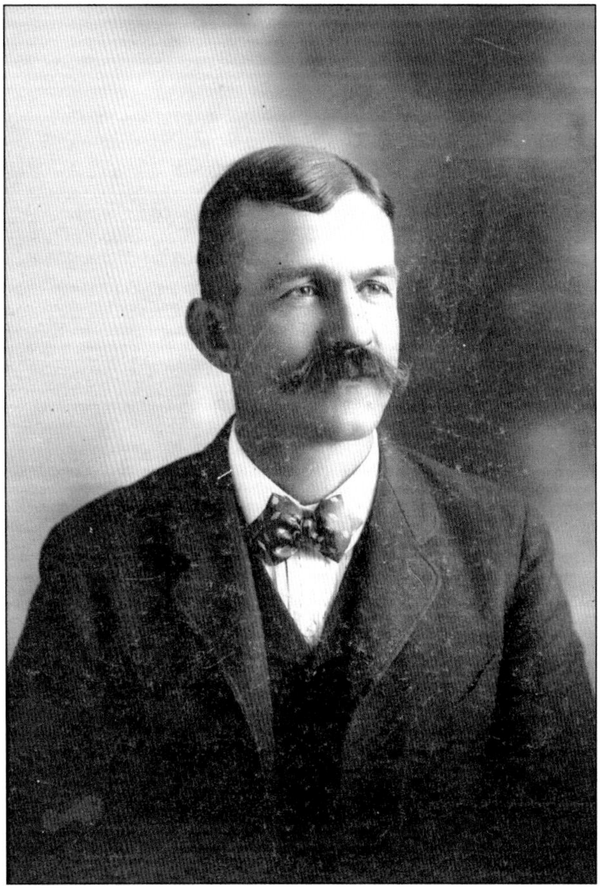

By the time this photograph was taken, it was near the end of Shelton's Camp, and the available timber no longer met the expectations of Sierra Lumber Company's executives. Timber was farther and farther away, and men grew tired of long weeks absent from families and luxuries. However, as the camp prepared to shut down, this photograph was taken on the spot that today bears the name Shelton Ridge.

This photograph, taken at the request of Sierra Lumber Company executives, was a gift to Ed Shelton for his many years of service. Ed worked quite a few years after Shelton's Camp ceased operation, and in later years, he rode his horse Brownie to many of the familiar places he had worked around Lyonsville. Ed lived alone in Lyonsville and Red Bluff until his death and reposes at the Shelton plot in Belle Mill Cemetery.

Five

Remembrances and Memories of People and Places

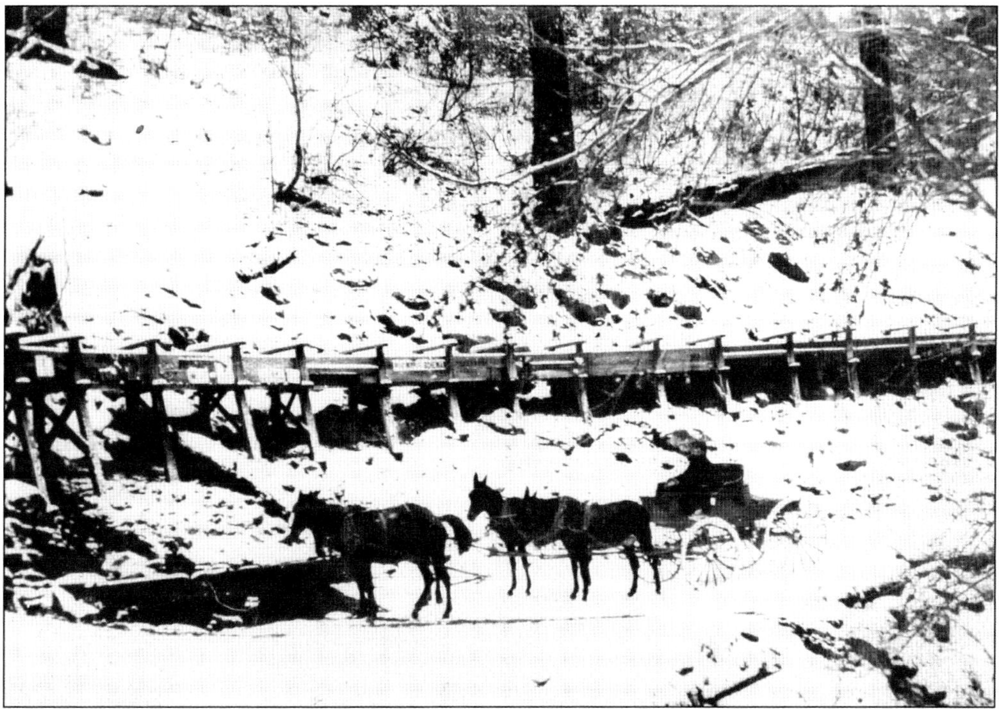

A gigantic ditch and flumes, including this one on the south fork of Battle Creek, snaked their way to Lyonsville in 1901 to supply the Champion Mill with water for boilers and the lumber flume to Red Bluff. One thousand miner's inches, approximately 11.6 gallons per minute per inch of water flow, channeled through this system. Bert Hampton's four-hitch wagon around 1900 is juxtaposed to the flume and the side advertisement for Bohemian Whiskey.

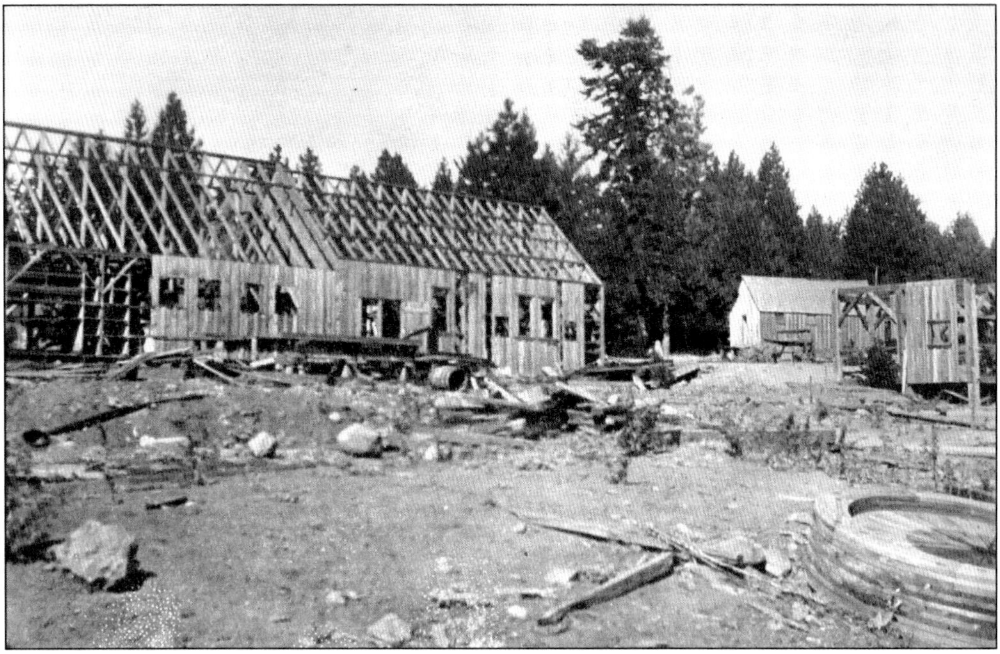

By 1922, when these pictures were taken, the Champion Mill had been stripped of most of its usable siding, windows, and metal roofing. In 1923, the final remaining rails at the mill were taken up and transferred for use in Stirling City. The shells of several hundred buildings were left to rot. The town had come and gone. It had supplied enough lumber to build several entire cities, and indeed many of California's historic buildings contain lumber from the Champion Mill. In 2007, the entire site, all the way from the sawdust pile to the base of Lyon Hill, is a thick pine forest with cedars and low-growing brush that conceals the stories and secrets of a town vanished, except for a road that runs through it.

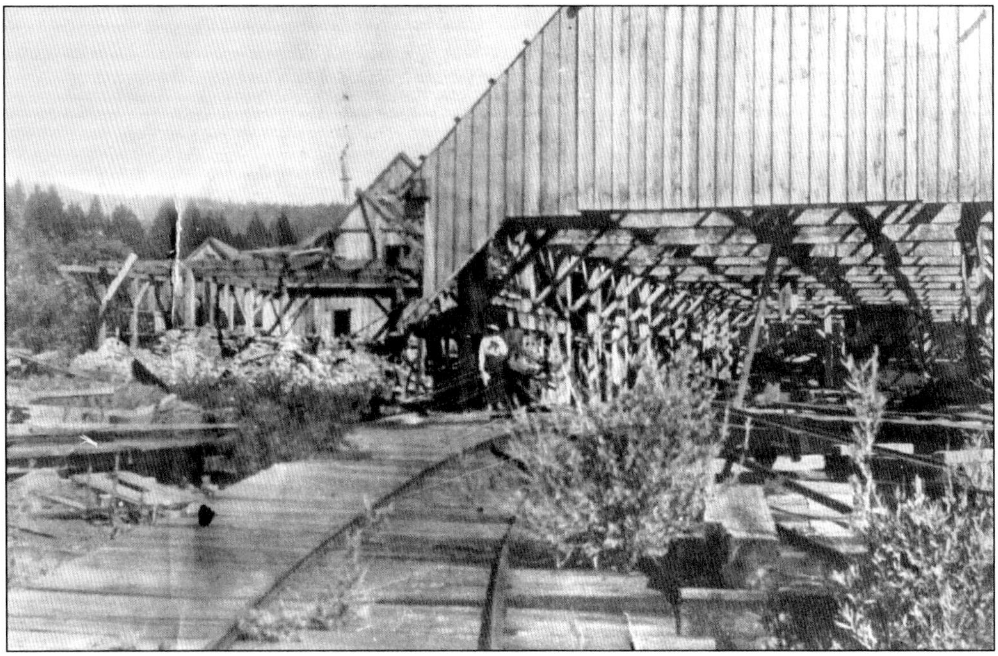

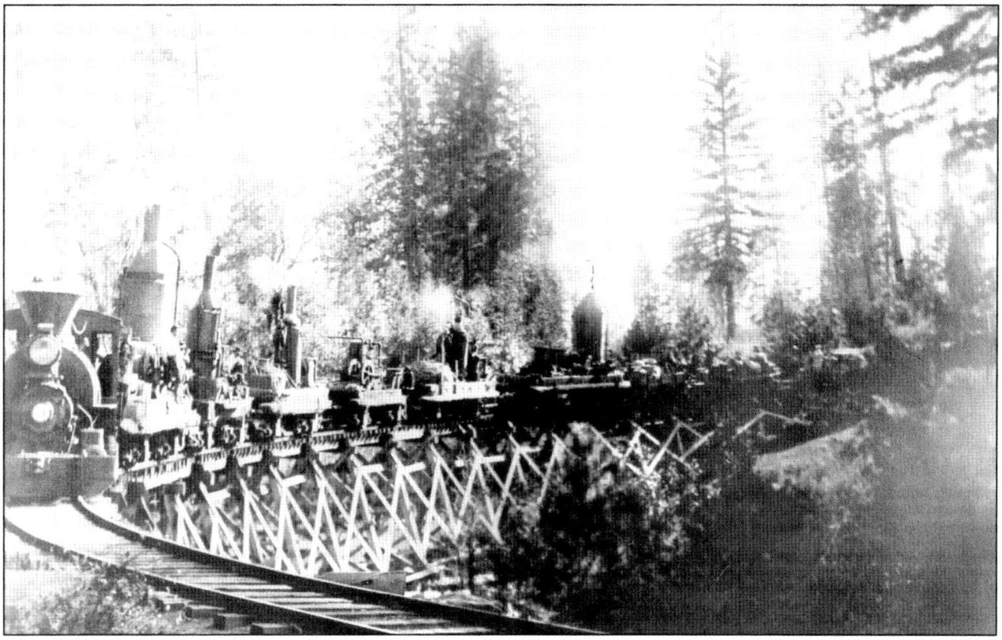

Closing down the camps as Lyonsville declined was a task in itself. Dolbeer Donkey engines, haul-back motors, winches, wheels, and every conceivable heavy piece of equipment had to be winched aboard flatcars and transported to Champion Mill, where it was either shipped to Red Bluff or Stirling City or dismantled for scrap. Here one such train hauls a load of donkey engines, still smoking, onto the cars.

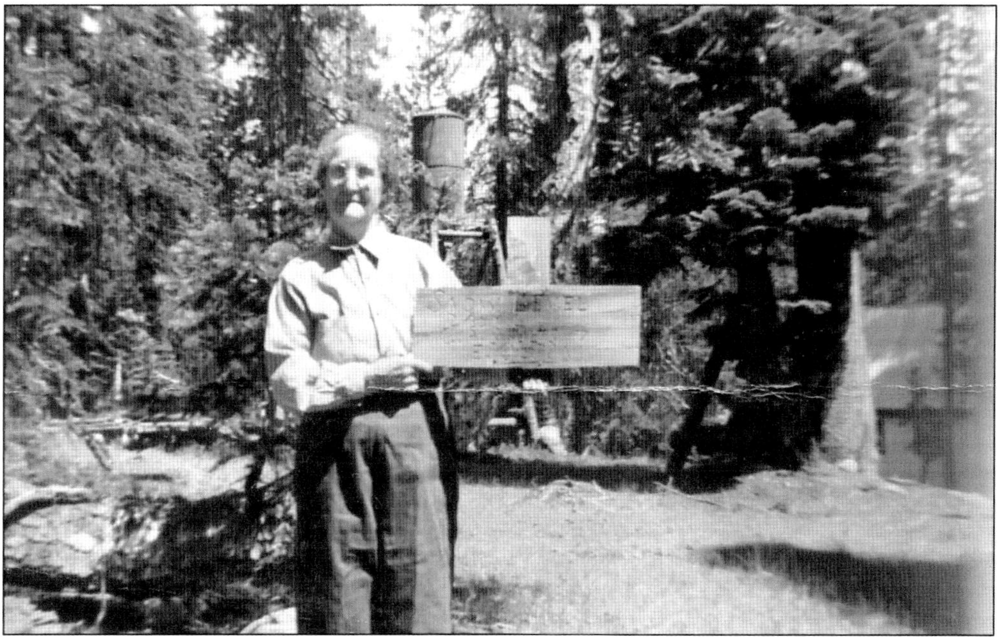

On August 28, 1957, Alice Olson was photographed for the last time at Grassy Lake by the cabin and at Juniper Lake, both on the same day. She wrote on the back of the photograph, "A sign Eddie carved in 1914 when Eddie and George Shultz were over." This sign still exists in the author's museum in Durham, California.

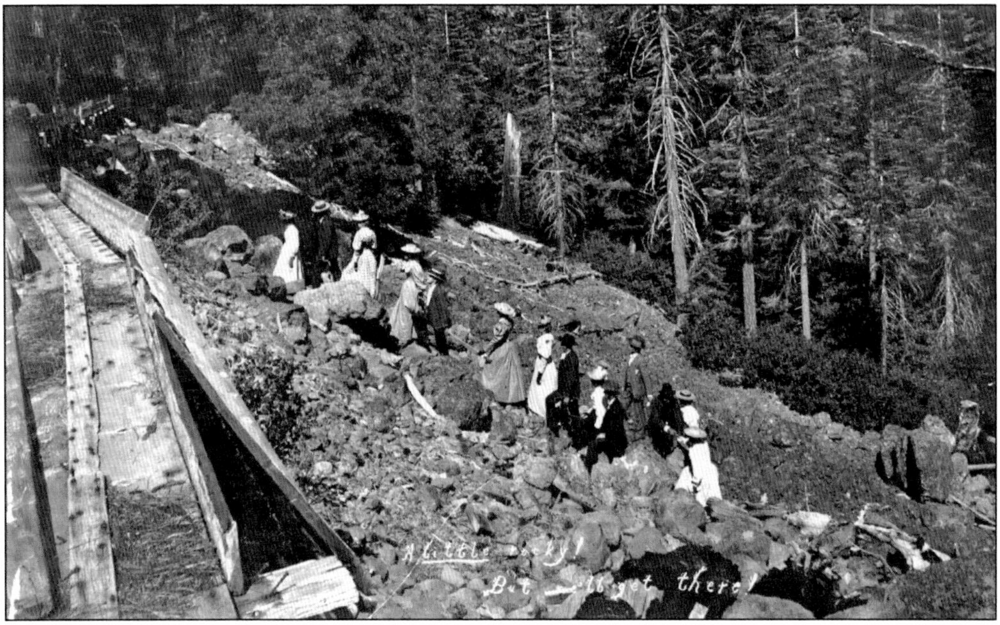

The original flume to the Shelton home, shown in ruins, was built entirely of square nails when this group of picnickers visited it in 1892. The ladies, who are dressed in their Sunday best, are assisted by gentlemen and the help of two-by-fours up the hill.

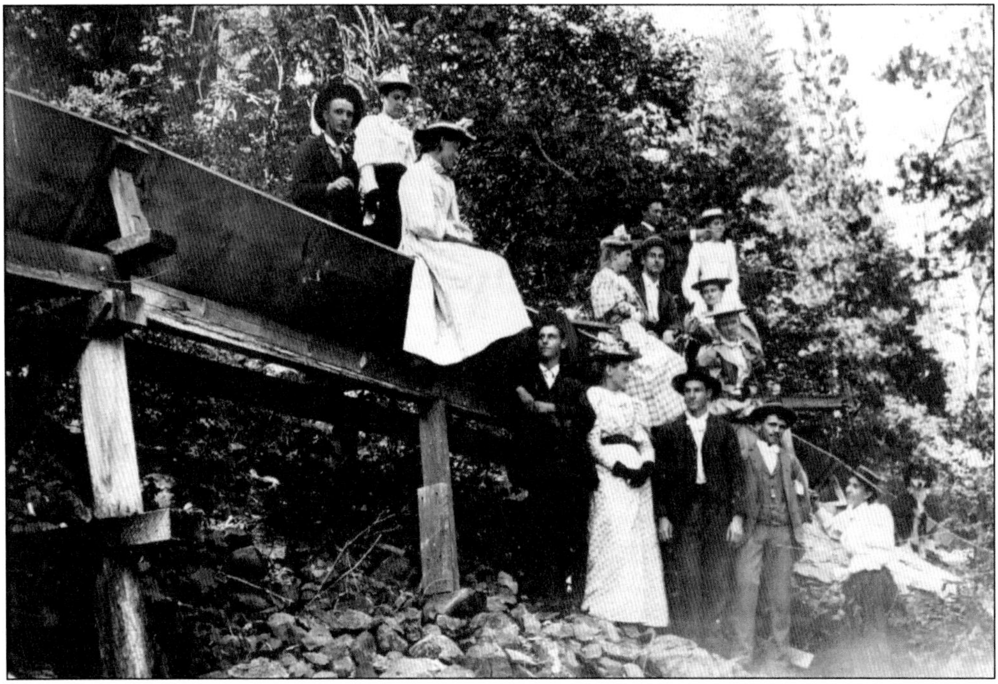

The earliest evidence of the town of Lyonsville was this long-abandoned flume that was bypassed to bring water to the town after the flume rotted away. A "Sunday Afternoon" group in 1892 is hiking up the pinnacle pile above the bank of Antelope Creek's south fork. These pinnacles were almost symmetrical and about three feet long and were often used to support the flume or for foundation stones for new buildings at Lyonsville.

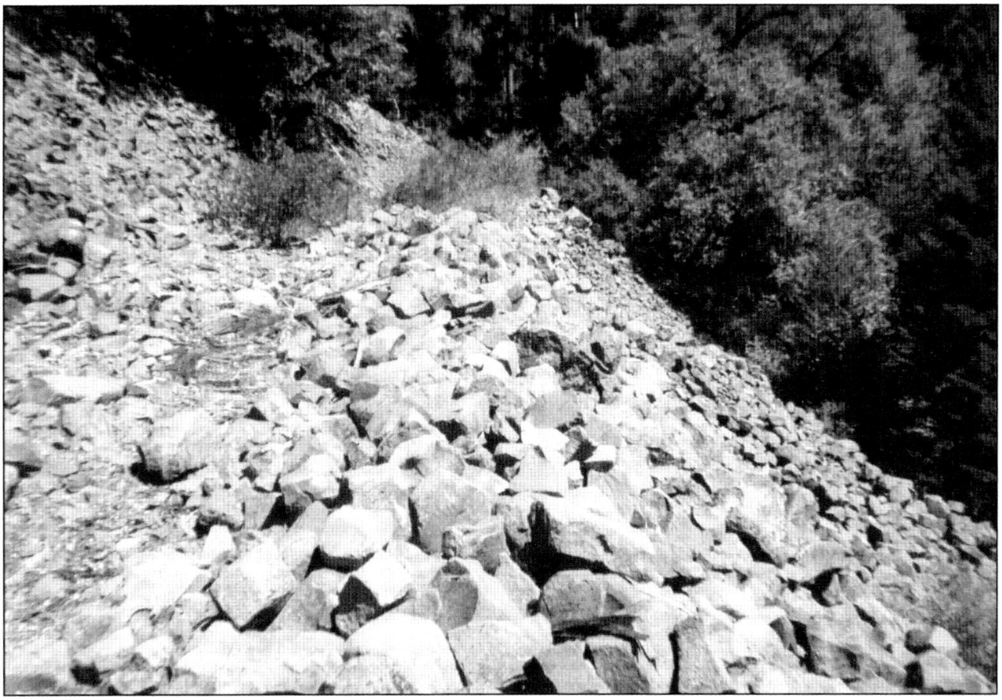

More than a century later, the flume track shows traces of the still-decaying timber in the contours of this perennial ridge in Lassen.

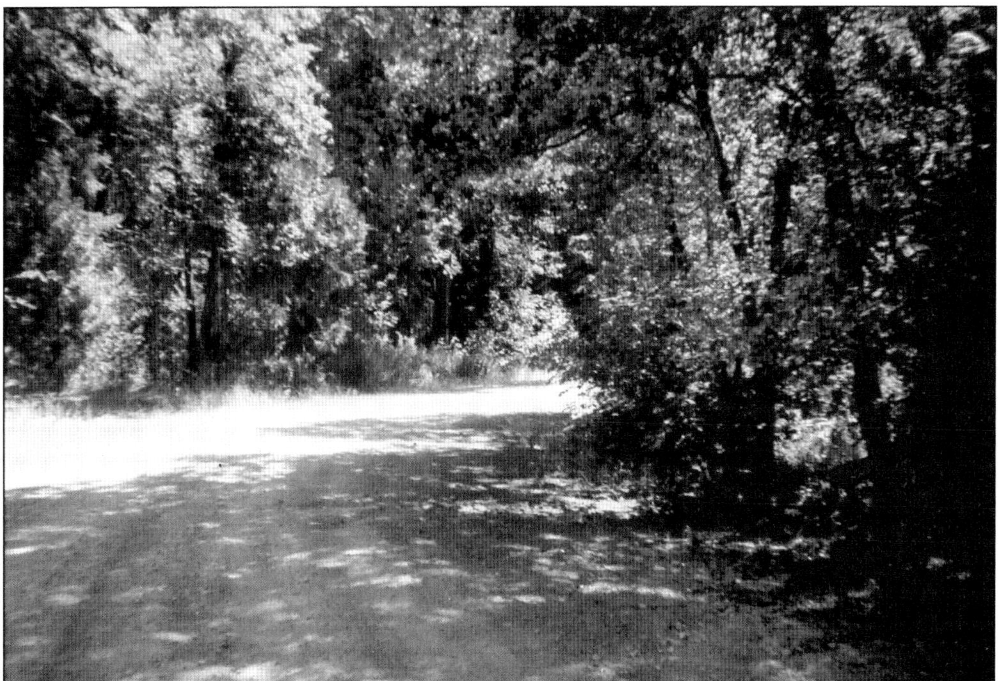

This September 12, 2006, image shows Boots' Bend today; the center of the photograph depicts where the north fork of Antelope Creek flows (see page 72 to compare the track of the original road to this present scene).

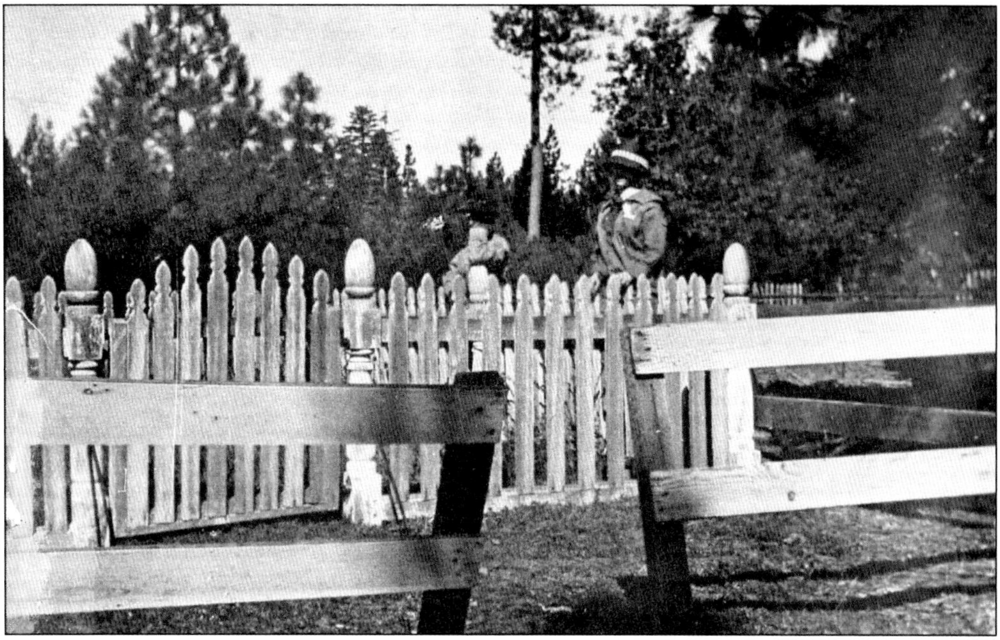

The original fence that encircled the Shelton graves at the Belle Mill Cemetery was identical to the fence around James Gray's grave. Both fences preceded a communal fence that now encompasses the cemetery. A recent dispute over graves that might be located beyond the fence, and the placement of new stones to replace many pioneer stones stolen in the 1960s, created a split between Native Americans and pioneer descendents and has caused the perimeter fence to be greatly expanded. The bottom photograph shows the same view 118 years later. Many iron fences that guarded small family plots were stolen at the time also. Many of these stones were spotted in Paynes Creek in the 1970s being used as a sidewalk, but soon they disappeared altogether.

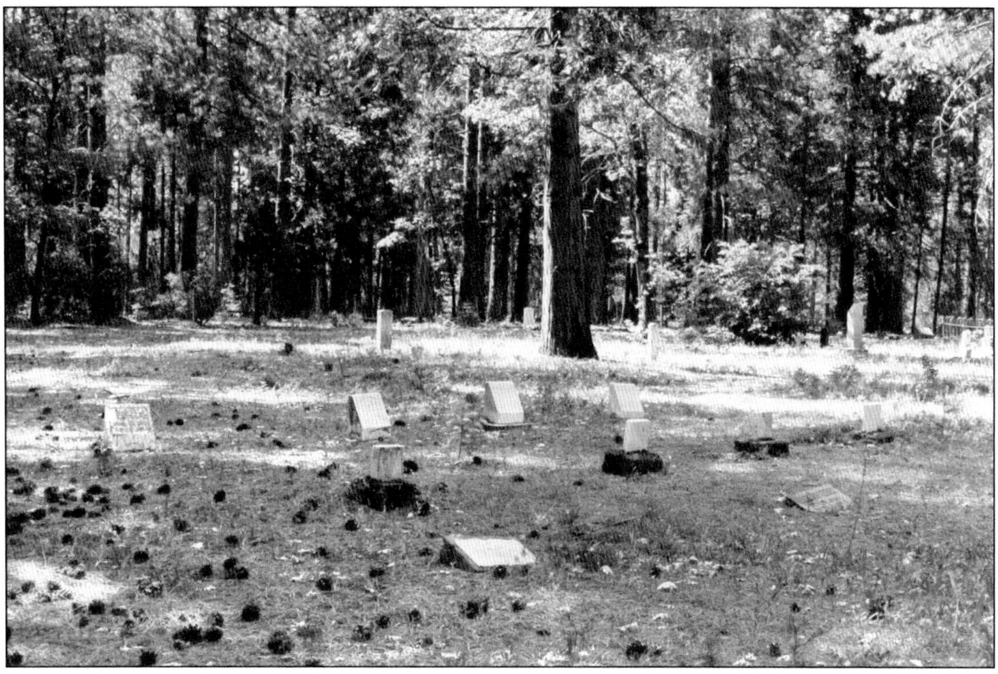

Shown in 1922 is Alice Olson standing by the gate of her Red Bluff home. The gateposts are none other than the original corner posts from the Shelton plot at Lyonsville's Belle Mill Cemetery. Alice, who was a collector and historian, was a loving, warm person who gave of herself to help others and preserve history by keeping alive the memories of those she loved.

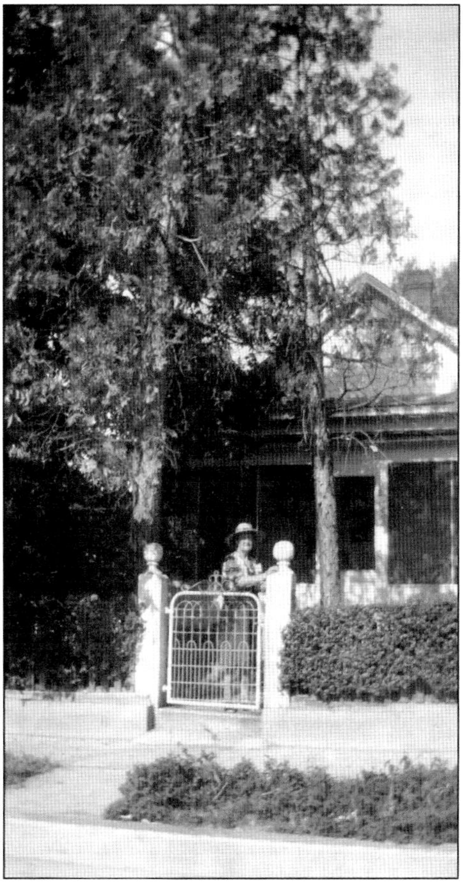

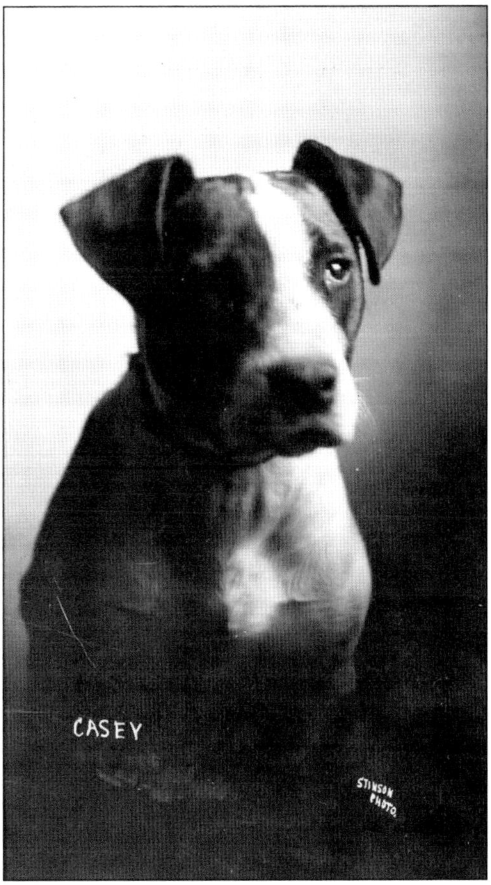

Jess Moulton went to Lyonsville School around 1910. The Moulton family would marry into the Shelton family. Prominent to any pioneer community were the pets and animals that were members of the families. Pictured is Jess Moulton's dog, Casey, who can be seen in Lyonsville School photographs from 1908 and in town photographs as late as 1917. After that, there is no further trace of Casey.

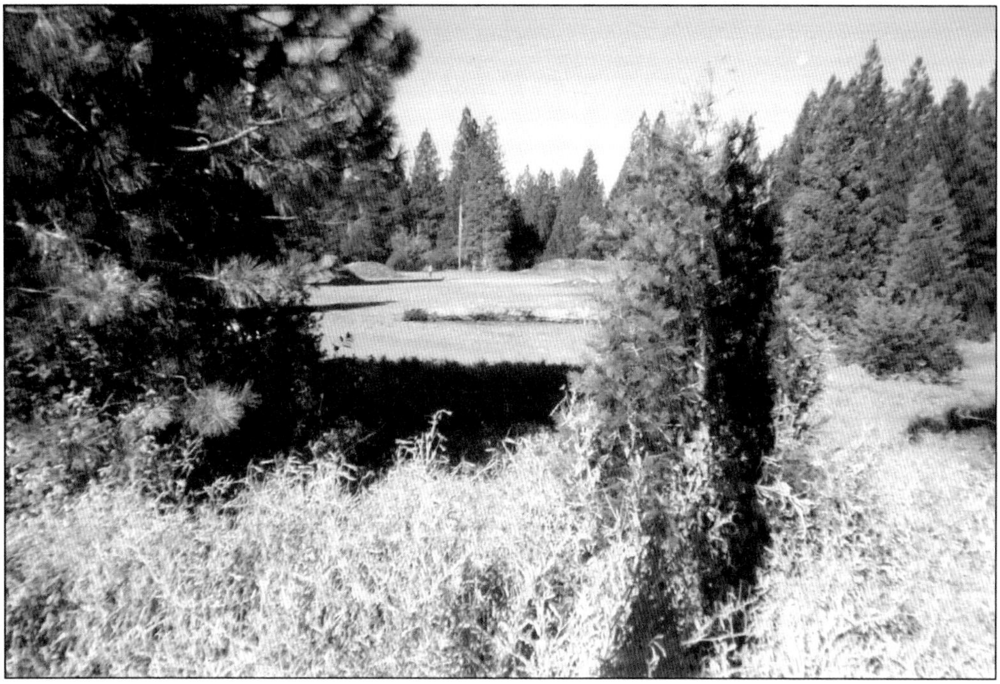

Today this is what the Lyman Springs millpond site looks like. The man standing in the far distance by the pole is Stanley Englebrite, formerly called the "Engebretsen" family a generation earlier. This is the same spot as the millpond of Belle Mill (see page 63 for an earlier view).

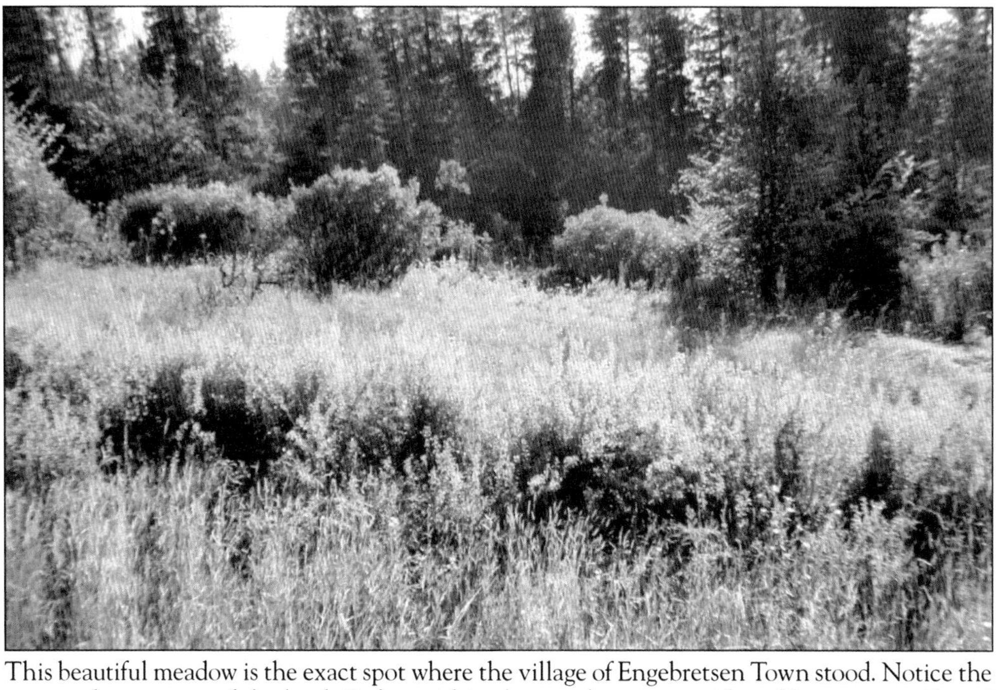

This beautiful meadow is the exact spot where the village of Engebretsen Town stood. Notice the present-day contour of the land. Today, within the meadow, iron artifacts like square nails and part of the original water pipe that supplied water to Adolf Engebretsen's home from the spring, can be found (see page 62 for an earlier view).

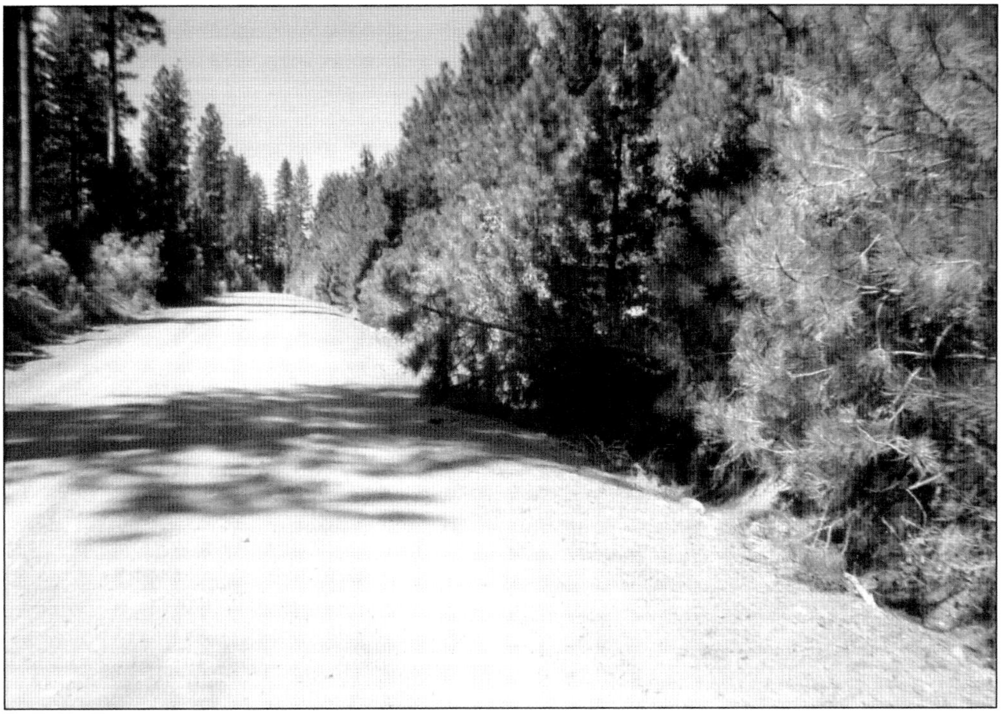

This September 12, 2006, photograph shows the roadbed looking up the hill from the south fork of Antelope Creek. At the upper left of the top photograph is the site of Eldus Johanssen's shack and the filing shed. The lower photograph on this page shows the cedar tree, which is still full of spikes and the nails where the saw filer's bench was attached. It is believed that this tree was spared by the loggers time and time again because of its use as a bench (see page 74 for an earlier view).

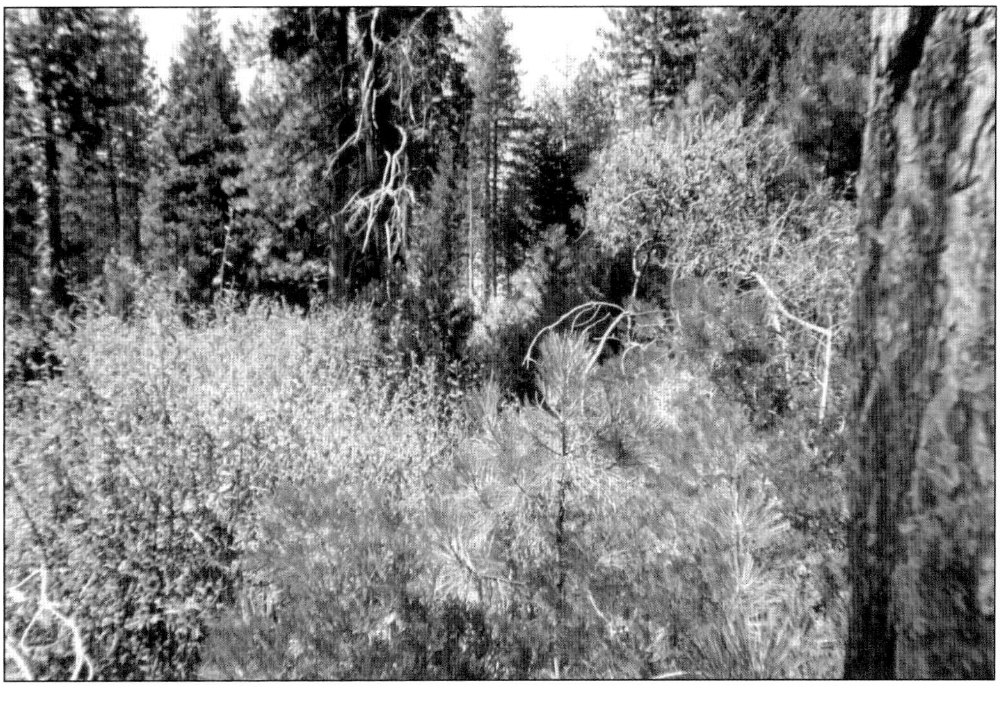

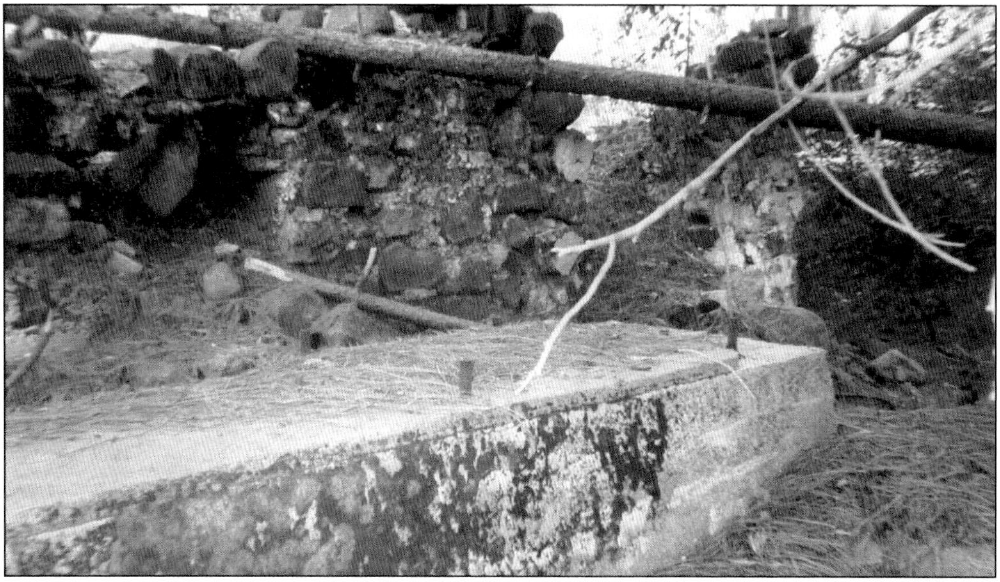

The boiler-feeding stations that fueled and powered the great Champion Mill are pictured as they appear today along with the exterior wall foundation. The fountain of the "Old Champ" and its massive, decaying sawdust pile are all that remain of Lyonsville, Sierra Lumber Company, and Darwin B. Lyon's dream community where recreation, life, and death went on for over 80 years. The photograph was taken September 12, 2006.

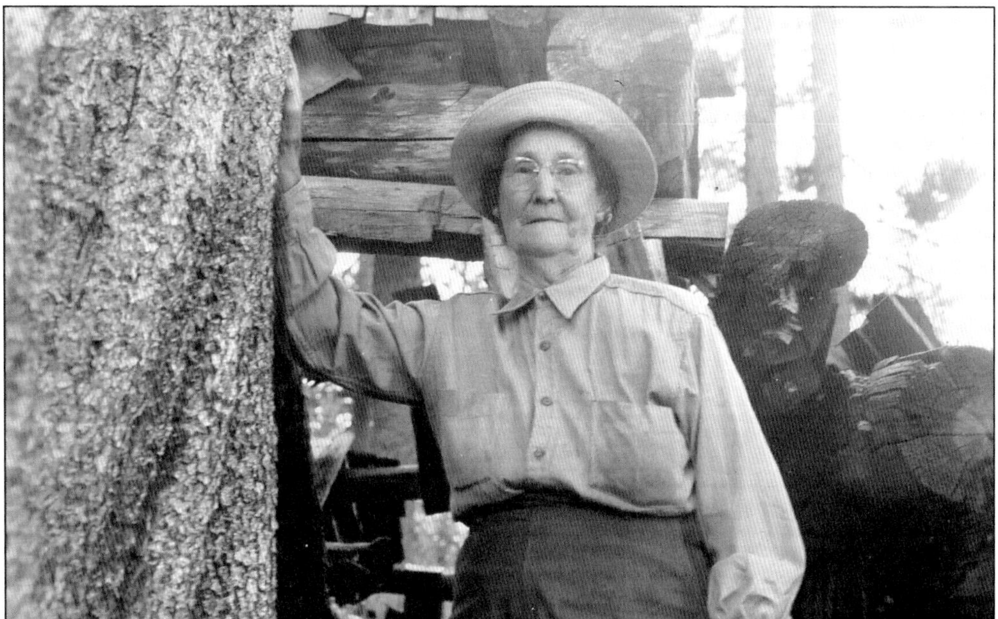

Appropriately titled "Alice in Wonderland Number 2," this photograph shows Alice Elizabeth Shelton Olson in the last photograph taken of her on August 28, 1957, as she left Grassy Lake for the last time. Shown leaning on a giant lodgepole pine, Alice stood and reflected about the lives of three generations of the Shelton, Olson, and Westrope families and their lives at "the cabin on Horseshoe Lake."

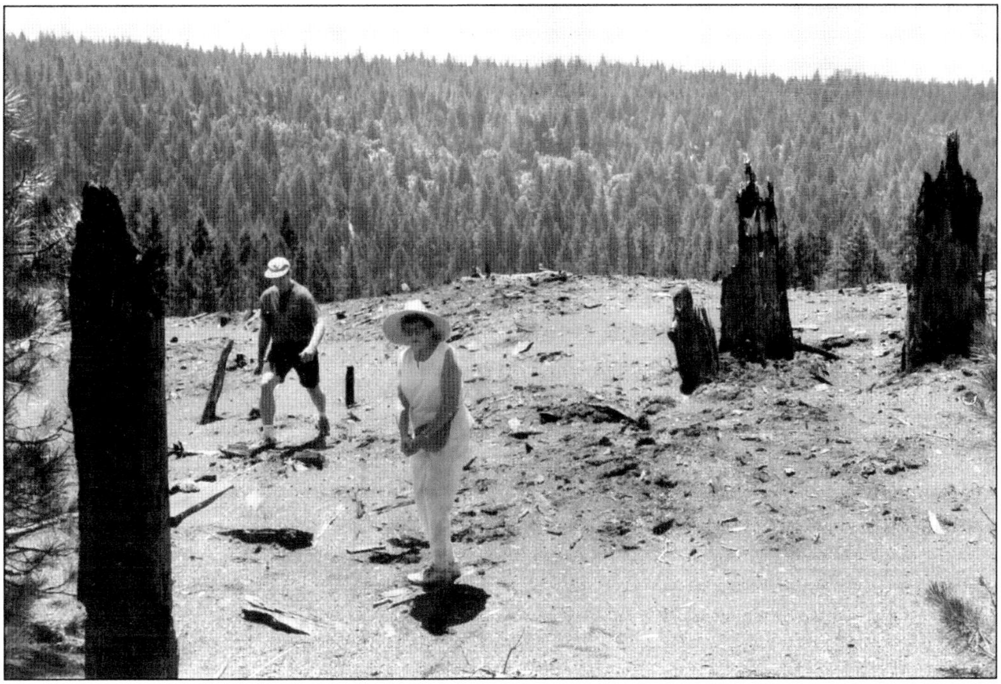

The sawdust pile for the old Champion Mill spills down over the grade and originally covered the old Native American footpath that ran along Antelope Creek, up to the top of Lyon Hill, and along the ridge to where it connected to the main trail that ran to *Waganupa*, or Mount Lassen. The blowing winds over the years have uncovered the butt stems of the giant trees that were gradually encased underneath 60 years of mill production sawdust. The sawdust actually preserves these artifacts and has been a historic treasure trove. In this 1996 photograph, author William Shelton and his cousin Linda Trudeau show how even pieces of perfectly preserved, century-old lumber get sifted from the sawdust. The greatest find over the years has been the old enameled sign from the saw works of Champion Mill and iron tools and implements.

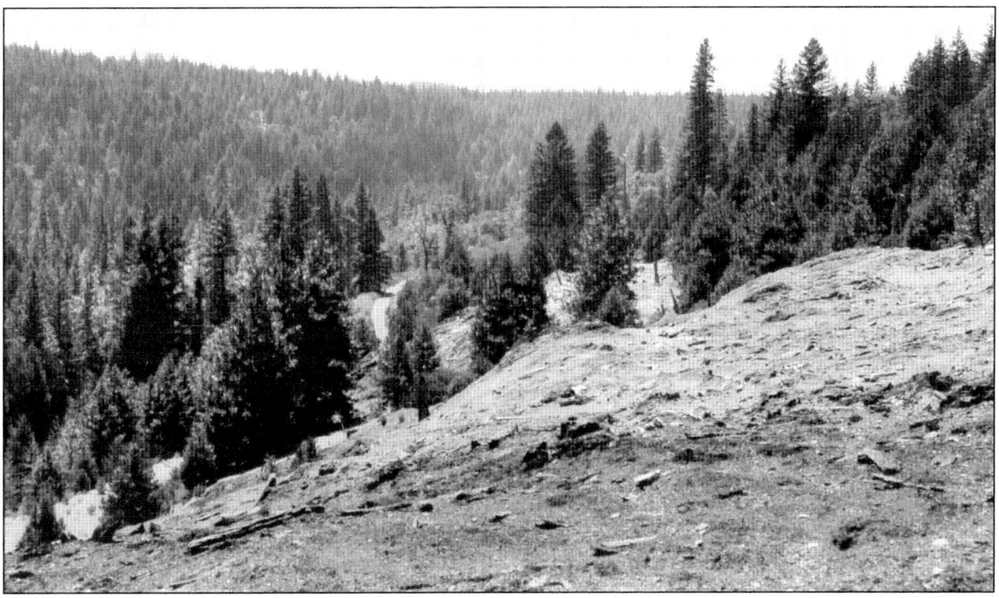

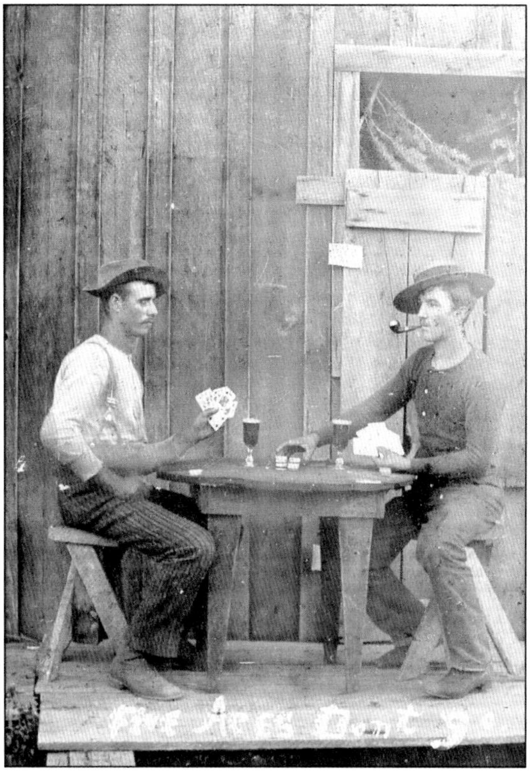

This fun cabinet card, "Five Aces Don't Go," was staged at Lyonsville on the deck of the Cliff House Saloon. Shown are Tom and John Shelton at an unknown date. This cabinet card was printed by Oscar Foss in San Francisco at a cost of $11 per 1,000. The treed area through the hatch was used to throw bottles and other refuse over the hill. Note the leather hinges.

Taken around 1907, just two years before they divorced, Madison Van Buren Shelton and wife Emma "Redwing" Shelton are shown here with three of their six children. In 1909, Emma could no longer live under the confines of her marriage, left her children with the Catholic sisters in Red Bluff, and struck out for Mill Creek Canyon to live with her people, The Maidu Indians.

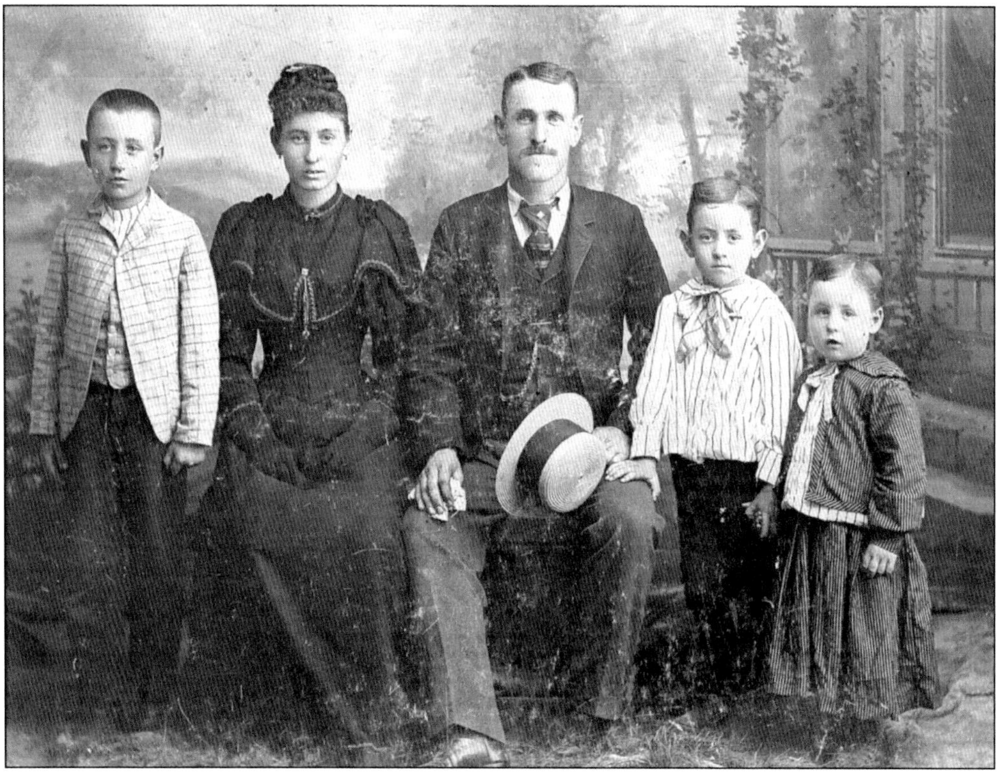

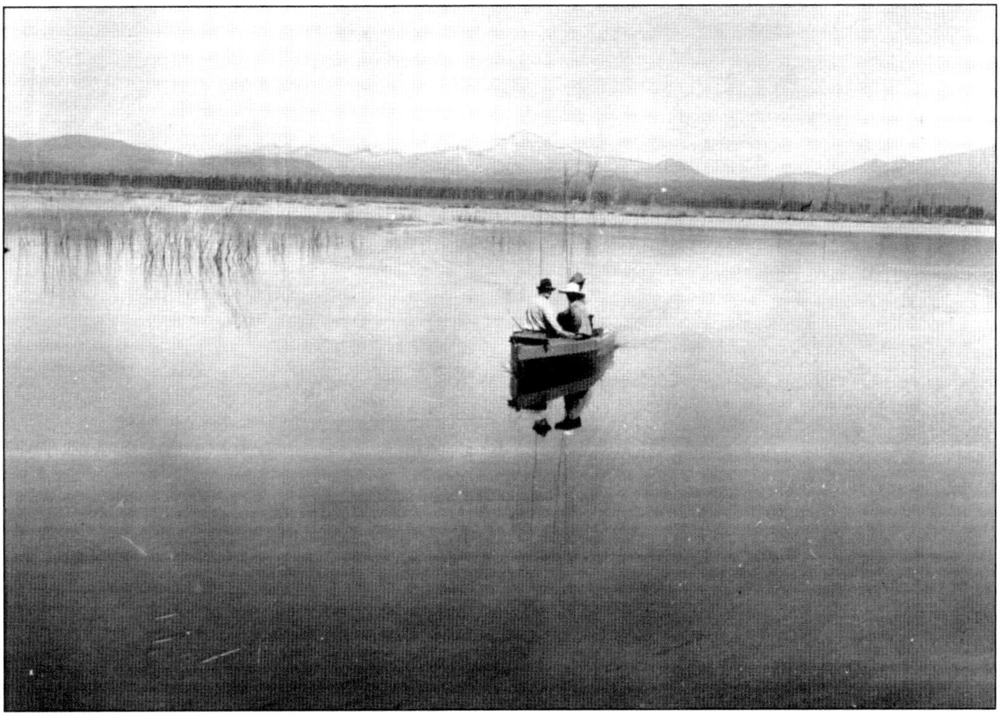

Alice Olson brought her split bamboo pole to fish both Grassy and Juniper Lakes on August 28, 1957. Not returning empty handed, both she and nephew Hobart Moulton caught their limits. Here they approach the far shore of Grassy Lake and the remains of the Olson cabin as Mount Lassen fades into the background. The park ranger is using the park rowboat (with a motor) to escort them to the reunion.

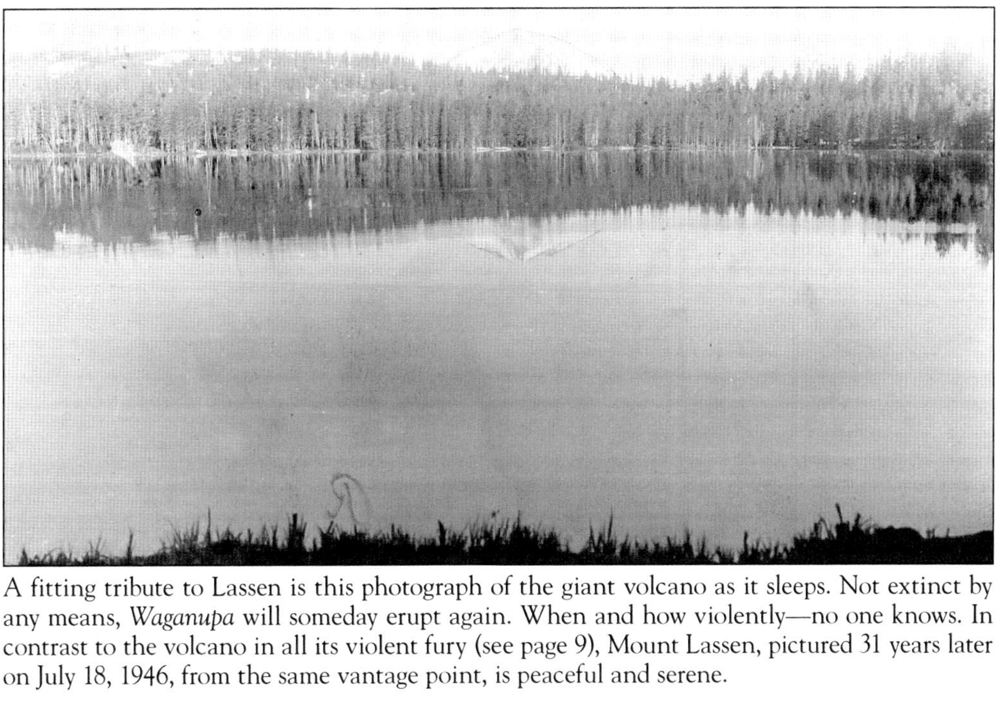

A fitting tribute to Lassen is this photograph of the giant volcano as it sleeps. Not extinct by any means, *Waganupa* will someday erupt again. When and how violently—no one knows. In contrast to the volcano in all its violent fury (see page 9), Mount Lassen, pictured 31 years later on July 18, 1946, from the same vantage point, is peaceful and serene.